Resolution of Conflict of Interest in Chinese Civil Court Hearings

Linguistic Insights

Studies in Language and Communication

Edited by Maurizio Gotti,
University of Bergamo

Volume 243

PETER LANG
Bern · Berlin · Bruxelles · New York · Oxford · Warszawa · Wien

Yunfeng Ge

Resolution of Conflict of Interest in Chinese Civil Court Hearings
A Perspective of Discourse Information Theory

PETER LANG
Bern · Berlin · Bruxelles · New York · Oxford · Warszawa · Wien

Bibliographic information published by die Deutsche Nationalbibliothek
Die Deutsche Nationalbibliothek lists this publication in the Deutsche Nationalbibliografie; detailed bibliographic data is available on the Internet at ‹http://dnb.d-nb.de›.

British Library Cataloguing-in-Publication Data: A catalogue record for this book is available from The British Library, Great Britain

Library of Congress Control Number: 2018932677

This work was supported by National Social Science Fund of China (Grant No. 16BYY064), 13th Five-Year Plan Scientific Research Project (2016) of National Language Committee (Grant No. YB135-5), and Social Science Project of Shandong Province (Grant No. 13CWXJ23).

ISSN 1424-8689 hb.
ISBN 978-3-0343-3313-9 hb.
ISBN 978-3-0343-3315-3 EPUB
DOI 10.3726/b13264

ISSN 2235-6371 eBook
ISBN 978-3-0343-3314-6 eBook
ISBN 978-3-0343-3316-0 MOBI

This publication has been peer reviewed.

Wabernstrasse 40, CH-3007 Bern, Switzerland
bern@peterlang.com, www.peterlang.com

Acknowledgement

This work is based on my Ph.D dissertation, which could not have been accomplished without the guidance, help, support and love of many people.

First and foremost, my deepest gratitude goes to my supervisor, Professor Jinbang Du, for his patient guidance and warm encouragement. Professor Du's knowledge and expertise in forensic linguistics and discourse analysis made my study a pleasant experience. I have greatly benefited from his systemic framework of discourse information theory. He also read every draft of the dissertation with great care and patience, and gave me detailed advice at every phase of the research. Without his priceless comments and constant encouragement, I would never have been able to finish the dissertation. He has also set me a good example with his profound scholarship and deep commitment to his students.

My heartfelt thanks also go to Ms. Xinrong Zhang for her kindness and generosity. She offered great help and care to me in the past few years.

I also feel greatly obliged to the committee members, Professor Jianxin Ding, Professor Qi Gong, Professor Shaogang Yang, Professor Junfeng Zhao and Professor Zhanghong Xu, for their insightful comments and valuable suggestions.

Last but not least, I am greatly indebted to my beloved wife, Dr. Hong Wang, and our dear daughter, Hanchen Ge, for their endless love and wholehearted support.

Contents

1 Introduction

With the rapid development of the economy of China, Chinese society has entered a transition period characteristic of various kinds of conflicts. These conflicts can be resolved in four different approaches: political approach, economical approach, ethical approach and legal approach (Wang 2010). As for the legal approach, two specific methods are frequently adopted: legislative control and judicial control (Bodenheimer 1962).

According to jurisprudence of interests, interest is the origin of law and the balancing of interest is one of the fundamental legislative principles (Bodenheimer 1962). On the other hand, law is the means by which interest is protected and realized when disputes arise. Therefore, both the legislative and judiciary organs of a nation are closely related to the interest of its fellow citizens. To be specific, the major function of legislators is, through legislation, to define the interest relations between different interest groups; and the ultimate aim of judicial officers – judges in particular – is to satisfy their different material or spiritual pursuit of interest. Actually, interest is regarded by Bodenheimer (1962) as the nucleus which both legislative and judicial activities center on. In this study, I will conduct the research on the conflict of interest (hereinafter referred to as COI) in Chinese civil court hearings. Particular attention will be focused on how participants of civil lawsuits commit themselves to the resolution of COI.

Needless to say, court hearings cannot be carried out without the use of language, and there is no exception as well when resolution of COI is concerned. Moreover, as a common practice of forensic linguistics, linguistic theories and methods contribute significantly to the revelation of the nature of legal issues (Levi 1990). Among the prevalent linguistic theories and methods, discourse analysis, with its comprehensive coverage and deep exploration of the nature of language, provides illuminating insights into the understanding of relevant activities in court hearings. This study, based on the discourse information theory and by integrating the context model schema and the relevant theories in cognitive grammar, will describe, analyze and interpret the language used in Chinese civil court hearings, with the expectation of revealing the process of how COI is resolved.

This chapter introduces the relevant studies on interest and COI, presents the general research objective and research questions, and outlines the structure of the book.

1.1 Studies on Interest

Human beings are not naturally born with the concept of interest. In early human history, the incidental and unsystematic interest theories were always shadowed by religious, ethical, and political influences, with people's pursuit of interest being suppressed and severely restricted. It was not until Renaissance that the concept of interest was explicitly proposed by the bourgeoisie, who, by inquiring into human nature and social need, advocated the rationality of people's pursuit of interest (Hao 2007: 49).

In the middle of the 19th century, with the increase of social wealth and people's awareness of protection of interest, jurisprudence of interests was rewarded and respected for their advocacy of legalization of pursuit of interest. However, people's pursuit of interest has moved from the extreme of being severely restricted towards the extreme of maximizing personal interest, which leads to complex interest conflicts and social problems (Hao 2007: 49). As a result, resolution of COI has become not only a social concern, but also a legal problem (Xia & Shi 2006).

This section introduces the basic terms related to interest theory, on the basis of which different approaches to resolution of COI are reviewed.

1.1.1 Interest and Classification of Interest

1.1.1.1 Definition of Interest

Sik (1962) defines interest as the demand of a subject to meet a long-lasting desire, which, if not satisfied, would initiate repetitive and even stronger pursuit. This definition, by regarding interest as a biological need of human beings, reveals the natural feature of the pursuit of interest (Zhang 2002). As is elaborated by Zhang (2002), it is just in the process of demanding and satisfying demand that human beings develop themselves as a natural existence. Sik's definition also reveals the subjective feature of interest, namely, the dominance and initiative of human beings in pursuit of interest, since "human beings, with cognitive and practical abilities, always create conditions to satisfy their interest demand for the sake of existence and further development" (Sun 2008: 16).

However, Sik's definition emphasizes too much of the natural need of interest and fails to take into account the social feature of interest (Sun 2008). Marx believes that although natural need is the drive of all kinds of human activities, the subjectivity of interest cannot be emphasized to such an extent that the social aspect of interest is ignored (Marx & Engels 1956). Marx treats interest as the fundamental concept in social analysis and regards pursuit of interest as the impetus for all social activities, in that "everything people struggle for is closely related to their interests" (Marx & Engels 1956: 82).

Accordingly, Wang focuses more on the social feature of interest by defining interest as "a form of social relation between interest subjects established during distribution of interest objects" (2010: 74). This definition, by identifying the need of human beings as the natural basis and the interrelation between interest subjects as the social basis, summarizes three fundamental features of interest: naturalness, subjectivity, and sociality, and can help us to have a comprehensive understanding of the nature of interest.

1.1.1.2 Classification of Interest

Interest is also a complex system which can be classified into different categories. The diversity of interest originates from the diversity of human need as a result of the development of the society. According to Sun (2008: 18), interest can be classified into different categories according to different standards, as is shown by the following table (Table 1–1).

Standard of Classification	*Types of Interest*
Subject difference	Personal interest, group interest, social interest
Object difference	Economical/non-economical interest Material/spiritual interest
Temporal-spatial difference	Current/long-term interest Local/global interest
Difference of Importance	Fundamental/non-fundamental interest
Difference of influence	Direct/indirect interest

Table 1-1. Classification of Interest.

Classification of interest can help us understand the relations between different interest types. And more importantly, in addition to examining more profoundly the interest orientations and goals of different interest subjects, classification of interest can help to reveal their attitudes and behaviors when they are confronted with interest disputes or conflicts.

1.1.2 Interest Relations

According to Marxist theory (Wang 2010: 147), man's production activity is the process of interest pursuit and acquisition from which interest relations originate. The relation between human beings is the relation of interest, on the basis of which society comes into being and develops. Therefore, human relations can be regarded as interest relations (Sun 2008: 18).

Theoretically, a society works best when all kinds of interest relations are kept in balance, especially when the personal interest motives of individuals conform to the maximal interest pursuit of the whole society. However, the absolute balance of interest relations is only a hypothetical optimum, and imbalance is the ordinary state, resulting in various kinds of interest differences which may develop into conflict of interest (Sun 2008: 24).

1.1.2.1 Interest Difference

In the process of social production and exchange, there always exists interest difference between individuals or groups. So interest difference is a kind of interest relation between interest subjects with different interest pursuits, and constitutes the basis of interest conflict. It is caused by the gap between the personal demand of individuals and the social demand of groups (Wang 2010: 155). Moreover, the distribution of social labor and the difference in possession of means of production are decisive factors that result in interest difference (Wang 2010: 156).

In his study of interest difference, Sun (2008) focuses more on personal interest. He (2008: 24) concludes that personal interest is the core component of interest relations, and therefore should be taken as the starting point in the analysis of interest difference.

In China, although interest difference is not a difference based upon class antagonism and interest is fundamentally consistent and compatible for all people, it is still likely, if not properly handled, to cause disputes or conflicts (Wang 2010: 159).

1.1.2.2 Conflict of Interest (COI)

Among the various kinds of interest relations, interest contradiction is the most stable and fundamental relation which is based on interest difference (Wang 2010: 159). The contradiction between man's interest demand and social production provides the primitive impetus for the development of human society. Since social production is always conducted in certain economical relations, the contradiction between man's interest demand and social production is certain to manifest itself in the form of personal interest contradiction (Wang 2010: 160). This position is very similar to Sun's idea (2008) that interest difference is the starting point of interest analysis.

Under certain circumstances, interest difference and interest contradiction between different interest individuals or interest groups may escalate and develop into COI (Zhao 1998, Wang 2010). COI usually manifests itself as a dynamic social process, underlying which is the inconsistency of motives, intentions, goals and demands of interest subjects (Wang 2010: 166).

Being either antagonistic or non-antagonistic, COI can be classified into conflict between individuals and conflict between groups and has three basic forms of manifestation: emotional conflict, verbal conflict and behavioral conflict (Wang 2010: 170).

Studies on interest relations can help us to have a better understanding of its regularity, thus finding out efficient ways to prevent, control or resolve COI when necessary.

1.1.3 Resolution of COI

As was mentioned previously, COI can be resolved in a political approach, an economical approach, an ethical approach and a legal approach (Wang 2010). The first three approaches can be grouped into interest coordination (Sun, 2008); the legal approach can be further classified into legislative method and judiciary method (Xia & Shi 2006).

1.1.3.1 Resolution of COI through Coordination

Interest coordination is usually concerned with the balance of the relation between interest subjects, and the adjustment of their concepts of interest and their related behaviors, and is usually of economic, political and ethical features (Sun 2008).

There are five specific means of interest coordination: economic, political, cultural, ecological, and social (Sun 2008). The economic approach resolves COI through economic policy, and is regarded as the major approach in interest coordination, for it fundamentally resolves the conflict between interest subjects and interest objects by satisfying as much as possible the need of interest subjects (Wang 2010). The political approach "resorts to the function of government and the authority of other political institutions for the resolution of COI" (Wang 2010: 244). The cultural approach refers to "the coordination of interest by means of traditional cultural protection, cultural innovation, construction of cultural facilities, etc. to satisfy various kinds of cultural demands of different groups" (Sun 2008: 29). The ecological approach emphasizes "the protection of non-renewable resources to achieve the balance of interest acquisition" (Sun 2008: 31). The social approach attempts to coordinate interest of different groups "by comprehensively considering such social factors as law, government policy, market and public service" (Sun 2008: 30).

These means of interest coordination are quite practical in the resolution of COI. However, interest coordination is not the panacea for all kinds of COI, and interest contradiction cannot be totally prevented and resolved only through coordination (Wang 2010). For the complex interest relations, there must be a diversiform mechanism to resolve the possible COI, among which, legal approach is a basic and indispensible one (Chen 2010).

Although studies on interest coordination always include the legal approach as an important component in the resolution of COI, few of them have conducted profound and systematic investigation into it. The legal characteristics in resolution of COI cannot be neglected since "in modern society, resolution of conflict is always closely related with law" (Fan 2007: 117). Therefore, "it is of great necessity to examine the enforcement, function and operation status of the legal mechanism from the perspective of judicial practice and conflict resolution" (Fan 2007: 117).

1.1.3.2 Resolution of COI through Legislation

The legal approach to resolution of COI has come from the idea of jurisprudence of interests under the influence of legal realism, which regards interest as the origin of law (Bodenheimer 1962). Jurisprudence of interests was first established in early 20th century in opposition to conceptual jurisprudence, according to which correct judgments can be reached on the basis of sufficient understanding of specific regulations of law via proper logical deduction reasoning (Bodenheimer 1962). Conceptual jurisprudence establishes law as an isolated system composed of legal concepts, in which the role of judges is confined to classification of cases and entering into judgments by appealing to logic (Du & Zou 2003).

Jurisprudence of interests, however, regards interest as the origin of law in that interest determines the creation of legal provisions and is the basic element of both legislative and judicial processes of law (Huang 2007). Therefore, the major function of legislators is to define the contradictory interest relations on the basis of their value judgment on the desired form of society (Lv & Sun 2000). Accordingly, the ultimate goal of judicial activities, which usually appear in the form of judgments entered into by judges, is to satisfy life needs, namely, the material and spiritual pursuit of individuals or groups. Therefore the foremost thing for the judiciary is to confirm the interests that legislators intend to protect (Du & Zou 2003).

Corresponding to the idea that law is a means to protect interest, the major function of the judge in court identified by jurisprudence of interests is to resolve various kinds of COI (Xia & Shi 2006). More importantly, since legal provisions are not always as profound and unambiguous as expected, it is desired that judges make their own value judgments on interests without conflicting with the values expressed in legislation (Bodenheimer 1962). Therefore, instead of being confined to literal interpretation and application of legal provisions, judges are encouraged to make their own valued judgments on the basis of which COI is negotiated and finally resolved (Bodenheimer 1962).

Based on the fundamental concept that law originates from COI, jurisprudence of interests emphasizes the application of law by focusing on interest in legislation and litigation. It contributes to the resolution of COI by proposing that the trial of cases and finally the judgments entered into by judges should be based on the consideration and balance of interests (Zhang 1999).

1.1.3.3 Resolution of COI through Litigation

Influenced by jurisprudence of interests, court hearing is taken as one of the major means to resolve COI. As is explained by Zhang (1999), the fundamental functions of law are realized by judicial activities during the process of resolution of COI. Therefore, court hearing is defined as a process of resolution of COI between interest subjects, which cannot be resolved otherwise, for example, by following regulations of law (Xue 2008).

As for the realization of resolution of COI through court hearings, a lot of research has been carried out. For example, Lu (2003) proposes that resolution of COI should be realized by both legislative and judicial means, with the latter being effected by judicial relief and intervention, so as to suppress illegal interest appeals and protect and balance legal appeals. Zhu (2008) focuses on resolution of COI between different social classes by claiming that resolution of COI between different social classes should be based on the construction of the mechanism to express, evaluate and balance different interests. These studies elaborate the general principles that should be followed in resolution of COI, but fail to explore in detail the nature of court hearings (Xia & Shi 2006).

Xia & Shi (2006) define court hearings as a process in which interest subjects negotiate and finally resolve disputes by reaching agreement. They propose that the nature of litigation has two prescriptive aspects, one being the social subjectivity, and the other, the will of state. The former manifests itself in its will to resolve disputes and the latter in the intervention of public power. Therefore, "litigation becomes the joint point that connects social subjectivity and the will of state […] which are in a waxing and waning relation" (Xia & Shi 2006: 98).

They further propose that although court hearing is characteristic of intervention of public power, its coercing feature should be treated with care. In fact, the will of interest subjects is the constant factor in the process of dispute resolution, and thus is the essential component of court hearings. Therefore, the resolution of COI is regarded by them as the most straightforward and ultimate goal of litigation: "Other goals such as protection of rights and establishment of social order are crucial but not as straightforward as resolution of COI" (Xia & Shi 2006: 100).

Xia & Shi (2006) also elaborate how litigation is effected during the resolution of COI. According to them, the resolution of COI is composed of three orientations: interest appeal, interest negotiation, and agreement reaching. Interest negotiation can be further analyzed into two kinds of interactions, vertical and horizontal communications of information. The former refers to the interaction between the judge and litigants, and the latter refers to the interaction between litigants themselves, which, is the central component of judicial procedures (Xia & Shi 2006).

Their findings conform to the fundamental ideas of jurisprudence of interests. And by defining court hearings as a process of interest negotiation and agreement reaching, their research is highly instructive to the study of courtroom discourse (Du 2009b).

However, most of the studies that regard court hearings as resolution of COI are conducted from a legal perspective and have ignored its communicative and dynamic features. They fail to notice that legal system is "a highly elaborated network of interrelationships between language use, on the one hand, and social, economic, political, and even moral forces on the other" (Levi 1990: 6). Therefore, it is necessary to examine court hearings under the instruction of linguistic theories and methods. Otherwise, we cannot have a thorough understanding of "how language is used and the uses of language are affecting the outcomes of legal processes" (Levi 1990: 4).

1.2 Research Objective and Research Questions

As mentioned previously, COI is an unavoidable social reality which, if handled improperly, may influence the stability of society. As one of the important ways to resolve these conflicts, court hearing is expected to make indispensable contribution to the efficient resolution of COI. In view of this, the research objective of this study is to explore the process how COI is resolved in Chinese civil court hearings from the perspective of discourse information theory. To achieve such a research objective, three specific questions are raised in this study:

1) What are the features of discourse information processing in interest appeal?

As mentioned earlier, interest relations appear in the form of interest difference, interest contradiction and COI. In court hearings, COI takes the form of verbal conflict since litigants appeal to language for the expression of their different interests. And in order to gain the maximal benefit, litigants tend to express their interest appeals as clearly as possible. Therefore, to investigate the features of discourse information processing in interest appeal lays a foundation for further research of the final resolution of COI.

2) What factors influence the negotiation of interest between participants in court hearings?

According to Wang (2010), COI is a dynamic relation between different interest parties which can be negotiated and balanced under certain conditions. Court hearings provide parties with a judicial occasion to negotiate their interests. The analysis of the factors that are involved during the negotiation of interest between different parties can help us to achieve a deeper understanding of the resolution of COI.

3) How is discourse managed to reach agreement for the resolution of COI?

Based on the results of interest appeal and interest negotiation, agreements can be arrived at during court hearings. Agreement in court hearings takes various kinds of forms ranging from conciliation settlement to final judgment imposed by the court.

Whichever form agreement takes, participants in lawsuits usually resort to discursive devices for the manipulation of the cognitive information processing to express, either explicitly or implicitly, their wishes to reach agreement. The analysis of these discursive devices can help us understand how discourse is managed to promote agreement for the resolution of COI.

It is hoped that the process of resolution of COI will be revealed by, apart from analyzing the discourse produced by participants in lawsuits, digging into the latent cognitive factors and information processing activities that underlie discourse production.

1.3 Structure of the Book

This book consists of seven chapters. Chapter 1 provides a general research orientation of the study, introduces studies on interest and resolution of conflict of interest, and the objective and research questions that will be answered. Chapter 2 presents a review of theories of discourse analysis and studies on courtroom discourse, including the cognitive approach to discourse analysis, discourse information theory and different analytical approaches to courtroom discourse. Chapter 3, based on the relevant theories reviewed in Chapter 2, constructs the theoretical framework for this study. Moreover, the methodology the book adopts is also elaborated. The following three chapters, from Chapter 4 to Chapter 6, focus on analysis of the collected data in order to address the three research questions respectively. Chapter 4 concentrates on features of discourse information in interest appeals. Chapter 5 elaborates factors that influence the process of interest negotiation between participants in lawsuits. Chapter 6 focuses on participants' discourse management strategies that help to promote agreements. Chapter 7, the concluding part of the book, summarizes the findings of the research and discusses the theoretical and practical implications. The limitations of the study and suggestions for future research are also included.

2 Discourse analysis and Courtroom Discourse

In this chapter of the book, I will introduce some of the important theories of discourse analysis, including discourse analysis in cognitive grammar, discourse information theory, and the discourse management model, and the recent discourse studies conducted in the courtroom context.

2.1 Theories of Discourse Analysis

The term "discourse analysis", since its appearance, has been used with lots of meanings which cover a wide range of activities. Traditionally, discourse analysis has been defined as the discipline "devoted to the investigation of the relationship between form and function in verbal communication" (Renkema 2004: 1). This approach tends to focus more on description of features of spoken or written texts.

Other researchers focus more on the communicative features of discourse and how texts are structured and used in communication (Conley & O'Barr 1998). They propose that discourse analysis can be used to "examine how humans use language to communicate and, in particular, how addressers construct linguistic messages for addressees and how addressees work on linguistic messages in order to interpret them" (Brown & Yule 1983: ix).

Different from the traditional practice where discourse analysis is confined to the study of linguistic forms and the regularities of their distribution, this approach puts interlocutors at the center of communication. It suggests that discourse analysis involves a consideration of the general principles of discourse production and discourse interpretation by which people normally make sense of what they say and hear.

2.1.1 Discourse Analysis in Cognitive Grammar

Among the different schools of discourse analysis, cognitive linguistics regard both the production and the comprehension of discourses as cognitive activities, with the structure of discourse and other discursive features being characteristic of human beings' cognitive patterns. In view of this, cognitive linguists suggest conducting discourse analysis from a cognitive perspective, with the aim of exploring the underlying factors that give shape to the different forms of discourses as they are. In this apart of the study, I will introduce and review, among others, Langacker's cognitive approach to discourse analysis.

2.1.1.1 Discourse Space

According to Langacker (2001: 143), "linguistic units are abstracted from usage events, retaining as part of their value any recurring facet of the interactive and discourse context". Discourse is thus the final product of cognitive activity which, based on the full understanding of the context, consists of one's comprehensive conceptualization of the event.

Langacker (2001) further proposes that the conceptualization that inheres in the usage event includes two important components: 1) the interlocutors' apprehension of their interactive circumstances; and 2) the very discourse they are engaged in. The former is termed ground (G), which consists of the speech event, the speaker (S) and hearer (H), their interaction, and the immediate circumstances--the time and place in particular. The latter is termed current discourse space (CDS) and defined as the mental space that comprises those elements and relations shared by the speaker and hearer as a basis for communication at a given moment in the flow of discourse. The ground and CDS further constitute the cognitive domains evoked as the conceptual base for the meanings of linguistic expressions. The various aspects of a usage event are demonstrated by Langacker (2001: 145) with the following figure.

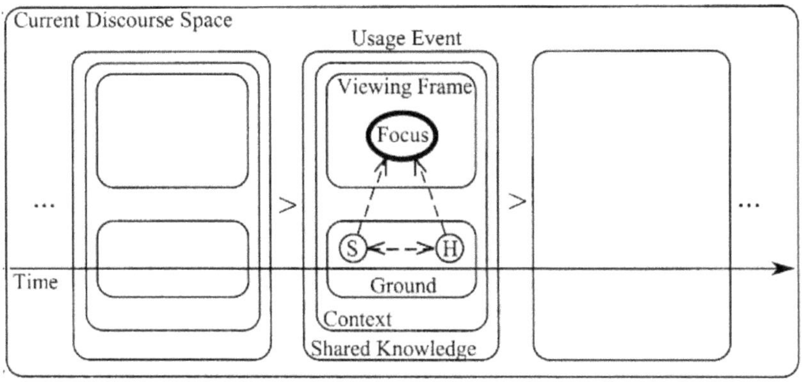

Figure 2-1. Current Discourse Space.

In this figure, a usage event refers to the action carried out by the speaker (S) and hearer (H), which involves the directing and focusing of attention. In successful communication, the speaker and hearer would coordinate this action and focus their attention on the same conceived entity. But because of the limitation of the visual field, the speaker and hearer can take in only a portion of the world at any given moment, which is called "viewing frame" by Langacker (2001, 2008). The immediate scope of the conception at any instant is limited to what appears in this frame, with the focus of attention--what an expression profiles--included in that scope.

Context is interpreted by Langacker (2001, 2008) as the circumstances in which a usage event takes place. It includes physical, mental, social, and cultural elements. At the center of the context of speech is the ground. One important element of the ground is that the speaker and hearer are engaged in a coordinated viewing of some facet of the world.

The speaker and hearer are supposed to share a body of knowledge, which includes their apprehension of the ongoing discourse itself, a series of previous usage events, and subsequent events that are expected to happen.

With the CDS theory, Langacker (2001) extends the application of cognitive grammar theory to the investigation of discourse. By putting other contextual factors into consideration, such as relation between the speaker and hearer, their shared knowledge and other social and cultural elements, the CDS theory regards discourse as a social interaction which should be studied in a broad social and cultural background (Wang 2003).

2.1.1.2 Viewing Frame

As an important notion in the CDS theory, a viewing frame is defined by Langacker (1987, 1991, 2001, 2008) as a usage event with bipolar compositions, including both conceptualizing and vocalizing activity. Each pole can be realized by multiple channels, as shown in the following figure.

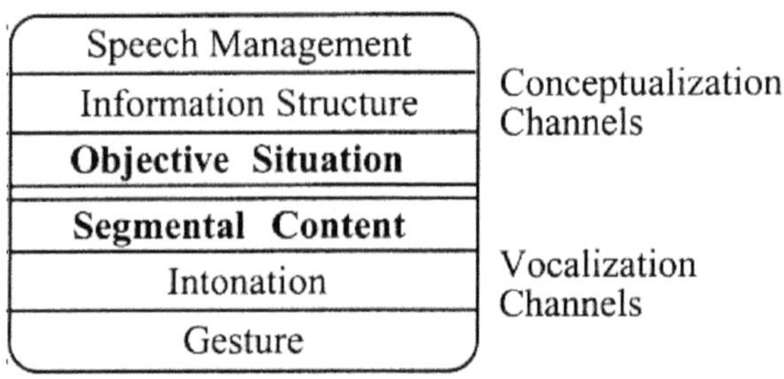

Figure 2-2. Viewing Frame.

At the conceptualization pole, objective situation, also called objective or conceptual content by Langacker (2008), refers to the concept that is formed based on the object or the event that speakers are engaged in. It is generally more substantive, more concrete, and more at the center of our attention than the other channels. Information structure includes such factors as emphasis, discourse topic, and status of information as given versus new. Speech management consists of such matters as turn taking and holding or relinquishing the floor. At the vocalization pole, segmental content is comparably salient, with such suprasegmental features as intonation and gesture auxiliary to it.

According to Harder (1996), linguistic structures of any size can be seen as instructions to modify the current discourse space. Each instruction focuses our attention on a particular entity within the viewing frame. Therefore, "a discourse comprises a succession of frames each representing the scene being 'viewed' and acted on by the speaker and hearer at a given instant" (Langacker 2001: 151). Each viewing frame corresponds to one updating of the CDS, as is shown by the following figure:

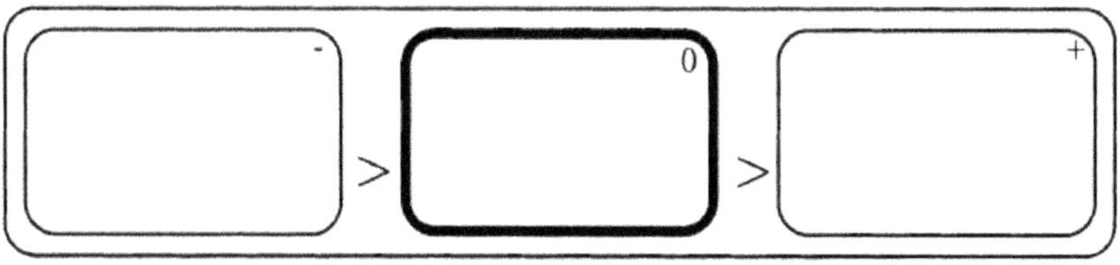

Figure 2-3. Succession of Viewing Frames.

In this figure, the heavy lines indicate the focus frame that is currently acted on, which can also be called the zero frame. It is preceded by a minus frame and followed by a plus frame. The size and nature of these frames may arrange from lexicon to discourse, depending on the level and dimension of linguistic units we examine.

By defining a viewing frame as a bipolar entity composed of conceptualization and vocalization channels, Langacker (2001) reveals the correlation between linguistic expressions and their conceptualizing activities. The elaboration on the components of these two channels also makes it possible to carry out more detailed analytical investigation. Moreover, the concept of the succession of viewing frames that constitute the flow of discourse reveals the dynamic features of discourse construction and highlights the importance of linguistic context in discourse construction (Wang 2003).

2.1.1.3 Construal

According to Langacker (2001, 2008), the meaning of a linguistic expression comes not only from the conceptual content it evokes, but also from how that content is construed. "In viewing a scene, what we actually see depends on how closely we examine it, what we choose to look at, which elements we pay attention to, and where we view it from." (Langacker 2008: 55) In other words, our focus of attention plays a significant role in construing the world around us. In order to explain how attention is reflected in language, Langacker (2008) classifies construal into four major types: specificity, focusing, prominence, and perspective.

Specificity

With specificity, Langacker (2008) refers to the level of precision and detail at which a situation is characterized. The term is often used in opposition to schematicity. According to Langacker (2008), highly specific expressions describe a situation in fine-grained detail, while expressions of lesser specificity only offer coarse-grained descriptions that reveal gross features and global organization.

Focusing

With focusing, Langacker (2008) refers to the phenomenon that we use linguistic expressions to access particular portions of our conceptual universe. It includes the selection of conceptual content for linguistic presentation and its arrangement which is termed as foreground versus background. Here is how Langacker (2008: 58) defines the relation between foreground and background:

> We can reasonably speak of background and foreground for any case where one conception proceeds and in some way facilitates the emergence of another. In this broad sense, we can say that expressions invoke background knowledge as the basis for their understanding.

Foreground and background relations also help to explain the composition of a complex linguistic structure, which is in a hierarchical arrangement and represented in tree-like diagrams, as is illustrated by Langacker (2008: 60) with the following example, which is reproduced here as Figure 2-4:

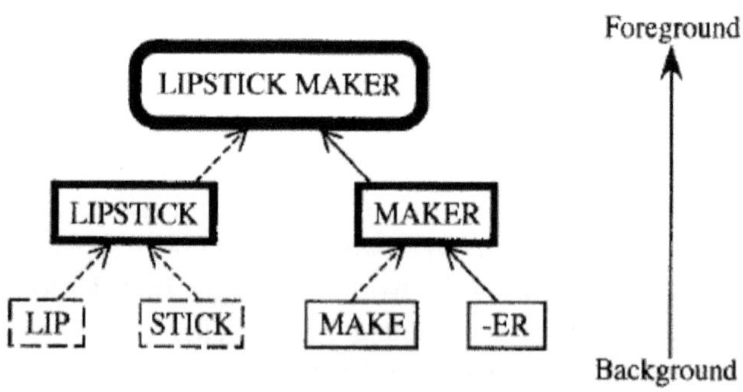

Figure 2-4. Composition of "Lipstick Maker".

In the figure, the thickness of lines represents the relative degree of foregrounding. When the composite expression *lipstick maker* is used, the individual meanings of *lipstick* and *maker* are invoked at the same time, which facilitate and background the emergence of the composite conception. By the same token, the conceptual components *lip* and *stick* are backgrounded in relation to *lipstick*, and *make* and *-er* in relation to *maker*.

Prominence

Langacker (2008: 66) proposes that "language structure displays numerous kinds of asymmetries that are reasonably considered matters of prominence". He identifies two particular sorts of prominence: profiling and trajectory/landmark alignment.

The core of the notion is that an expression selects a certain body of conceptual content as its conceptual base, which can be construed either broadly as its maximal scope or narrowly as its immediate scope. "An expression's profile stands out as the specific focus of attention within its immediate scope." (Langacker 2008: 66) This explains why two or more expressions evoking the same conceptual content still differ in meaning. It is because they profile different substructures within the common base. For example, *hub, spoke*, and *rim* all evoke the conception of 'wheel' as their base, but contrast semantically because they designate different parts of wheel, as is shown by Langacker (2008: 67) with the following figure, which is reproduced here as Figure 2-5:

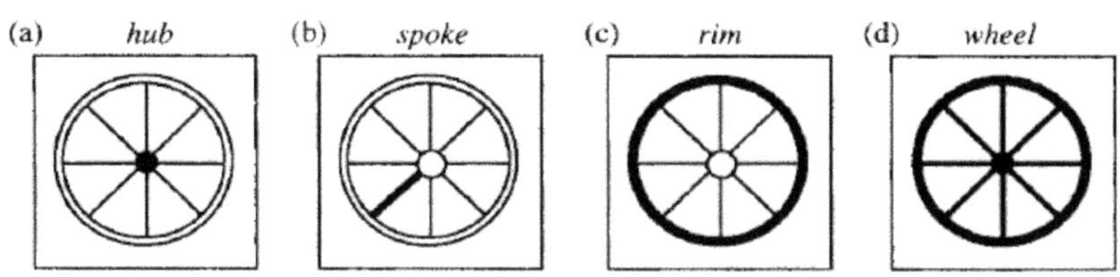

Figure 2-5. The Profiling of *Hub*, *Spoke*, *Rim* and *Wheel*.

When an expression profiles a relationship, varying degrees of prominence can be conferred on its participants. The most prominent participant is called 'trajector' (tr) and attracts the primary focus within the profiled relationship. The participant that attracts a secondary focus is called 'landmark' (lm). "Expressions can have the same content, and profile the same relationship, but differ in meaning because they make different choices of trajector and landmark." (Langacker 2008: 70) The notions of trajector and landmark can help to explain the semantic difference between the following two sentences.

(1)
(a) *The other guests all left before we arrived.*
(b) *We arrived after the other guests all left.*

Before and *after* profile the same relationship of temporal precedence between two events, but contrast semantically. The difference in meaning does not reside in content or profiling, but in their choice of trajector and landmark, as demonstrated by the following diagram:

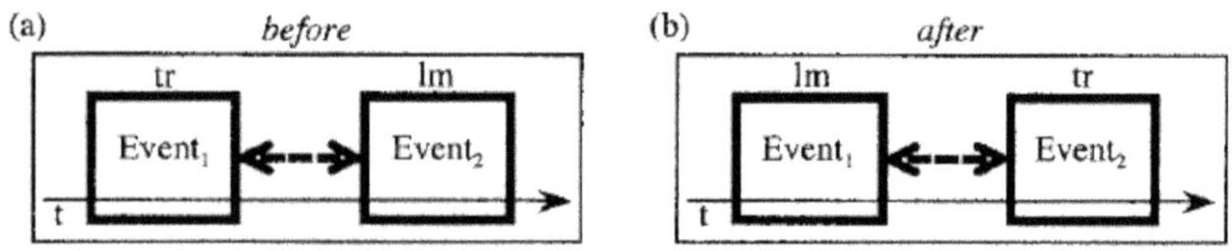

Figure 2-6. Trajector and Landmark of *Before* and *After*.

Perspective

Perspective refers to the viewing arrangement, which is the overall relationship between the *viewers* and the situation being *viewed*. According to Langacker (2008), viewing arrangement is usually in default-case status where interlocutors are in a fixed location and thus is invisible to us. One component of the viewing arrangement is a vantage point, by which Langacker (2008) refers to the actual location of the speaker and hearer. Vantage points play a significant role in construing a situation in that the situation "can be observed and described from any number of different vantage points, resulting in different construals which may have overt consequences" (Langacker 2008: 75).

Another important aspect of perspective is its dynamicity, which concerns how a conceptualization unfolds through processing time. According to Langacker (2008), there is a natural tendency to identify the order in which events are described with the order in which they actually occur, as can be illustrated by the following examples:

(2)
(a) *I quit the job, got married, and had a baby.*
(b) *I had a baby, got married, and quit my job—in reverse order, of course.*

Sentence (2)-(a) would normally be interpreted as indicating that the resignation happened before marriage which then was followed by the birth, although the sentence does not explicitly say this. Sentence (2)-(b) indicates that we can describe events linguistically in a sequence that diverges from their actual order of occurrence. The differences can be illustrated by the following figure (Langacker 2008: 80):

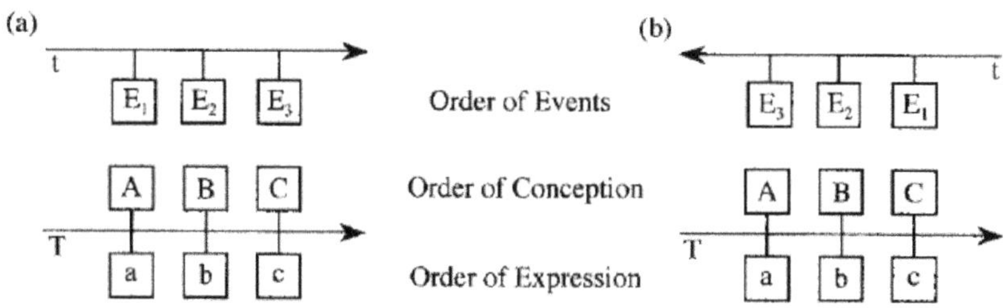

Figure 2-7. Order of Events, Conception and Expression.

Langacker's notion of construal has revealed more diversifying features of conceptualization from comprehensive dimensions. It explains how linguistic expressions reflect our difference in construing the world around us. As is emphasized by Langacker (2008), linguistic difference inheres in our different apprehension of the world, not in the world per se, and ultimately, it is up to the speaker to decide on the choice of linguistic expressions. Therefore, the prominence of an entity "depends on the construal imposed by the linguistic elements employed, in accordance with their conventional semantic values" (Langacker 2008: 80).

Instead of focusing only on the semantic relation between linguistic units, Langacker's theory (2008) has taken such contextual factors as speaker's intention into consideration and conducted the analysis more dynamically. Furthermore, based on one of his fundamental ideas that linguistic units constitute continuity from lexicon to discourse (Langacker 1987, 1991), Langacker's research on construal can be further extended to the study of discourse.

However, although Langacker's theory incorporates contextual factors as important components of discourse analysis, he focuses more on the effects of linguistic context that takes different viewing frames as its components. His explanations of other contextual components such social and cultural factors are too general to be applied to discursive analysis. The notions of information structure and speech management in the concept of viewing frame are defined too broadly and need to be further specified.

Moreover, by claiming that "the speaker and hearer view the profiled process in relation to their own circumstances" (Langacker 2001: 154), Langacker indicates that even for the same usage event taking place in the same viewing frame, the speaker and hearer may form different discourses. However, he fails to investigate the underlying social, psychological or cultural factors that may cause that difference.

Furthermore, for the convenience of analysis, the notion of viewing frame is analyzed within the linguistic unit of clause. This practice, influenced by Chafe (1994) and also embraced by Halliday (Halliday & Matthiessen 2004), seems to be problematic and inadequate when dealing with linguistic units larger than clauses. The following section will be devoted to the review and comment on the relevant approaches to the study of discourse information.

2.1.2 Linguistic Information and Discourse Information

As was discussed in the above section, due to the limitation of cognitive capacity, our attention can only be focused on one small portion of discourse abstracted from a particular usage event. The discussion of viewing frame in discourse processing has inevitably led to the study on how information is defined and presented. In this section of the research, two major approaches to information study – linguistic information and discourse information – will be introduced. The former is represented by the dichotomy of old/new information, and the latter, the discourse information theory.

2.1.2.1 Old Information and New Information

The linguistic study on information was initiated by the Prague School and then was developed by the London School. According to Halliday

(1967), old information refers to the information that the addressor believes is known to the addressee, whereas new information refers to the information that the addressor believes is not known to the addressee.

As for the differentiation between old information and new information, Halliday (1967) follows the Prague School by proposing that intonation is the proper candidate to mark off which information the speaker is treating as new and which information as given (Brown & Yule 1983). Therefore, the organization of information unit relates to how old and new information is distributed by phonological chunks. "With respect to information structure, intonation operates like an on/off switch." (Brown & Yule 1983: 169)

When written texts are examined, the information structure is believed to be manifested in syntactic form, with new information introduced by indefinite expressions and old information referred to by definite expressions (Brown & Yule 1983). This approach has led to the discussion of the meaning of the status "given" and "new", since information status is regarded as "irrevocably assigned by the form of expression used" (Brown & Yule 1983: 177).

Halliday (1967) claims that although syntactic form is the parameter to identify information status, it is speakers who signal what kind of information it is. This idea is challenged by Sanford & Garrod (1981) who claim that information status is neither attributed by the speaker nor by the syntactic form, but evoked by the scenario. Sanford & Garrod's research (1981) has led to the discussion of the structuring of background knowledge and the taxonomy of information status. Abandoning the given/new dichotomy, Prince (1981) provides an extended taxonomy by classifying information into three basic groups: new, inferable and evoked.

Although Halliday (1967) has attributed information status to speakers or writers, he actually suggests that "the 'Given-New' partition can apply to any sentence in a discourse and is signaled both in its syntax and intonation" (Sanford & Garrod 1981: 92). Moreover, Halliday's discussion of background knowledge and taxonomy of information fails to establish an information structure which "can be appealed to in analysis independently of the forms which the speaker produces" (Brown & Yule 1983: 187).

2.1.2.2 Discourse Information Theory

In contrast to the common practice to regard information as a sentence-level notion that corresponds to such sentential constituent as clause, Du (2007, 2012, 2014) defines information as proposition. It is the minimal integral meaningful unit used for communication that has relatively independent complete structure. He further proposes that the process of communication is information processing. In the flow of discourse, information is woven into a network in which information in different parts of discourse relates to each other and bears such relations as primary and secondary, upper and lower, former and latter, etc, which ultimately takes the form of a tree (Du 2007, 2014).

Information Units and Information Knots

According to the discourse information theory (DIT), discourse is composed of information units, each of which acts as the smallest meaningful unit based on a proposition. Information units relate to each other and each develops its immediate subordinate information units from a certain aspect.

(3)
(a) I didn't participate in the discussion.
(b) Firstly, I wasn't mentally equipped.
(c) Secondly, I was unfamiliar with the topic.

The relationship between the three information units (a), (b) and (c) can be described as follows:

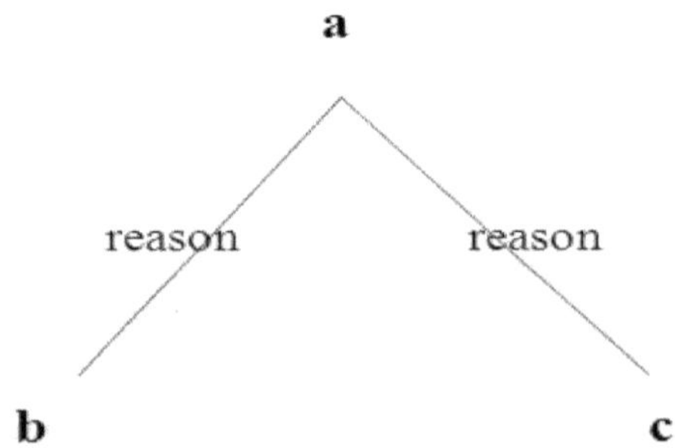

Figure 2-8. Relation of Information Units.

As subordinate information units, (b) and (c) give reasons for (a), which is their immediate superordinate unit. Thus, the relation between information units (a) and (b), and that between (a) and (c) form two information knots of reason, which is represented by WY (why). So an information knot is different from an information unit, in that the former refers to relations between information units whereas the latter designates the content of information. In discourse information theory, there are altogether 16 kinds of information knots to define different relations between information units (Table 2-2).

No.	*Information Knot*	*Abbr.*	*No.*	*Information Knot*	*Abbr.*
1	Kernel Proposition	KN	9	Where	WR
2	What Thing	WT	10	How	HW
3	What Basis	WB	11	Why	WY
4	What Fact	WF	12	What Effect	WE
5	What Inference	WI	13	What Condition	WC
6	What Disposal	WP	14	What Attitude	WA
7	Who	WO	15	What Change	WG
8	When	WN	16	What Judgment	WJ

Table 2-2. Types of Information Knots.

Information Sharing Categories

Du (2014) has proposed a classification of six information sharing categories for the convenience of discourse analysis. These information sharing categories are classified according to whether participants of discourse know the information, as shown in the following table:

Context	*Categories*	*Notes*
Monolog	A, B, C, E, O, D	A: known to A, but not B B: known to B, but not A C: known to both A and B E: unknown to both A and B O: known to everyone present D: known to be disputable
Question	a, b, c, e, o, d	From left to right corresponding to knowledge categories in monolog
Dialogue	R, S, T, Y, Z, U	From left to right corresponding to knowledge categories in monolog

Table 2-3. Information Sharing Categories.

By defining information as proposition, the discourse information theory (Du 2007, 2012, 2014) regards information as the basic constituent of discourse, and thus establishes information as the basic unit of discourse analysis. Furthermore, by defining such notions as information unit and information knot, the discourse information theory assigns discourse information with a hierarchical structure, which is more flexible for discourse analysis compared with the notions of clause and sentence.

More importantly, the discourse information theory has extended the study of discourse to the level of cognition by classifying discourse information into different information sharing categories. It reveals that the cognitive status of information is a very important factor that may influence communications between speakers and hearers, and thus should be taken into consideration during our analysis of discourse.

2.1.3 Context in Discourse Analysis

2.1.3.1 Context in Functional Grammar

In discourse analysis, the notion of context has attracted a lot of attention and has been elaborated from different perspectives. Van Dijk stresses that "discourse analysis and conversation analysis need to make explicit what contexts are and how exactly the relations between contexts and text or talk are to be analyzed in ways that explain how language users do this" (2008: 3).

The traditional approach to context assumes a direct relationship between the environment of text and talk, on the one hand, and the structures of discourse itself, on the other. For example, Systemic Functional Linguistics (SFL) emphasizes the social nature of language and claims that language use is an integral part of the experience of the members of a society and culture (Halliday 1978). The most important notion of context in SFL is register. It is further analyzed into a triad that includes field, tenor and mode, with field referring to institutional setting, activities, subject matter, tenor referring to relations between participants, and mode, medium and the role of language in the situation (Halliday & Matthiessen 2004: 27).

SFL has revealed the close relationship between language use and society, and thus extended the study of language from structuralism in which language is regarded as an isolated and autonomous entity to functionalism in which language use is taken as closely related to social context (Nuyts 2007). However, the concept of context in SFL is only a general classification of its possible components. It fails to consider the underlying mechanism of how context really functions and how these potential components of context are connected with the production and comprehension of discourse.

As a result, by attributing a direct relation between discourse and the environment where discourse is produced and consumed, SFL reduces context to *objective* and *observable* properties of situations (van Dijk 2008). Moreover, although SFL includes participants as one of the components of context, it refuses to consider the function of cognitive factors in abstracting, interpreting and constructing context. Halliday suggests that: "Language is part of the social system, and there is no need to interpose a psychological level of interpretation" (1978: 39).

Therefore, the notion of context in SFL is more or less a product of social empiricism that prevents a serious explanation of how elements of social situations can possibly affect the production or comprehension of discourse, thus totally disregarding the problem of the mediation between society and language use (van Dijk 2008: 37).

2.1.3.2 Context as Participant Construct

Apart from SFL's definition of register, more and more researchers have noticed the dynamic features of context. For example, Martin (1985) defines context as a situation that is constantly changing. But he does not account for where such dynamics come from. Van Dijk (2006) emphasizes the important role of participants in context construction by proposing that context should be non-deterministic and allow speakers in the same situation to speak in different ways. He refuses to treat contexts as objective or deterministic constraints of society or culture and instead defines contexts as "subjective participant interpretations, constructions or definitions of such aspects of the social environment" (van Dijk 2006: 163). Van Dijk (2008: 44) also elaborates his considerations for defining context as participant construct:

> Only when language users are able to represent social conditions of the situation in a personal way (for instance, in their mental models of the communicative situation), are they able to adapt to the social situation as they wish, following the norms or not, and in their own way--and it is for this reason that not all language users in the same situation speak exactly in the same way even when they have the same social characteristics.

Van Dijk's definition of context emphasizes the fact that the production or comprehension of discourse is not controlled directly by such objective factors as gender, ethnicity or power but by participants themselves, because it is participants who interpret, represent and make use of such external constraints.

More importantly, by defining context as participant construct and emphasizing the cognitive power of discourse participants, van Dijk's notion of context echoes with Langacker's cognitive approach in discourse analysis in which the role of the speaker and hearer is also highlighted.

2.1.4 Discourse Management Model

Discourse production and comprehension involve a complex range of both linguistic and non-linguistic processes. Among those researches that have been contributed to the study of discourse processing (Levelt 1989, Lambrecht 1994, Tomlin et al. 1997), Tomlin et al. (1997), based on the relevant studies on information flow carried out by Chafe (1979, 1980, 1987, 1994), has summarized a comprehensive model of discourse management.

Tomlin et al. embraces the basic idea of cognitive linguistics that discourse is the result of "some sort of conceptual representation of the subject matter under discussion" (1997: 68). The conceptual representation, most of the time in form of propositions, provides the fundamental meaning for the speaker in constructing a discourse. However, the conceptual representation itself is not the meaning of discourse, because before the final outcome of discourse the speaker must select information from the overall conceptual representation and build a discourse out of that selected information.

As a consequence, how the speaker manages information plays a crucial role in discourse production and comprehension. According to Tomlin et al. (1997), discourse management involves four threads: rhetorical management, thematic management, referential management, and focus management.

Rhetorical management mainly concerns the goals and intentions of the discourse interaction, which can be analyzed on both macro and micro levels. The realization of goals and intentions of discourse interaction is not only dependent on its propositional content but also dependent on the global linguistic structures or discourse organization as well.

Thematic management is concerned with "how the speaker lets the listener know what information is more central to the discourse" (Tomlin et al. 1997: 93). The underlying reason for thematic management is that, for the speaker or hearer, certain concepts or propositions are more central or important to the development of the discourse.

The key insight within referential management is that certain concepts are presumed to be held in common by both the speaker and hearer, while other concepts are not. Therefore, referential management is closely related to knowledge status because it is on the basis of knowledge status that the speaker chooses to use referential expressions or not.

In contrast to thematic management which concerns the prominence of information at discourse level, focus management involves prominence of information elements, in that it is concerned with how the speaker lets the hearer know what in particular should be noticed about the central information.

The discourse management model proposed by Tomlin et al. provides a comprehensive framework for the analysis of discourse processing at both micro and macro levels. More importantly, by taking information as its basic unit of discourse processing, this model makes it more operational in doing discourse analysis. Last but not least, by taking into account the knowledge status in referential management, this model helps to reveal the underlying cognitive activities in discourse management.

2.2 Studies on Courtroom Discourse

As was mentioned in Chapter 1, under the influence of jurisprudence of interests and legal realism, law is no longer characterized as an autonomous system of rules and principles that courts can logically apply in an objective fashion to reach judicial decisions (Bodenheimer 1962). Rather, the adjudication is an inherently subjective system which is largely based on the political, social, and moral predilections of judges (Simon 2001). Therefore, the social conditions and their influences on the making and application of law have become a focus of study ever since.

The shift of epistemology in jurisprudence leads to the emergence of the study of courtroom discourse, which involves a variety of social factors. Courtroom discourse is regarded as unique because it is an intersection between legal issues and the use of language (Coulthard & Johnson 2007). Accordingly, courtroom discourse is defined as a typical type of institutional discourse with distinct communicative features under the influence of judicial functions and social culture (Ge 2011).

According to Levi & Walker (1990), there are three orientations in the study of courtroom discourse. The first is to take language as the primary focus of research while considering the complex world of the law as a context where patterns of linguistic organization and use are explored. The second takes language as an instrument for understanding the legal system rather than the object of inquiry. The third emphasizes society, culture or human psychology through the study of human language in the context of the law. Whichever orientation is adopted, the study of the language in courtroom activities is essential to achieve a better understanding of the judicial process, in that "language is the vehicle by means of which law is transmitted, interpreted, and executed in all cultures" (Levi & Walker 1990: 4).

In this section, I will introduce the major areas where analytic attention has been focused in the study of courtroom discourse.

2.2.1 *Sociological Research on Courtroom Discourse*

2.2.1.1 *Language in Evidence*

The study of courtroom discourse was initiated with the need of expertise that can help to solve the legal issues where language is used as evidence (Gibbons 2003). In recent years, a lot of linguistic research has been conducted with their findings used in court to prove or disprove a specific fact which is important to the outcome of a case (Levi & Walker 1990).

Based on the analysis of tape-recorded social conversations, Green (1990) has proposed theoretically that linguistic analysis of conversation does qualify as a proper subject of expert testimony. According to Green (1990), expert witness can help to examine both the forms and content of discourse in order to interpret conversations introduced into evidence, since the discourse behavior reflects the attitudes, beliefs, and agendas of speakers. Prince (1990), on the other hand, while approving of the feasibility and reliability of addressing legal issues on the basis of expert testimony, points out the severe legal consequences of unskilled transcription of recorded talk or uninformed interpretation of how social conversation works.

Green (1990) and Prince (1990) are two of the initiators who apply the achievements of conversation analysis to the investigation of courtroom discourse and demonstrate that social conversations are qualified as evidence of speakers' intentions under careful examination (Levi & Walker 1990: xviii). Following that, a great number of forensic linguists (e.g. Shuy 1993, Eades 1997, Jensen 1995, Coulthard & Johnson 2007) have contributed to the investigation of expert testimony in the courtroom context.

In court hearings, eyewitness testimony is another important variable that may change the outcome of litigation. Earlier research (e.g. Munsterberg 1908, Brigham 1981, Brigham & Wolfskeil 1983, Wells & Loftus 1984) has mainly been concerned with eyewitness identification.

Based on the research of experimental psychology, especially achievements in human perception and memory, Loftus (1996) has developed a theoretical framework that views eyewitness testimony in terms of a three-stage process: acquisition where an event is perceived and information about it is initially stored in memory; retention where information is resident in memory; and retrieval where memory is searched and pertinent information is retrieved and communicated.

The findings of Loftus (1996) have proved that language can play a very important role in affecting the memory of eyewitness especially during stage one and stage two (Gibbons 2003). More importantly, Loftus (1996) has contributed to the study of witness testimony by integrating a variety of psychological factors that may influence the reliability of the testimony (Gibbons 2003). "The work by Loftus and others on the psychology of eyewitness memory has important potential application to legal practitioners and to psycholinguists alike." (Levi 1990: 16)

Another empirical research has been conducted by Sun (2013), who, based on Jef Verschueren's theory of linguistic adaptation, Labov's narrative theory, and Gibbons' genre structure for police interviews, has investigated the structure and nature of witness statements and examined the main factors which influence the accuracy of witness statements in Chinese criminal cases.

2.2.1.2 Narratives and Narrative Structure

The pioneering study of trial as narrative or storytelling was initiated by Bennett & Feldman (1981), who propose that "in a criminal trial a jury interprets the evidence presented to it from the opposing sides and constructs a story" (see Maley 1994: 34). Maynard (1984: 1) makes the same claim that attorneys often present facts by telling stories about "what happened". Maynard (1990: 66) makes it more clearly what significant role narratives play in cour hearings:

> The claim is not that narrative structure is itself a casual "variable" that explains bargaining outcomes. Rather, through narratives and narrative structure, as elements of a robust and impermeable interaction order, participants bring to life such factors as the law, organizational "roles", and even the identity of a defendant, as part of mundane negotiational discourse. It is through narrative that actors make decisions and effect "outcomes".

According to the research done by Bennett & Feldman (1981), the jury makes its verdict based on whose story is most convincing, in terms of its completeness, consistency and the credibility of supporting witnesses. Similarly, Jackson (1991) proposes that narrative has three crucial elements: temporality/sequence, action/purpose, and intelligibility/experience. Another important framework of narrative structure is from Maynard (1990), who, after analyzing 10 hours of recording in 52 cases, has constructed a narrative structure of courtroom plea bargaining which consists of three components: story entry devices by which participants warrant the telling of a story, the story itself, and a defense segment usually in the form of denial or excuse. Jacquemet (1996) analyzes the narrative structure in Italian courtroom and notes that judges usually follow three fundamental factors in deciding the credibility of informers: consistency, good knowledge of details, and ability to provide contextual embedding for their testimony.

O'Barr & Conley (1990) investigate how the informality of small claims court procedures affects the ways in which litigants tell their stories. They (1990: 129) have made important findings about narrative structures and their influence on the legal adequacy of the testimony:

> Small claim courts, operating without the formalities of the rules of evidence, do indeed allow accounts to be given in a relatively unconstrained manner so that people generally feel that these courts allow them the storytelling opportunity denied in more formal courts. However, a new and potentially more serious problem emerges when plaintiffs fail to give accounts that deal adequately with issues of blame, responsibility, and agency and to present them in a deductive framework that the court can test against the evidence presented.

O'Barr & Conley's study (1990), by examining the narratives for elements of internal structure and comparing them to standards for legally adequate narratives, has broadened to add the legal to the linguistic approach (Levi & Walker 1990: xvi).

Another detailed theoretical study of narrative in court comes from Amsterdam & Bruner (2000), who, after discussing the two main theories of narrative, namely, the endogenous approach that regards narrative as inherent in the nature of human mind, and the plight-modeling approach that regards narrative as culture-driven, focus on the indispensability of narrative for law. Amsterdam & Bruner's study (2000) reveals the lawyers' strong desire to argue for their clients by presenting his version of story which results in a vivid picture of information chains and chunks in the minds of the courtroom participants.

Gibbons (2003) focuses on the role of genre when discussing trial as narrative. He argues that genre structures underlie both the realities that are in constant interaction in the legal process and the secondary reality that is the reason for the legal process, including crimes and disputed events. He then constructs a framework to display the relationship between the primary reality, the secondary reality and the legal frame. Gibbons' framework (2003) contributes to a deeper understanding and conceptualization of legal processes and legal discourse.

2.2.1.3 Language and Power in Court Hearings

Another significant issue in the study of courtroom discourse is the relation between language and power, or how power and authority are exercised through language. According to Gibbons (2003: 75), "the justice system is arguably the most directly powerful institution in societies subject to 'the rule of law' [...] An important manifestation of power relations is language behavior".

Earlier studies on the relation between language and power were conducted from an empirical perspective. Conley et al. (1978) are the initiators to notice the powerful influence of language in the legal process. Their comparison of *power* versus *powerless* language demonstrates that the distinction of modes of speech can have significant influence on the reactions of subjects to testimony, even when the apparent substance of the testimony is held constant (Levi & Walker 1990: ix). Drew (1990) has investigated the power distribution in cross-examination and demonstrated how patterns of asking questions may be adopted to diminish the credibility of witness testimony in court. Berk-seligson (1990) focuses on the role of interpreter in bilingual court proceedings and has discovered that "the presence of an interpreter creates powerful effects not present in monolingual litigation [...] [and] the neutrality of the interpreter, which is assumed by courts, is rejected by the study" (Levi & Walker 1990: x).

In recent years, however, the majority of research into language and power has assumed a critical orientation and "has resulted in findings which both identify and exemplify the role of language in the creation and maintenance of institutionalized power and asymmetry" (Cotterill 2003: 7). Wodak (1985) has investigated judge-defendant discourse and argued that the power in the form of socio-economic variables appear to influence the outcomes of the defendant's interactions with the judge.

Greatly influenced by Systemic Functional Linguistics, the critical orientation in the investigation of language and power has often been integrated with lexico-grammatical analysis. Harris (1989, 1994) examines the judicial discourse in UK magistrate's courts and finds that judges can express their ideological stance through such lexico-grammatical mechanisms as mood and modality choices. Conley & O'Barr (1998) in *Just Words: Law, Language and Power* also investigate the linguistic strategies of the judge and demonstrate the close relationship between linguistic choice and power. Conley & O'Barr's contribution (1998) "sets out to show how close linguistic analysis of legal language can help to illuminate broader social inequities" (Cotterill 2003: 8). Gibbons (2003: 88) summarizes the linguistic indicators of power in courtroom discourse by classifying them into two groups: powerful attributes and less powerful ones. The former includes such variables as interrupting, loudness, fluency, coherence, etc, and the latter, hedges, uncertainty, intensifiers, mitigation, etc.

2.2.2 Courtroom Discourse from Cognitive Psychology

The last few decades have witnessed a marked increase in the degree of interest and involvement in the legal process on the part of cognitive psychologists (Johnson 1990: 291). The methods and concepts used in the disciplines of psychology and law have been integrated (Foley 1993: 25).

As early as in 1906, Sigmund Freud (see Foley 1993: 3) first proposed that psychology could assist the legal system in delving into the truthfulness of reported events. In 1908, Munsterberg published his book *On the Witness Stand*, which discussed psychological factors that can affect the outcome of a trial. He questioned the accuracy of witness testimony and argued that witnesses are prone to suggestions. After that, psychologists were encouraged to extend their research to address real life concerns to reveal the effects of legal process on society. Therefore, law, psychology and society are integrated as a multi-disciplinary study. Tapp (1977: 3) has concluded three overriding themes for this new perspective: the union of psychology and law can promote justice and science; psychology can and has offered ways of systematically documenting a social-legal and psychological event; and the phenomena of both psychology and law require new views of science and society.

However, the earlier investigation of the relationship between psychology, law and society is of behavioral and experimental characteristics (Kapardis 2010). It was not until the 1970s that such cognitive concepts as perception, memory, problem solving and language were introduced to the study of law (see Kapardis 2010: 6). Brewer & Williams (2005) has summarized the recent developments of cognitive research into judicial process, which include such topics as interviewing of witness, testimony and memories of eyewitness, deception detection, decision making of jurors, and comprehension of judicial instructions, etc. The contributions included in Brewer & Williams (2005: 1) have illustrated how theoretical advances in psychology can provide valuable directions for applied research which in turn "can be used to make meaningful contributions to the solution of everyday or real-world problems".

Du (2008) has constructed an interactive cognitive model for judicial discourse on the basis of which the features of implicit persuasion in legal discourse has been examined. Du (2008) finds that implicit persuasion can be realized in such discourse features as evaluation, hedging, presupposition, intertextuality and conversation implicature. Du's study (2008) reveals the cognitive, interactive and discursive features of court hearings. And more importantly, it suggests that the application of cognitive research into judicial process is complementary and comparable to linguistic analysis.

In the same vein, Chen (2011), Xu (2013) and Li (2013) contribute to the solution of legal problems in court hearings by revealing the cognitive process underlying the linguistic activities.

2.2.3 Corpus Research on Courtroom Discourse

The study of language in the judicial process benefits greatly from two major developments. The first one is the development in theories of linguistics, especially the breakthrough of studying language in the real-life contexts rather than as a formal and self-contained system. The second is the development and increased accessibility of sophisticated recording techniques, both audio and video, as is put by Levi (1990: 10):

> These technological developments have tremendously enhanced the ability of language scientists to perform quite complex multidimensional microanalysis of linguistic behavior (in legal settings as well as elsewhere) and to have their primary data remain accessible to colleagues for potential replication and verification of their findings.

Prince (1990) has investigated the problems of data mistranscribing that exist in the FBI when social conversation is used as evidence in a court of law, and has found that although tapes are played for the jury, "jurors rely entirely on the transcripts in front of them and would virtually never notice any discrepancy between the tape and the transcript" (1990: 282). Inconsistency also exists when social or courtroom conversation is analyzed to reveal the legal fact behind it. Therefore, it is of great necessity to investigate "how to listen to speech, how to transcribe it, and how to interpret it [...] [following] basic linguistic and sociolinguistic principles of how social conversations work and of how individuals interact verbally" (1990: 289).

Although the past few decades have seen a rapid development in corpus linguistics (e.g. Sinclair 1991, Biber et al. 1998, Kennedy 1998, Gries 2003), a systemic corpus study of courtroom discourse is still in its infancy. Onesti & Ge (2012) have introduced the construction of an Italian legal corpus, which consists of three subcorpora: regulative, judicial, and parliamentary. One peculiarity of the corpus is that the data are POS-tagged to retrieve part-of-speech information based on the Corpus Query Processor. Another peculiarity is the manual textual markup to reveal the macrostructure of the discourse. Onesti & Ge's research (2012) is a tentative study on the construction of legal corpus and is enlightening in the approach to take care of both the lexical and discursive analysis of the data. However, although the corpus includes a judicial section, the dada collected are mainly such written documents as judgments, which are far from adequate to reveal the dynamic feature of courtroom interaction. Moreover, the tagging device it employs only focuses on part of speech of specific words and such macrostructure as "title", "body", "motivation", etc. which may, as it claims, offer some instruction to legal translation, but fails to reveal the hierarchy of discourse structure and the mechanism of information flow and distribution.

The theoretical framework, *the Tree Information Structure Model* (see section 2.1.2.2) constructed by Du (2007, 2012, 2014), has filled up the deficiency in discourse information study both at home and abroad. Following the Tree Information Structure Model, other relative models such as information flow, information elements, information processing etc. can be further developed and applied in the analysis of courtroom discourse.

Based on the theoretical models developed by Du (2007, 2012, 2014), a Corpus for the Legal Information Processing System (CLIPS) has been constructed and put into operation in the past few years. CLIPS covers a comprehensive range of legal data such as legislative texts, judicial discourse, legal language teaching material, etc. The most prominent feature of CLIPS is its attention to courtroom interaction and its way of tagging.

Besides the comprehensive coverage of legal materials in CLIPS, the tagging of discourse has centered on information which is regarded as the basis of discourse processing and discourse analysis (Du 2014). In addition to that, the tagging reveals very valuable information about social conditions of information units, such as information source, knowledge type, etc. More importantly, the tagging displays the hierarchical relationship of information units and therefore is very convenient for discourse analysis since it demonstrates how information flows from one level to another and enhances our understanding of information processing and discourse production.

In this section, I have reviewed the recent developments in the study on courtroom discourse. Under the influence of legal realism, studies on courtroom discourse have paid increasing attention to such social conditions that influence the application of law, among which language is of particular importance. Besides, since court hearing is a process that involves participants of different interests, the judicial outcome is inevitably influenced by their psychological activities. For that consideration, the achievements in cognitive psychology have been applied to the analysis of court hearings.

As a result, such familiar topics as narration, witness testimony, deception, etc. have received new explanations that either deepen or challenge our previous understandings of courtroom discourse. These studies reveal a more close relationship between law, language, society and cognition.

2.3 Summary

This chapter has introduced the relevant theories and notions of discourse analysis, among which the cognitive approach to discourse analysis, the discourse information theory, the notion of context and the discourse management model have been explained in details. The relevant studies on courtroom discourse have also been reviewed, which help us understand how researches on such topics as evidence, power in court hearings, etc. are conducted linguistically.

The theories of discourse analysis and studies on courtroom discourse can help us to have a better understanding of the dynamic features and mechanism of discourse in the legal context. In the folllowing chapter, I will construct the analytical framework for the analysis of the resolution of COI in the Chinese courtroom context.

3 Theoretical Framework and Methodology

This chapter is devoted to the construction of the theoretical framework for the study. Based on the previous discussions on discourse analysis and studies on courtroom discourse, I will first introduce the theoretical background of the present research. Then, by integrating the concepts and relevant theories in discourse analysis, I will construct an operable theoretical framework that will be applied to the resolution of COI in Chinese civil court hearings.

3.1 Theoretical Background

3.1.1 The Tree Information Structure Model

Information refers to the minimal integral meaningful unit used for communication that has relatively independent complete structure (Du 2007, 2014). It is regarded as the direct outcome of cognition, on the basis of which discourse is managed and produced.

According to Du (2007, 2014), discourse information is a hierarchical network which centers on a kernel proposition (KN), which is further developed by detailed information at subordinate levels. Therefore, discourse information network can be described as a tree structure, as is shown by the following figure.

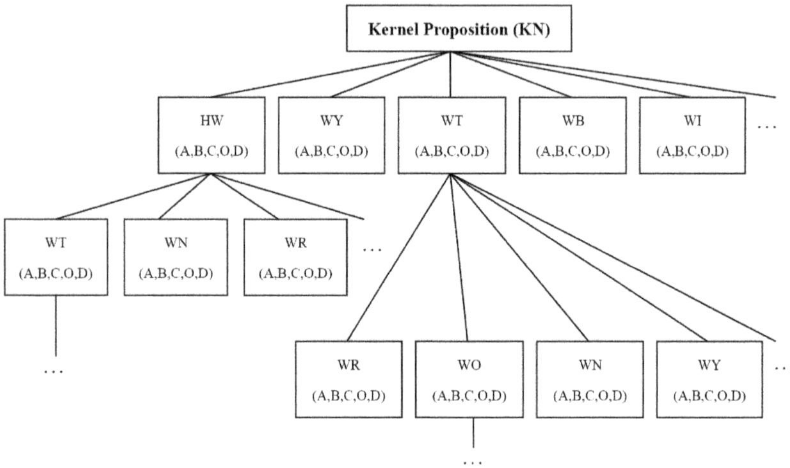

Figure 3-1. Tree Information Structure of Legal Discourse (Du 2007: 43)

Note: HW (how), WY (why), WT (what thing), WB (what basis), WI (what inference), WN (when), WR (where) and WO (who) are information knots (see Table 2–2). A, B, C, O and D refer to information sharing categories (see Table 2-3).

In Figure 3-1, the kernel proposition is the nucleus of discourse, which is usually the topic of discourse. Kernel proposition is developed by information units below, which may be further developed by information units at the next lower levels. The lines that link the kernel information with information units at the lower levels represent their relationships, which are termed as information knots.

With information processing being one of the prominent features of courtroom interaction (Du 2009b), the Tree Information Structure Model can help reveal more of the dynamic nature of Chinese civil court hearings. Besides, other basic DIT notions like information unit, information knot, information element, information flow, information sharing category and their applications (e.g. Zhao 2011, Chen 2011, Xu 2013, Li 2013, Du 2012) in the analysis of courtroom interactions have enriched and developed information as an independent level on which discourse can be analyzed and processed.

3.1.2 Conceptualization

Based on the CDS theory and the notion of viewing frame (see section 2.1.1), Langacker (2001) proposes the notion of conceptualization, which refers to the result of cognition. Conceptualization consists of three layers: objective situation, information structure and speech management.

Objective situation, also called conceptual content, refers to the concrete or substantive concept that is formed based on the communicative event that speakers are engaged in (Langacker 2001). Information structure in conceptualization is defined more broadly by Langacker (2001, 2008) as given/new information, which is adequate in analyzing such linguistic unit as clause, but is obviously insufficient in investigating units larger than that. As mentioned above, the Tree Information Structure Model provides a more applicable tool to analyze such larger linguistic units as courtroom discourse. Speech management is defined by Langacker (2001, 2008) as consisting of turn taking and floor holding. But it does not have a comprehensive coverage of speech management strategies used in discourse production. The discourse management model (see Section 2.1.4) proposed by Tomlin et al. (1997) provides a more comprehensive framework for analyzing discourse processing at both micro and macro levels.

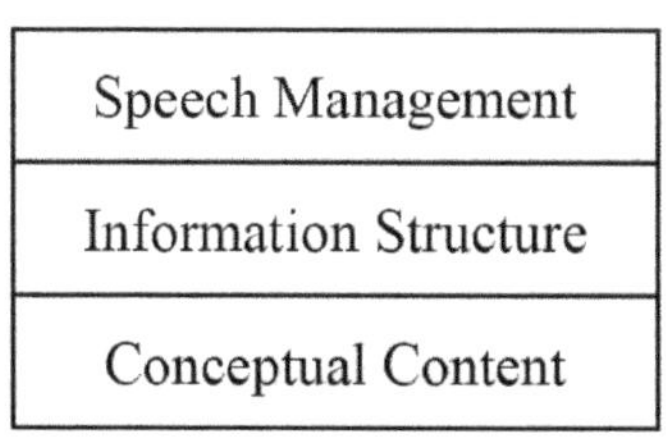

Figure 3-2. Conceptualization.

Since courtroom activities are entirely conceptual in nature (Brewer & Williams 2005), conceptualization can help to reveal how participants in lawsuits resolve their COI on the layers of conceptual content, information structure and speech management and thus can facilitate our understanding of how court hearings are constructed by participants through language.

3.1.3 Context Model Schema

Conceptualization is formed on the basis of context, which is the circumstances where a communicative event takes place (Langacker 2001, 2008). Based on the idea that context is a socially based but subjective construct of participants (see Section 2.1.3.2), van Dijk (2008) develops a theory of context model which is assumed to control the production and comprehension of discourse. As explained by van Dijk (2008: 59), "as well as talking about events, language users also need to model themselves and other aspects of communicative situation in which they are currently engaged". Therefore, context models have become the important interface that connects mental models of events and the discourses about such events. In this way, "context models organize the ways our discourse is strategically structured and adapted to the whole communicative situation" (van Dijk 2008: 71).

On the basis of the definition of context as participant construct and earlier studies on context categories, van Dijk (2008: 76) proposes the following context model schema:

- Setting: Time/Period, Space/Place/Environment;
- Participants (self, others):
  communicative roles (participation structure);
  social roles types, membership or identities;
  relations between participants (e.g. power relationship);
  shared and social knowledge and beliefs;
  intentions and goals;
- Communicative and other Actions/Events

The context model schema places participants at the center of context and highlights the cognitive characteristic of context construction. In other words, context models are crucially egocentric, with *self* being the central and orienting category in that it organizes the relations between participants and is responsible for the construal of other categories such as knowledge, goals, etc. (van Dijk 2008: 77).

The context model schema can contribute to the analysis of courtroom discourse since participants in lawsuits would place their own interests at the center of litigation and organize their language accordingly. More importantly, taking a socio-cognitive perspective, the context model schema has focused more on the social dimension in clarifying the context categories, thus providing a solid social basis for the analysis of resolution of COI in court hearings.

3.1.4 Construal Phenomena

As a participant construct, the context model is the result of speakers' cognition and is therefore closely related to their construal phenomena. Langacker (2008) identifies four basic construal phenomena: specificity, focusing, prominence and perspective.

Specificity is used in opposition to schematicity and can help to define the level of precision or detail at which a situation is characterized. Focusing distinguishes between foreground and background and can help to decide what conceptual content may appear in the subjective viewing frame. Prominence highlights the difference between trajector and landmark, which can profile the relationship between participants and imply different meanings. Perspective refers to the viewing arrangement between *viewers* and the situation being *viewed*, which can be analyzed on the dimensions of location and time.

By highlighting the differences in how we understand the world around us, the notions of construal phenomena provide a cognitive basis for the construction of context model and the processing of discourse information, and thus can be regarded as the fundamental layer in the production and comprehension of discourse.

Moreover, the notions of construal phenomena can help us understand how participants in lawsuits, driven by different appeals of interest, may construct different context models and form conflicting conceptualizations of the same incident that leads to the litigation.

3.2 Theoretical Framework

Based on the theories and notions elaborated above, the relationship between construal phenomena, context model schema and conceptualization can be illustrated by Figure 3-3.

According to the figure, discourse analysis can be analyzed into three layers: construal, context model schema, and conceptualization. Construal is at the deepest level of human cognition and is responsible for what perceptions we form of the world around us and how we perceive the same world in different ways. Context model schema is the first cognitive outcome of construal which is formed as a result of the speaker or writer's construction of the ongoing communicative situation (van Dijk 2008: 103). On the basis of construal and influenced by context model schema, conceptualizations are finally constructed which usually take the form of spoken or written discourses.

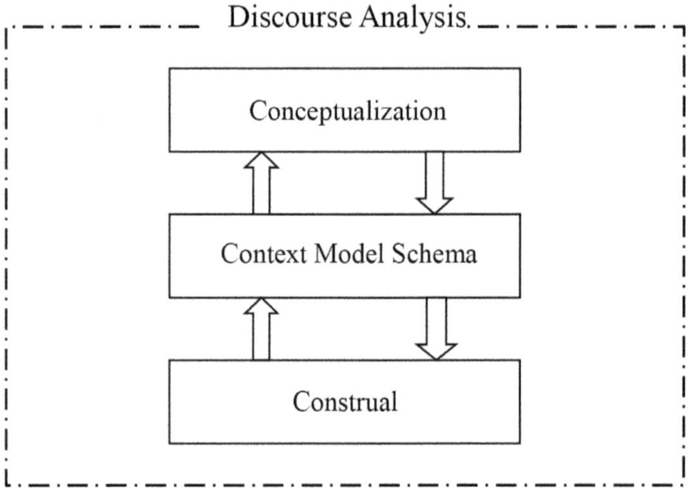

Figure 3-3. Theoretical Framework.

As indicated by the looping arrows, the tree layers in discourse analysis are interdependent of each other. It means that conceptualization may become part of context model schema which in turn imposes influence on speakers' construal phenomena.

The nucleus of this theoretical framework is that discourse, as one of the major forms of human activities, is the outer manifestation of human cognition in that the expressions in discourse conform to their cognitive structures in human mind (Langacker 2001, 2008).

3.3 Analytical Framework

Under the guidance of the theoretical framework constructed above, and considering the fact that court hearings take resolution of COI as their most fundamental goal (Xia & Shi 2006, Du 2009b), in this section I will develop the analytical framework for this study.

The analytical framework is made up of four levels. The first level is resolution of COI, the fundamental goal of court hearings. The second level is conceptualization, which consists of three components: conceptual content, information structure and speech management. The third level is context model schema, which includes participants, setting, discourse space and knowledge status. The fourth level is construal phenomena, which can be analyzed into specificity, focusing, prominence and perspective. The downward arrows show further analysis based on the analytical tools at the levels of discourse, information and cognition. The upward arrows indicate that the result of the analysis at the three levels eventually float up to the first level to the legal problem (see Figure 3-4).

In Figure 3-4, the first level is the core dimension of solving the legal problem: COI and its resolution. It is the starting point of the analysis since the production of courtroom discourse and processing of information all center on participants' efforts to solve disputes. It is also the terminal stage since this study aims to reveal the process of how COI is resolved based on the multi-dimensional analysis of courtroom discourse.

Court hearings can be analyzed into three basic stages (Xia & Shi 2006, Du 2009b): interest appeal, interest negotiation, and agreement reaching. Interest appeal is the most fundamental stage where litigants express their basic positions or attitudes in lawsuits (Du 2009b).

Interest negotiation is mainly carried out under the guidance of judges, and mainly takes place at two axes: the horizontal axis and the vertical axis (Xia & Shi 2006). The former refers to negotiation between opposing parties; and the latter refers to negotiation between judges and litigants.

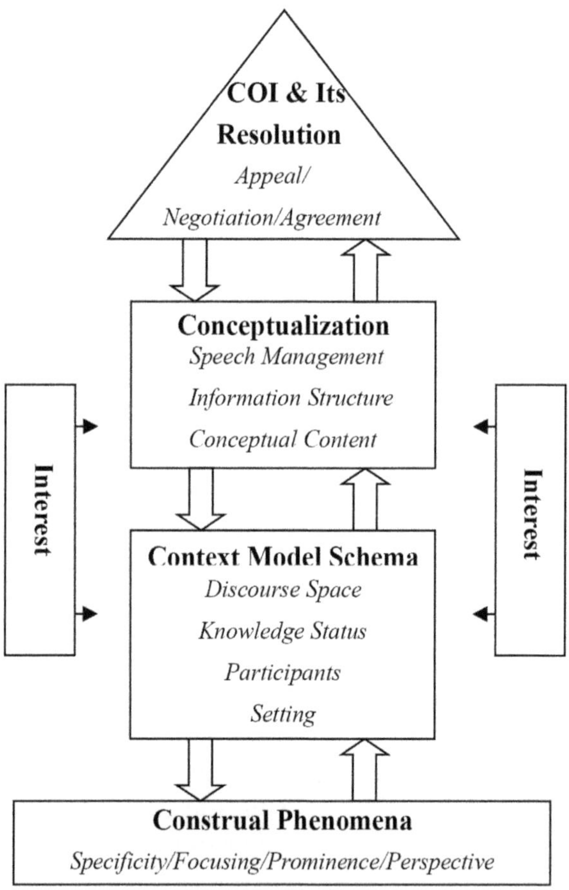

Figure 3-4. Analytical Framework for Resolution of COI.

The third stage of court hearings is, on the basis of interest appeal and interest negotiation, to arrive at agreement between opposing parties. According to Xia & Shi (2006), court hearing is a process, which, by adjusting litigants' inconsistency in their expectations of each other's behaviors, reformulates a relationship that is satisfactory to both sides. With the development of negotiation of interests, the divergence between the two opposing parties is being diminished and a certain kind of agreement is arrived at, which may take forms of conciliation or judgment (Xia & Shi 2006). With judgment, although an ultimate agreement fails to be reached as in conciliation, it has already included some compromise in fact-finding and consensus in the application of law, which are the direct results of court hearings.

The second level of the diagram, namely, conceptualization, has three components. Conceptual content is the general idea or basic position litigants adopt in the lawsuit. It is the primary result of cognition on the basis of which information structure and discourse are formulated and produced. Information structure is analyzed into information units, information knots, information elements, and tree information structure. How information flows is also examined in order to reveal the development of courtroom discourse. Speech management mainly concerns language strategies, which, apart from the cognitive management and information management, includes the discourse management strategies summarized by Tomlin et al. (1997), namely, rhetorical management, thematic management and referential management.

The third level, context model, is the environment from which the three components of the second level are generated. Context model is analyzed into four components: participants, setting, discourse space and knowledge status. Participants are treated as the nucleus factor since context model, as a mental construct, is established by the collaborate effort of litigants and judges. Participants can be further analyzed into four subcategories: identities, social relations, participants' behaviors and the related intentions/goals in the behaviors. Setting is mainly concerned with the physical and social environment of court hearings, with the former being analyzed into temporal and spatial settings and the latter, cultural, institutional and evidential settings. Knowledge status can be analyzed into information shared among participants and information source. Discourse space refers to the linguistic context of the communicative event, which is mainly concerned with how things that have already been talked about or will be talked about influence the ongoing discourse.

The fourth level is concerned with different construal phenomena, which include specificity, prominence, focusing and perspective. They are the fundamental abilities all cognitive activities are based on.

In this analytical framework, there is one factor that runs through all the levels discussed, namely, interest, which is highlighted at the two sides of the diagram. It is based on the difference of interest that construal phenomena are selected, context model constructed and conceptualization generated.

The three stages of court hearings – interest appeal, interest negotiation, and agreement reaching – are examined respectively to find out how they are realized on the three levels of discourse analysis.

The diagram of the analytical framework is very similar in appearance to a rocket, with resolution of COI at the top of the diagram being like a satellite or spacecraft to be launched. The second and third levels are like a multistage rocket with interest at both sides as rocket boosters, which is used to send the satellite or spacecraft into space, metaphorically referring to the solution of the legal problem. The fourth level, the basic cognitive abilities, is the platform on which the rocket is launched. So the analytical framework can be metaphorically named the "rocket model".

3.4 Research Methodology

In virtue of the analytical framework constructed in the preceding section, this study is to carry out a corpus-based qualitative analysis of how COI is resolved in Chinese civil court hearings. In this section, I will introduce the general considerations of the analysis, how data are collected and in particular how data are analyzed to fulfill the research objective of the study.

3.4.1 General Considerations of Analysis

According to the analytical framework, the resolution of COI in court hearings consists of three stages: interest appeal, interest negotiation and agreement reaching. Interest appeal is the preliminary stage where participants in lawsuits express their basic positions or attitudes towards the infringements that lead to the litigation. While giving consideration to all the three layers in the theoretical framework, I mainly focus on the analysis of features of discourse information in litigants' interest appeal, including information knots, content of information units and their distribution, combination and development.

On the basis of litigants' expression of their positions in interest appeal, interest negotiation is conducted for the sake of preparing for the potential agreement that will be arrived at between participants in lawsuits. Therefore, interest negotiation is mainly a cognitive process that concerns not only participants' personal option of construal phenomena but also their consideration of the social factors that may lead to the change of their attitudes. Thus, in the analysis of the data concerning interest negotiation, the attention will mainly be focused on the investigation of the factors that influence the process of interest negotiation.

Compared with the fist two stages, agreement reaching is a more comprehensive stage since it can only be realized on the basis of interest appeal and negotiation and is mainly conducted deliberately by participants through discourse management. Therefore, for the analysis of agreement reaching, I will mainly focus on the discourse management strategies employed by participants to generate consensus between them.

3.4.2 Data Collection

In order to ensure the reliability of the study, the data analyzed are from the CLIPS (Corpus for the Legal Information Processing System), which consists of transcripts of Chinese civil court hearings of more than 300 cases. The data collected are mainly recordings of observed court proceedings, which were collected with professional digital voice recorders with the permission of the court and the consent of both parties. These recordings were then transcribed according to the commonly used transcription conventions (see Appendix I for Transcription Conventions). The extracts used in the book were translated by the author himself.

In this study, texts of court hearings from 36 civil trials are used for analysis, covering disputes of tort, breach of contract, family relation, partition of real estate, etc.

3.4.3 Data Analysis

In CLIPS, all the transcribed materials are tagged following the tagging convention specified in the Tree Information Structure Model (Du 2007, 2014), which contains different symbols to describe features of information, as is in the following extract.

(4)

01[法官]：<2,3,3,21,WA^{1},P,0,J,Z,b,0,0,0,0,是否同意原告陈述>被告是否同意原告的陈述？	01[J]: Does the defendant agree with the plaintiff on his statement?
02[被告]：<2,3,3,21,WA^{2},P,0,B,Z,a,0,0,0,0,不同意原告陈述>不同意。	02[D]: No.

The numbers before the square brackets refer to the turns of speech. "法官(J)" and "被告(D)" in the square brackets refer to the speakers of the two turns. The symbols in the angle brackets are descriptions of the features of information units, which are tagged and can be retrieved with the help of computer software. Numbers "2,3,3,21" represent the level of the information unit in the whole discourse, namely, the 21st unit of the 3rd level ("3,21"), with its super-ordinate unit being the 3rd unit of the 2nd level ("2,3"). Symbols of information level can help us to locate specific information units in the whole discourse. "WA" refers to the type of information knot, namely, "what attitude". The superscripts above "WA" ("WA^{1}" and "WA^{2}") are used to indicate the sequence of the information unit in the discourse. Letter "P" and number "0" following "WA" describe the value of the information knot. "P" means favorable, namely, the current information unit proposed by the judge in question form is favorable to the development of the following discourse. “J” and “B” refer to the judge and attorney for the defense, the source of information unit. “Z” indicates that the information unit is not cited from the previous discourse, with the following “0,0,0,0” indicating the lack of repetition. Letters “a” and “b” stand for the information sharing category of the information units. The following Chinese characters are the keywords of the content of the information unit.

It should be noted that, for the convenience of analysis and for space’s sake, in the analysis of the following chapters only symbols describing features of information which are necessary for the study will be extracted, with others being omitted.

4 Features of Discourse Information in Interest Appeal

4.1 Introduction

Interest appeal in civil court hearings mainly centers on the four constitutive elements of tort: facts of harm, unlawful act, intentional or negligent fault, and the cause-effect relationship (Yang 2005, Zhang 2010). Apart from that, litigants also have to make clear their attitudes or express their opinions on those issues concerning trial procedures or facts of the case, offer evidence or make necessary explanations about their positions or statements.

The above-mentioned activities have a clear manifestation on the level of discourse information, which, according to Du (2009b), can be classified into three general groups in light of its functions in discourse: subjective information, objective information and explanatory information. These three groups of discourse information may help participants to make claims or counterclaims, provide basis for litigation, ensure reasonableness of their interest appeal and help the judge to define facts and disputes of lawsuits.

Under the guidance of the analytical framework constructed in Chapter 3, this chapter embarks upon the exploration of features of discourse information in interest appeal in civil court hearings. During analysis, such cognitive activities as participants' communicative intentions or goals that underlie the information processing will also be touched upon. But the exploration of features of discourse information in interest appeal will be conducted mainly from a functional perspective.

4.2 Subjective Information: Making Claims or Counterclaims

Article 124 of China's Civil Procedure Law prescribes that litigants have the right to make claims or counterclaims in court hearings. To make claims or counterclaims is a process for litigants to take a position on the issues involved in the ongoing lawsuit. Apart from that, litigants are entitled to rebut the facts or reasons proposed by the opposing party (Jiang 2010), manifest their attitudes or provide answers to the questions initiated by the judge (Li 2011).

Therefore, the process of making claims or counterclaims can be concluded as a subjective process for litigants to manifest their intentions or requests. According to the different purposes litigants desire to fulfill in court hearings, the process of making claims may be further divided into three phases: to claim damage compensation, to attribute fault and to assert unlawful act.

These purposes may be fulfilled mainly by subjective information, the basic functions of which are to make judgments or inferences, to declare attitudes, to generate expectations, to make selections, and to exhibit orientations (Du 2009b). The analysis of the data has revealed that, among the various kinds of information types, WA, WI, WP and WJ are the most frequently used subjective information units when litigants make claims or counterclaims.

4.2.1 Claiming Damage Compensation

Damage compensation, as an important means to protect the rights of subjects, refers to the civil liability a party has to take to compensate the losses incurred to others because of his or her infringement or non-performance of duties. Articles 117 to 120 of the General Principles of the Civil Law of PRC prescribe three types of damage compensation: physical damage compensation, property damage compensation and mental damage compensation.

In civil litigation, the claiming of damage compensation is a topic that runs through the whole process of court hearings. The process to claim damage compensation is mainly an expression of litigants' subjective attitudes or wills. In court hearings, damage compensation is usually expressed clearly and precisely by subjective discourse information.

4.2.1.1 Making Compensation Requests

Compensation requests are usually first made by plaintiffs at the beginning of a court investigation, immediately after the judge's instruction for them to make the opening statement. In compensation requests, litigants usually propose that certain measures should be taken by the opposing party to compensate the losses they have suffered. During the process, WP units are found to be the most frequently used discourse information type, as in the following extract.

(5)

01[法官]：<WT^{1},A>现在进行法庭调查。<WT^{2},A>首先由原告陈述具体的诉讼请求。
02[原告]：<WP^{1},A>一、判令被告停止侵害，<WP^{2},A>即刻撤除其商业网站上原告夫妇肖像，<WP^{3},A>并消除影响，<WP^{4},A>连续60日在知名网站和各大报纸公开说明实情、赔礼道歉；<WP^{5},A>二、判令被告赔偿原告精神损失费200万元；<WP^{6},A>三、判令被告负担诉讼费及公证费1000元。

01[J]: Now proceed to court investigation. The plaintiff shall first make compensation requests.
02[P]: Firstly, we request the defendant to stop its infringement by removing the photos of the couple of the plaintiff on its business website and take effective measures to eliminate the ill effects; apologize to the plaintiff and reveal the truth of the photos on well-known websites and newspapers for 60 days. Secondly, we request the defendant to pay 2 million yuan for the plaintiff's mental damage. Thirdly, we request the defendant to pay 1000 yuan for the litigation and notary fees.

This extract is from a case of reputation infringement, in which the plaintiff claims that the defendant has infringed his portrait rights by using his photos without being permitted. In the extract, after the initiation of the procedure of court investigation by the judge with two WT units (WT^{1} and WT^{2}), the plaintiff claims damage compensation with six WP units, which constitute the main information structure in the plaintiff's conceptualization.

The first WP unit activates in the context model schema the discourse space of the general request for the defendant to stop infringement. It is then further developed by the following three WP units (WP^{2}, WP^{3} and WP^{4}), which work as the space constituents to specify the detailed requirements. These WP units reflect specificity in the plaintiff's construal of the dispute. Unit WP^{2} requests the defendant to remove the photos of the plaintiff from the website. With this unit, the plaintiff also presupposes that the using of the plaintiff's photos has constituted infringement and therefore measures should be taken to eliminate the ill effects (WP^{3}). Although no specific fact is offered by the plaintiff to demonstrate the unfavorable effects, unit WP^{3} has laid a foundation for the following requests for compensation. Unit WP^{4} asks the defendant to make apologies on well-known websites and newspapers.

Units WP^{5} and WP^{6} state the second and third compensation requests, which activate two discourse spaces of compensation for mental damage and litigation costs respectively. Unlike the first discourse space activated by unit WP^{1}, these two discourse spaces include no constituent information units and therefore are not fully developed, as is illustrated by figure 4-1.

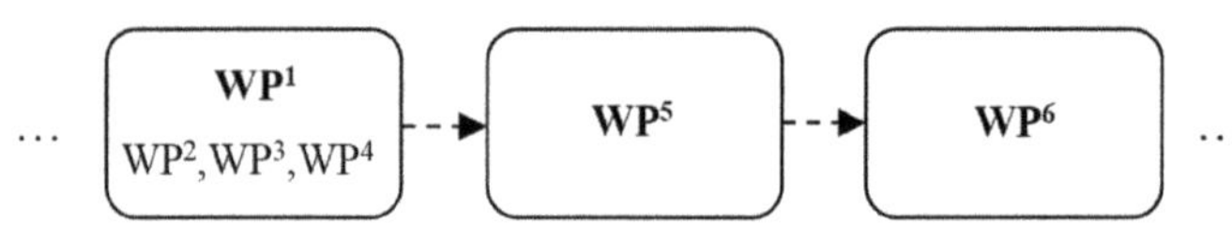

Figure 4-1. Discourse Spaces in the Plaintiff's Compensation Requests.

These discourse spaces are the starting points where the plaintiff attempts to exert influence on the construal of the judge and the defendant, who may be persuaded into forming favorable attitudes towards the plaintiff's interest appeal.

Moreover, the speech of the plaintiff in the extract is well managed to form a parallel distribution of the WP units, which can help litigants express their compensation requests in a clear and precise way.

However, WP information units usually do not appear alone when litigants make compensation requests. In most cases, they are combined with units of other information types to achieve a better effect.

(6)

01[法官]：<1,1,2,1,WT,A>原告请陈述你的诉讼请求以及依据的事实和理由。

02[原告]：**<2,1,3,1,WP^{1},A>**一、请求依法分割本市普善路某室房屋。<3,1,4,1,HW^{1},A>具体分割方式如下：<4,1,5,1,WC^{1},A>若被告不要求取得房屋，<4,1,5,2,WP^{2},A,>则由原告取得产权，<4,1,5,3,WP^{3},A>并向两被告各支付房屋价值三分之一的补偿款；<4,1,5,4,WC^{2},A>若被告要求取得房屋，<4,1,5,5,WP^{4},A>则由被告取得产权，<4,1,5,6,WP^{5},A>两被告向原告支付房屋价值三分之一的补偿款。**<2,1,3,2,WP^{6},A >**二、请求判令两被告向原告支付上址房屋出租的租金。<3,2,4,2,HW^{2},A>自2007年9月1日起至2012年3月20日，每月1,500元，<3,2,4,3,WP^{7},A>原告主张其中三分之一。

01[J]: Now the plaintiff shall make a statement about compensation claims and relevant facts and reasons.

02[P]: **Firstly, we request for the partition of the apartment on Pushan Road of the city in the following way**. If the defendants do not ask for the property right, the plaintiff will get the apartment and will pay one third of the total value of the apartment to each of the two defendants. If the defendants ask for the property right, the defendants will get the apartment and will pay one third of the total value of the apartment to the plaintiff. **Secondly, we request the two defendants to pay the plaintiff the income from the renting of the apartment**, namely, one third of 1,500 yuan per month from September 1st, 2007 to March 20th, 2012.

In this extract, the plaintiff claims for ownership of an apartment and payment of the relevant rent. The claims in the plaintiff's conceptualization are realized by 11 information units. Different from example (5) in which only WP units are used, other information unit types are employed by the plaintiff to help strengthen his claiming.

The first WP unit activates the discourse space of the plaintiff's request to partition the ownership of the apartment. However, the request is too general to be applicable even if it is granted by the court. Therefore, it is further developed by seven information units at the lower discourse information levels, which substantiate the discourse space. First, unit HW^{1} introduces the two principles by which the partition is realized. At the lower levels, unit WC^1 presents the condition of the first principle *被告不要求取得房屋 (If the defendants do not ask for the property right)*; units WP^2 and WP^3 make it clear how the partition will be realized. At the parallel level, unit WC^2 presents the condition of the second principle *若被告要求取得房屋(If the defendants ask for the property right)*, and the following two WP units (WP^4 and WP^5) introduce the second proposal to partition the apartment.

Unit WP^6 activates the second discourse space of the plaintiff's request for the payment of the relevant rent. The components of this discourse space manifest a very similar information structure with the first. In order to make the request more specific, units HW^2 and WP^7 are employed to explain the calculation of the rent and the specific amount of money the plaintiff claims on it. The composition of the two discourse spaces can be shown by figure 4-2.

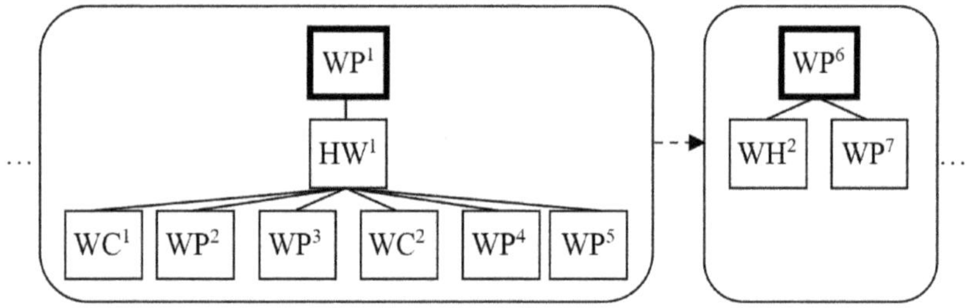

Figure 4-2. The Hierarchical Structure of Information Units in Discourse Spaces.

It can be seen that the distribution of the discourse information in this extract conforms to our common cognition pattern of construing the world from schematicity to specificity (Langacker 2008). The information units which work as constituent components of the discourse spaces assume a hierarchical structure, with the schematic top-level units (WP^1 and WP^6) further developed by units at the lower discourse information levels (WC, HW and WP). This hierarchical structure develops from the general compensation requests (WP^1 and WP^6) to the more specific ways to realize them (WH, WC and WP units), thus making the compensation requests more practical and easier to accept.

4.2.1.2 Defining Compensation Liability

Another important aspect that goes along with compensation request is the definition of compensation liability. In court hearings, litigants would declare their unambiguous attitudes towards the definition of responsibility for damage compensation. Among the various types of subjective information units, WA units may be the most frequently used type in the definition of compensation liability since they mainly concern the expression of attitudes (Du 2009b). However, in order to make their propositions more acceptable, litigants may combine WA units with other information types, as is in the following extract.

(7)

[原告]：<3,1,4,1,WF^{1},A>我方在修车过程中花去了修理费。<4,2,5,1,WY,A>且由于修理厂没有配件，<3,1,4,2,WF^{2},A>我方被迫在修理厂外买了配件。**<2,1,3,1,WA^{1},A>**这部分的花费，应由被告承担。<3,2,4,3,WF^{3},A>车辆在修理厂修理50天，<4,3,5,2,WE^{1},A>无法履行与第三方的合同，<4,3,5,3,WE^{2},A>我方支付了20,000元的违约金，**<2,1,3,2,WA^{2},A>**也是车辆修理的原因。<3,3,4,4,WF^{4},A>原告是请司机开车的，**<2,1,3,3,WA^{3},A>**雇请司机的费用也应计算在其中。**<1,3,2,1,WA^{4},A>**综上，这几个方面的损失应依法由被告赔偿。	[P]: We paid for the maintenance of the vehicle. And due to the garage's lack of vehicle accessories, we had to buy them from other places. **These expenses should be assumed by the defendant.** During the 50 days when the truck was repaired, we failed to fulfill the contract with the third party and had to pay 20,000 yuan for breach of contract. **This cost was also incurred due to the vehicle maintenance.** The plaintiff has been hiring the driver for transportation. Therefore, **the driver's salary should also be included in the compensation. To summarize, according to the relevant regulations, the economic losses of these aspects should be compensated by the defendant.**

The plaintiff, who is the owner of a truck, claims that he has suffered great economic losses due to the defective vehicle accessories provided by the defendant. In the plaintiff's conceptualization, speech is managed to define the compensation liability of the defendant from three aspects: a) vehicle maintenance and accessory costs, b) damages for breach of contract for a third party, and c) salary of the driver.

The discourse consists of 11 information units, among which the four WA units are used to attribute compensation liability to the defendant, one of the participants in the context model. The last WA unit (WA^4) is the nucleus unit of the whole discourse and is the most prominent. It declares clearly that three aspects of compensation liability should be attributed to the defendant.

The relation of the WA units also reflects the plaintiff's way of construal in defining compensation liability. For example, the nucleus unit (WA^4) is foregrounded by other three WA units (WA^1, WA^2 and WA^3) in the background, which define the defendant's compensation liability for costs of vehicle maintenance and vehicle accessories, a third party and the salary of the truck driver. At the lower level, the three WA units are further foregrounded by several objective information units such as WF and WE to support the plaintiff's definition of the compensation liability.

For example, unit WA^1 is supported by three units (WF^1, WF^2 and WY), which introduce the situation of the fixing of the truck and explain how the costs have been incurred. The claim made in WA^2 is supported by the preceding WF and WE information units (WF^3, WE^1 and WE^2). Unit WF^3 introduces the time spent on the fixing of the truck (50 days), which leads to the consequent breach of contract by the plaintiff (WE^1). Then unit WE^2 presents the specific amount of compensation the plaintiff has paid to the third party for his breach of contract. The foreground-background relation of the information units in the extract can be illustrated by figure 4-3.

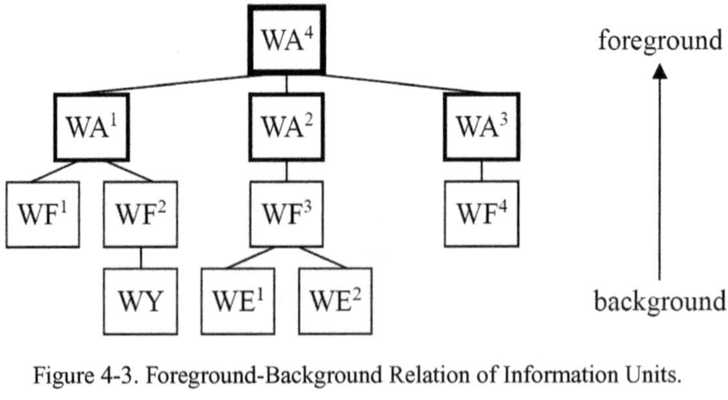

Figure 4-3. Foreground-Background Relation of Information Units.

The WA units and their supporting objective units not only form different information patterns such as "WF-WA" and "WE-WA", but also shape into different function patterns, with WA units declaring the party's basic positions or attitudes and WF or WE units offering facts or effects as their basis. This inductive pattern of cognition can help make the plaintiff's interest appeal in his definition of compensation liability better-grounded and more reasonable.

When facing the charges of the plaintiff, the defendant would also make his position clear by declaring whether he agrees or disagrees with the plaintiff's position. During this process, WA information may also be expected to play a major part. But considering the fact that the defendant is usually placed in a comparatively passive position in court hearings (Liu 1999), since he is usually limited by the plaintiff's speech content, the defendant's discourse information may assume quite different features.

(8)

[被告二]：<2,2,3,1,WF^1,C, Q>针对本次交通事故发生的过程以及责任认定，<2,2,3,2,WA^1,A, Z>我们的意见和被告一是相同的。<2,2,3,3,WA^2,A, Z>同时，**XX**保险公司也同意在交强险的责任限额内承担先行赔偿的义务。<2,2,3,4,WF^2,C, P>对于原告的部分诉请，<2,2,3,5,WA^3, A, Z>我们是有异议的。<3,5,4,1,WP, A, Z>具体要等到质证阶段针对原告所提供的证据，我们再逐项的进行核对。<2,2,3,6,WA^4,A, Z>最后一个就是，本案的诉讼费用不应当由保险公司来承担。

[D2]: **We agree with the first defendant** on the facts about how the traffic accident took place and the definition of liability. Meanwhile, **the XX insurance company is also willing to make prior compensation within the scope of mandatory liability insurance. We object to** part of the plaintiff's compensation claims, which will be specified when the plaintiff's evidence is checked at the cross examination. Lastly, **the litigation expenses of the lawsuit should not be assumed by the insurance company.**

Note: Letters "P", "Q" and "Z" refer to the source of quotation, with "P" referring to Party A, "Q", Party B, and "Z", no Party.

In this extract, the second defendant's conceptualization of the dispute is mainly expressed by four WA units, which reveal his basic positions. Unit WA^1 conveys the defendant's attitude to agree with the position of the first defendant[1] on the definition of accident liability; unit WA² expresses his willingness to make prior compensation within the scope of mandatory liability insurance; and units WA³ and WA⁴ reveal his opposition to the compensation requests made by the plaintiff.

As in (7), apart from the WA units, the defendant also employs such supporting units as WF and WP to advocate his position in interest appeal. However, the supporting units in this extract have demonstrated quite different features of knowledge status in context model. Firstly, the two WF units (WF^1 and WF^2) are both category C, namely, information shared by both parties. It indicates that the two defendants have formed a similar conceptual content about the compensation liability as a result of their common construal of the traffic accident.

Secondly, these WF units are presented with different speech management strategies. They are both information quoted from other parties. As indicated by the symbol "Q", unit WF^1 is quoted from the first defendant, while unit WF^2 is quoted from the plaintiff ("P"). However, the two quoted units have quite different functions in the discourse. Unit WF^1 is quoted to show the defendant's consensus with the first defendant, while unit WF^2 is quoted to rebut the plaintiff's request for mental compensation.

Moreover, as for how the plaintiff's request for mental compensation will be rebutted, a WP unit is employed by the defendant for further explanation. Although no detailed information is provided in the WP unit except the proposition that the evidence will be challenged during cross-examination, the WP unit activates a new discourse space of evidence rebuttal in context model. The new space creates discourse expectations for further discussion of the compensation liability in the subsequent discourse, thus leaving more room for the defendant's interest appeal.

To sum up, WP and WA units are the most frequently used subjective discourse information during litigants' claiming of damage compensation. Firstly, they usually assume different functions: WP units can help litigants express their compensation requests clearly and precisely; and WA units can help reveal their attitudes or positions

1 According to the previous discourse, the first defendant counterclaims that the plaintiff himself should be liable for the traffic accident.

in lawsuits. Most of the time, WP and WA units are combined with other information types such as WF, WC, WH and WE to form more complicated information patterns. These patterns can help to make litigants' requests reasonable and well-grounded. Moreover, with WP and WA units usually being category A, some of their supporting information units are category C, which can help to increase their acceptability. Lastly, the information units in litigants' discourses have assumed different information structures. This usually results from the difference in their construal phenomena or their efforts in management of the speech to achieve a better effect in making interest appeals.

4.2.2 Attributing Fault

According to Article 106 of the General Principles of the Civil Law of the PRC, citizens and legal persons who, through their fault, breach a contract, fail to fulfill other obligations or encroach upon the property of other persons, shall bear civil liability. Fault refers to the psychological state of the subject of infringement which manifests itself as outside infringement actions (Yang 2005). Generally, there are two forms of fault that are recognized in civil litigation: negligent fault and intentional fault.

Negligent fault refers to the psychological state of the actor who, despite his ability to predict the consequence of his action, fails to do so, or who credulously believes that the consequence can be avoided (Yang 2005). Intentional fault refers to the psychological state of the actor who, despite his prediction of the consequence of his action, expects its happening or does not interfere with its happening (Yang 2005).

From the above definitions of the two kinds of fault, it can be seen that fault attribution is a process to prove the intention or psychological state of the litigants when infringement occurs. Therefore, it is expected that subjective discourse information may also be the major information type employed by litigants to make judgments, draw inferences or declare attitudes when attributing fault to the opposing party. However, due to the special requirements in fault attribution, the subjective information may display quite different features from those in claiming damage compensation.

4.2.2.1 Intentional Fault

In most cases, litigants would declare clearly and simply that the opposing party has committed intentional fault in his infringement act. Apart from that, litigants would also produce relevant facts as a basis for his declaration, because in judicial practice the rule of presumption of fault has been followed in fault attribution (Yang 2005). Presumption of fault is the process to infer the intentional fault of the infringer from facts of harm. Therefore, the attribution of intentional fault involves not only the simple process of making declarations, but a complicated process of making inference. Thus it may be expected that WI units may be the major subjective discourse information used in attribution of intentional fault.

(9)

01[原告]：<2,1,3,1,WF^1,A>被告生产XX服装的行为和在宣传材料上突出使用XX商标未经原告许可，**<1,1,2,1,WI^1,A>**已经侵犯原告商标权。<2,1,3,2,WF^2,A>被告虽然注册了商标，<2,1,3,3,WF^3,A>但与其在涉案商品上实际使用的商标不一致。

01[P]: The defendant's acts of producing XX clothes and using XX trademark in the advertising materials were not authorized by the plaintiff and **therefore have constituted trademark infringement**. Although the defendant has registered a trademark, yet the registered trademark does not conform to the trademark used on the clothes involved in the lawsuit.

02[原告]：**<1,1,2,2,WI^2,A>**被告的行为是故意侵权。<2,2,3,4,WF^4,A>原告已经向被告发出相应的通知，<2,2,3,5,WE^1(N),A>但XX市的公证书表明至少到2009年11月20日XX商标仍在进行大规模的宣传，<2,2,3,6,WE^2(N),A>产品也在进行销售。

02[P]: **The defendant's acts have constituted intentional infringement**. As indicated by the notarization, the defendant had been using the XX trademark for large-scale publicity and sale of the products at least till November 20th, 2009, despite the plaintiff's notification to stop the infringement.

Note: "(N)" refers to the value of unit WE, namely, negative or with no effect.

The plaintiff has formed a conceptualization that the defendant has committed intentional fault. The conceptualization includes two kinds of conceptual content: 1) the acts of the defendant have infringed his trademark right; and 2) there is intentionality underlying the defendant's infringement acts.

Unit WI^1 in 01, which defines the nature of the defendant's act as infringement, is first foregrounded in the plaintiff's construal. This inference is supported by three backgrounded WF units (WF^1, WF^2 and WF^3). Unit WF^1 describes the specific infringement acts of the defendant: to produce XX clothes and to use XX trademark in advertising materials. Units WF^2 and WF^3 highlight the inconformity of the trademark actually used with that registered by the defendant. These WF information units provide a good basis for the inference drawn in WI^1 that the defendant has committed trademark infringement.

The plaintiff's proving of intentionality in the infringement mainly draws on the construction of the context model, the intention factor in particular. With unit WI^2 in 02, the plaintiff makes it clear that "the defendant's acts have constituted intentional infringement". The intentionality is further demonstrated by a WF unit (WF^4) and two WE units (WE^1 and WE^2). Unit WF^4 describes the proper measures taken by the plaintiff to notify the defendant to stop the infringement, indicating that the defendant was already aware of the infringement. Units WE^1 and WE^2 reveal the corresponding effects of the notification. The value ("N") of the WE units indicates that the plaintiff's notification has yielded no positive effects, since the defendant continues with his infringement act in both advertising and sale processes despite of his awareness, thus constituting intentionality.

On the level of discourse management, in order to make the fault attribution reasonable, the extract is organized in such a way to have the information units well combined by strong internal logical relations. Each fragment of the discourse has a WI unit as its core unit, supported by either WF or WE units, which make the plaintiff's fault attribution well grounded. Moreover, the two fragments are in a progressive relation, in which the plaintiff moves from the discussion of the defendant's acts of infringement to his intentionality in the infringement, increasing the acceptability of the fault attributed to the defendant.

In some cases, however, intentional fault cannot be inferred as easily as extract (9) demonstrates. Especially in cases concerning breach of contract, the inference that the opposing party has committed intentional fault has to be drawn on the basis of different kinds of discourse information types.

(10)

[被告]：<3,9,4,1,WN,C>2010年10月7日，<3,9,4,2,WT,C>经中介双方签订房地产居间买卖协议，<3,9,4,3,WF^1,C>收了原告定金2万元。<3,9,4,4,WB^1,C>根据协议，应于5日内，即2010年10月12日前签订正式的房地产买卖合同，<3,9,4,5,WB^2,C>合同签订时原告应支付房款30万元。<3,9,4,6,WY,A>但是因为原告没有准备好首付款，<3,9,4,7,WE^1,A>无法与被告签订买卖合同。<3,9,4,8,WF^2,A>10月12日前被告多次与中介及原告沟通，<3,9,4,9,WF^3,A>多次给原告打电话希望其前来签约，<3,9,4,10,WE^2,A>被告只能退掉原来准备购买的XX房屋。<2,3,3,9,WI,D>所以是原告违约导致交易未能达成。

[D]: On October 7th, 2010, the defendant entered an agreement with the plaintiff for sale of the real estate through an intermediary agent and took 20 thousand yuan from the plaintiff as deposit. According to the agreement, the formal real estate contract will be signed five days later, namely, before October 12th, 2010, when the plaintiff should make a first payment of 300 thousand yuan. However, the contract was not signed due to the plaintiff's failure to make the first payment. Before October 12th, the defendant talked to the intermediary and the plaintiff several times. The defendant also phoned the plaintiff several times, hoping that he may come to sign the contract. As a result, the defendant had to reject the offer for sale of an apartment in XX. Therefore, **it was the plaintiff's breach of contract that led to the failure of the transaction.**

In response to the plaintiff's request to refund the deposit, the defendant counterclaims that it is the plaintiff who is responsible for the breach of contract, which has resulted in economic losses of the defendant. The conceptual content is realized by 11 information units, with the WI unit in the last sentence being the nucleus unit that attributes intentional fault to the plaintiff.

The inference in the WI unit is based on two factors in the context model schema: discourse space and knowledge status. In the extract, two related discourse spaces are activated: the discourse spaces of legal background and litigants' performance of the contract.

The discourse space of legal background is constructed as a result of the defendant's specific construal of the signing of the contract. For instance, units WN, WT and WF^1, which reveal information about the signing of the contract, provide background for the defendant's claims and define the legal relationship between the two parties. Units WB^1 and WB^2 are the specific provisions of the contract, which clarify the obligations the plaintiff is supposed to fulfill: to sign a formal real estate contract and make a first payment of 300 thousand yuan.

The discourse space of litigants' performance of contract is based on the defendant's construal of the trajectory-landmark relation between the two parties. According to the defendant, the plaintiff is the trajectory participant since, as indicated by units WY and WE^1, it is the plaintiff's non-performance of contract that led to the breach of contract. The plaintiff's non-performance is highlighted by the two negation elements *没有 (failure)* and *无法 (not)* in the two information units, which attribute intentional fault to the plaintiff for failing to sign the formal contract.

In contrast, the defendant is placed on the position of landmark in the construal of participant relation, which is a minor status and may be influenced by the trajectory. The defendant's landmark status is first realized by units WF^2 and WF^3, which describe the effort the defendant has made to save the uncompleted contract: talk to the intermediary and the plaintiff, and phone the plaintiff several times. With these WF units, the defendant intends to tell the court that, instead of committing any fault, he has tried every effort in the performance of the contract and that it is the plaintiff that should be blamed. In the following WE^2 unit, the defendant magnifies the intentional fault of the plaintiff by counterclaiming subsequent economic losses.

As for the knowledge status, it can also be seen that the information units have assumed different sharing categories. Those units concerning the background of the contract (WN, WT, WF^1, WB^1 and WB^2) are category C, since they are shared by both parties when the contract was signed. Therefore, the plaintiff's obligations revealed by the two WB units become indisputable information based on which the defendant blames the plaintiff for his non-performance of the contract. The units concerning the acts of the two parties (WY, WE^1, WF^2, WF^3 and WE^2) are category A, since they are only personal account to be challenged or accepted in the subsequent discourse. The category of the core information unit WI is D, since as a counterclaim that challenges the proposition of the plaintiff, the WI unit here has constituted a dispute of the case.

Therefore, the whole discourse manifests a syllogistic cognitive pattern, with the C-category units being the major premise, the A-category ones the minor premise, and the WI unit the inference, thus making the fault attribution more reasonable and acceptable.

4.2.2.2 Negligent Fault

Negligent fault is usually caused by negligence or laches, which refers to the actor's violation of reasonable duty of care (Wang 2004). Therefore, when attributing negligent fault, litigants would try to highlight the negligence or laches committed by the opposing party in his or her infringement acts.

Different from the practice that a litigant would declare clearly that the opposing party has committed intentional fault, the attribution of negligent fault is conducted in a more implicit way. Instead of adopting a combination of "WI-WF" or more complicated information pattern with WI units being the nucleus of the discourse information, litigants aiming to attribute negligent fault tend to rely on WF information units to fulfill their purposes.

However, instead of conveying neutral information about objective facts, these WF units are usually deliberately engaged by litigants to convey their subjective judgments or attitudes.

(11)

[原告]：<WN^1,C>原告到被告开办的北京XX小吃店就餐期间，**<WF^1,A>**被告不履行安全义务，**<WF^2,A>**没有及时将破碎在地上的酒瓶碎片清扫，**<WF^3,A>**其提供的三条腿小圆凳也存在安全隐患。<WN^2,A>原告在就餐中间去洗手间回到餐桌落座时，<WG,A>圆凳侧翻，<WE^1,A>导致我摔倒在地，<WE^2,A>被地上的酒瓶碎片扎伤。

[P]: When the plaintiff took meals at the defendant's XX restaurant in Beijing, **the defendant failed to fulfill his duty of safety care, who didn't clear the broken wine bottle on the ground and provided three-leg round stools with safety hazard.** During the dinner, when the plaintiff tried to sit down after his return from the bathroom, the stool turned on its side. The plaintiff fell to the ground and was injured by the broken wine bottle.

The plaintiff claims that it is due to the defendant's laches that leads to the injury of the plaintiff, thus attributing negligent fault to the defendant. The plaintiff's conceptual content of negligent fault is demonstrated mainly by three WF information units. Unit WF^1 defines the nature of the defendant's behavior. Unit WF^2 blames the defendant for his non-performance in clearing the broken wine bottle on the ground. Unit WF^3 demonstrates the long-existing safety hazard in the restaurant.

The information structure in the plaintiff's conceptualization is mainly formed on the basis of the setting component in the context model, in which the three WF units are employed to define the unsafe environment of the restaurant. In the WF units, certain constituent elements are mediated and profiled to reflect the plaintiff's particular way of construal, since, according to Kress & van Leeuwen (2006: 9), "all linguistic form is used in a mediated, non-arbitrary manner in the expression of meaning".

To be specific, unit WF^1 has incorporated a prominent negation *不(failed)* to define the quality information element *履行(fulfill)*, which in turn reveals the defendant's non-performance of his due obligations. In unit WF^2, again the negation *没有(didn't)* is highlighted to describe the defendant's negligence in failing to clear the broken wine bottle. In unit WF^3, the dative element *安全隐患(safety hazard)* is made prominent to reveal the potential safety hazard in the stools provided.

We can see that, instead of conveying neutral information about objective facts, the WF units are deliberately engaged by the plaintiff to incorporate subjective judgments in his construal of the setting component in the context model. These mediated or engaged WF units can be called "pseudo-WF" units. In this extract, these "pseudo-WF" units are further supported by the subsequent units WG, WE^1 and WE^2, which reveal the severe consequence as a result of the pseudo-WF units.

Furthermore, the plaintiff in this extract has delicately managed his speech in order to achieve a desired result in the conceptualization of other participants. The speech management is realized with a strategy of implicit persuasion (Du 2008). In this extract, rather than state clearly with such subjective units as WA or WI that the defendant has committed negligent fault and therefore should be responsible for compensation, the plaintiff encodes his attitude into the pseudo-WF units, achieving an effect of implicit persuasion, which can be more powerful or effective in attributing negligent fault.

Due to the difficulty of the proving of negligent fault, fault attribution usually becomes the focus of courtroom debate, in which the two opposing parties may mediate the same disputable information. But the mediation by the two opposing parties may reveal their contradictive positions or attitudes towards the same issue.

(12)

01[原告]：<WN^1,C>厨师在作火焰冰激凌时，<WF^1,D>不慎将酒瓶掉到了台上，<WE^1,C>原告的脖子和脸都被烧伤了。
02[被告]：<WF^2,A>（我）提示客人不要站起来，<WF^3,A>要坐好靠后。<WN^2,C>可在制作过程中，<WF^4,D>原告由于好奇心站起来，<WF^5,D>探身张望，……，<WE^2,C>烧到了原告。

01[P]: During the cooking of Flame Ice Cream, **the chef accidentally toppled the wine bottle on the operation area** and burned the neck and the face of the plaintiff.
02[D]: (I) warned the customers not to stand up and to sit back. However, during the cooking, due to his curiosity, **the plaintiff stood up and leaned forward to take a look**...and therefore was burned.

In this extract, the two opposing parties have formed conflicting conceptual contents about the negligent fault. They accuse each other of committing negligent fault during the cooking of Flame Ice Cream.

The dispute is first demonstrated in the knowledge status component in the context model. As is shown by the information sharing category (category D), units WF^1, WF^4 and WF^5, which concern the direct cause of the plaintiff's injury, are the focus of dispute. As in (11), these WF units are mediated by both parties to incorporate their particular construal phenomena of the incident.

The plaintiff's conceptualization in 01 is based on three information units (WN^1, WF^1 and WE^1), among which units WN^1 and WE^1 are category C to introduce the situation of incident and facts of harm respectively. With the defendant being the actor, unit WF^1 presents his acts in the cooking of Flame Ice Cream. Unit WF^1 is mediated by the plaintiff, with two information elements *不慎 (accidentally)* and *掉(toppled)* being highlighted. As a result of the mediation, the two parties are placed to different positions in the plaintiff's construal, with the defendant being the trajectory and the plaintiff, the landmark. The plaintiff indicates that it is the chef's carelessness that leads to his operational errors in the cooking of Flame Ice Cream, which in turn causes the burn of the plaintiff's neck and face (unit WE^1). The trajectory-landmark relation in the plaintiff's construal can be shown by Figure 4-4.

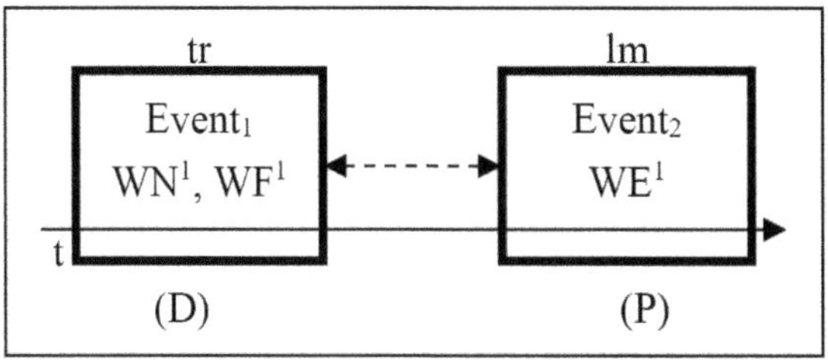

Figure 4-4 .The Trajectory-Landmark Relation in the Plaintiff's Discourse.

The defendant's conceptualization in 02 is composed of six information units. In the context model constructed by the defendant, the information sharing category of units WN^2 and WE^2 are category C, which indicates that the defendant agrees with the plaintiff on the situation of the incident and the facts of harm. But the following information units have assigned quite different participant relations to the two parties in the context model. The two parties assume a trajectory-landmark relation which is opposite to that constructed in the plaintiff's construal.

For example, units WF^4 and WF^5 are mediated by the defendant to describe negligence of the plaintiff. The environment element *由于好奇心 (due to his curiosity)* in unit WF^4 is clearly a presumption of the plaintiff's state of mind. Moreover, in contrast to *站起来 (stand up)* in unit WF^2, the process information element *探身张望 (learned forward)* in WF^5 highlights the plaintiff's negligence of the potential hazard in the cooking of Flame Ice Cream. The cause-effect relationship in 02 can be illustrated by Figure 4-5.

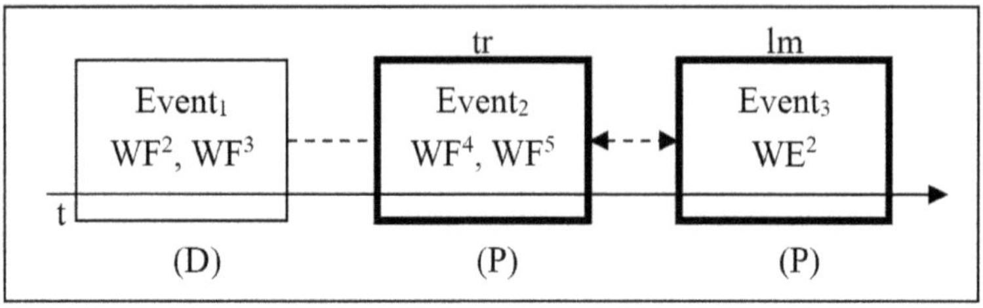

Figure 4-5. The Trajectory-Landmark Relation in the Defendant's Discourse.

The figure shows that three events are involved in the discourse, with the first event concerning the defendant and the other two, the plaintiff. With the first event in background, the defendant indicates that he is not involved in the cause-effect (trajectory-landmark) relationship between the second and the third events. In contrast, the thick lines of the last two events indicate that they are the prominent factors in defining the cause of the injury of the plaintiff, which, according to the defendant, should be attributed to the plaintiff himself.

To summarize, in the attribution of intentional fault, WI unit is the most frequently used discourse information type, whose information sharing category is usually either category A or D. Because of their subjectivity, WI units tend to be combined with such supporting units as WF, WE or WB to form such information patterns as "WI-WF" or "WB-WE-WF-WI", with the information sharing category of the supporting units being either C or A to increase the acceptability of the WI units. In the attribution of negligent fault, WF units are often employed and encoded by litigants with their subjective judgments to form pseudo-WF units to achieve the effect of implicit persuasion.

4.2.3 Asserting Unlawful Act

As one of the constitutive elements of tort, unlawful act refers to the performance or non-performance of citizens that leads to the violation of the law or legal obligations (Yang 2005). Unlawful acts usually manifest themselves in two forms: performance of unlawful act and non-performance of legal obligations.

Similar to fault attribution, assertion of unlawful act is also a subjective process in which litigants draw conclusions based on the facts presented in court hearings. Therefore, subjective information is also frequently employed as a major means to reveal the unlawfulness of the acts of infringers.

4.2.3.1 Performance of Unlawful Act

Performance of unlawful act refers to the violation of the law or regulations that results in the infringement of the health, property or reputation of others. The proving of unlawful acts is usually based on two integral factors: act of the infringer and the unlawfulness of the act.

In court hearings, it is a common practice for litigants to first present the specific acts performed by the opposing party with WF information units and then make conclusions about their unlawfulness with WJ information units.

(13)

[被告]：<WF^{1},A>原告停放车辆的路口设置有"禁止车辆停放"的交通禁令标志牌。<WF^{2},A>原告无视交通禁令标志牌，<WF^{3},A>将自己的车辆停放在该路段巷口路面内，<WF^{4},A>被监控录像摄录。<WB,A>其行为违反了《中华人民共和国道路交通安全法》第五十六条、《中华人民共和国道路交通安全实施条例》第六十三条第(一)项的规定。**<WJ,A>**其违法行为事实存在。

[D]: There is a "no-parking" warning board at the crossroad where the plaintiff parked his car. The plaintiff ignored the warning board and parked his car on the street, which was videoed by the monitoring camera. The plaintiff's behavior has violated Article 56 of the Law of The People's Republic of China on Road Traffic Safety and Paragraph 1 in Article 63 of Regulation on the Implementation of the Road Traffic Safety Law of the People's Republic of China. **Therefore the plaintiff has committed unlawful acts when parking the car.**

In this case, the defendant declares that the plaintiff's parking of the car is unlawful. The defendant's conceptual content is demonstrated by four WF and one WB units based on the context model schema of the event.

Unit WF^{1} introduces the "setting" component of the context model, namely, the spatial environment where the plaintiff parked his car. It states clearly that there is a "no-parking warning board" at the crossroad. The following two WF units (WF^{2} and WF^{3}) introduce the "participant" component, namely, the plaintiff, whose specific acts are presented. According to Halliday & Matthiessen (2004), unit WF^{2} involves a mental process where the plaintiff has totally ignored the no-parking warning board, and unit WF^{3} presents a material process where the plaintiff has committed the fault of parking his car on the street.

Units WF^{4} and WB constitute another dimension of the setting component, namely, the evidence in the institutional setting the defendant relies on to prove the fault of the plaintiff. Unit WF^{4} introduces the video evidence that can be used to prove his fault; unit WB introduces the specific provisions that the plaintiff has violated for his parking of the car.

On the level of speech management, the information units in the extract are well managed to form a distribution that can demonstrate their inherent logical relationship. The defendant starts with the prohibitory traffic sign (WF^{1}) to state the legal requirements of car parking on the street, and then moves on to describe the plaintiff's unlawful car parking behavior (WF^{2} and WF^{3}) which can be further demonstrated by the monitoring video (WF^{4}). In order to make it more convincing, the defendant cites specific provisions from relevant laws to prove the legality of the punishment imposed on the plaintiff.

In this extract, the discourse manifests a "WF-WJ" information pattern, with WJ being the core information unit and WF, the supporting unit. In this pattern, WJ units state the final conclusion and WF units offer basis for the conclusion. Moreover, the WF units in this pattern may assume different functions, varying from offering background information, attributing fault, to presenting evidence.

In most cases, litigants would take less disputable information as the basis for their conclusions. Apart from such objective information as WB or WF units, litigants also prefer to quote information from more reliable sources to support their conclusions, since information of this kind can help to minimize the subjectivity of WJ units in the realization of persuasive reasoning (Du 2014), as is shown in the following extract.

(14)

[被代]：<WB,C>根据交警出具的这份事故认定书，<WJ,A>可以认定原告在事故发生的时间节点上存在违法行为，<WF^{1},C>因为在一个红灯的状态，他在通行和横穿马路，<WF^{2},C>而出租车则是在绿灯状态下通行。

[DA]: According to the Report of Traffic Accident, **we have good reasons to believe that the plaintiff did perform unlawful act at the time of the accident.** He was walking and crossing the street when the traffic light was red, while the taxi was going at a green light.

In response to the plaintiff's claim that the defendant should take all the responsibility for the cause of the traffic accident, the defendant proposes that the plaintiff has also committed unlawful acts and therefore the defendant's liability for compensation should be mitigated.

Before arriving at the above conceptualization, the defendant first activates one of the components of the context model schema: the evidential setting of the conclusion, namely, the police's report of traffic accident (unit WB). In the unit, the information source *交警 (the police)* is also revealed, which is "normal information source" (Du 2012) and hard to be challenged. In order to give a sufficient demonstration of the unlawful act of the plaintiff, the content of the WB unit is then explained by two WF units (WF^{1} and WF^{2}).

Moreover, the information sharing category of unit WB and its supporting WF units is C, since the police's report of traffic accident has already been cross-examined previously and no objection was raised by the plaintiff against its legality, thus offering a solid basis for the conclusion.

On the speech management level, in order to achieve a better rhetorical effect, the two WF units are put together by the defendant to form a contrastive local structure. Unit WF^{1} reveals the specific unlawful act of the plaintiff, namely, to walk through a red light, which is obviously against the traffic law. In contrast, unit WF^{2} is used to describe the lawful behavior of the defendant, namely, to drive when the light is green. As a result, the unlawful act of the plaintiff is highlighted and the conclusion in the WJ unit is further strengthened.

4.2.3.2 Non-performance of Legal Obligation

Non-performance of legal obligation refers to the violation of obligation or duties prescribed by the law. The determination of non-performance of legal obligation is based on two prerequisites, one being legal obligation a party takes, the other, violation of that obligation.

In court hearings, legal obligation is usually demonstrated by WF information units since it is usually prescriptions of the law or facts agreed upon by litigants, e.g., in contract provisions. The declaring of violation of legal obligation is mainly a subjective process and therefore can be realized by subjective discourse information, with which the mishandling or misprocessing of the infringer may be proved.

(15)

[原告]：<4,5,5,6,WF^1,C>双方约定由原告向被告销售塑料桶。<4,5,5,7,WF^2,A>……原告于2008年为支持被告市场发展借给被告10万元现款，<4,5,5,8,WF^3,A>被告2008年所欠货款149,275元，<4,5,5,9,WF^4,A>除去退回破桶款93,650元。<4,5,5,10,WF^5,A>剩余155,625元欠款。<2,3,4,4,WP^1,A>原告多次向被告催要，<2,3,4,5,WP^2,A>但被告至今未还。

[P]: As stipulated in the contract, the plaintiff sells plastic buckets to the defendant. …In 2008 the plaintiff loaned 100 thousand yuan to the defendant for his development of new markets. Altogether in 2008 the defendant owed 155,625 yuan to the plaintiff (149,275 yuan's worth of the buckets minus 93,650 yuan for returned broken buckets). **The plaintiff has urged the defendant to make the payment for several times but still got no satisfactory response.**

In this extract, the plaintiff claims that the defendant has violated his obligation stipulated in the contract to make the payment. The plaintiff's conceptualization of the dispute is based on three discourse spaces in the context model, with five WF and two WP information units being their space constituents.

Unit WF^1 activates the discourse space of the contractual relationship between the plaintiff and the defendant. Although the space closes immediately after its activation, its single component unit WF^1 is a C-event, which legalizes the compensation claims of the plaintiff in the following discourse.

Units WF^{2}, WF^{3}, WF^{4} and WF^{5} constitute the second discourse space: the money owed to the plaintiff by the defendant. These WF units are the outcome of the plaintiff's specific construal of the legal relation between the two parties. To be specific, unit WF^{2} presents the first sum of money (100 thousand yuan) loaned to the defendant for his development of new markets; units WF^{3} and WF^{4} present the second sum of money unpaid by the defendant in the form of arrears; unit WF^{5} summarizes the total sum of money that the defendant still owes to the plaintiff based on units WF^{2}, WF^{3} and WF^{4}. The constituent units in the second discourse make detailed calculation about the money the defendant owes to the plaintiff, thus providing a solid foundation for the subsequent accusation reflected in the following WP units.

With units WP^{1} and WP^{2}, the plaintiff activates the discourse space of the defendant's non-performance of his obligations, which is the most prominent in the plaintiff's construal of the whole dispute. The two WP units constitute the nucleus information units of the whole discourse. Unit WP^{1} introduces the plaintiff's effort to urge the defendant to make the payment, while unit WP^{2} demonstrates the defendant's failure in his fulfillment of his obligations.

On the whole, the discourse displays a "WF-WP" information pattern. In this pattern, the WP unit, usually category A, is the core information unit of the discourse. It is employed to expose the non-performance of the legal obligations of the opposing party. The WF unit, either category A or C, is the supporting information to introduce such background information as the legal relationship of the two parties and their specific legal obligations.

Similar to the information pattern in (6), the WP units in (15) also work as the core information and are supported by other information types. But they perform quite different functions in the two discourses. The WP units in (6) are requests proposed to the court to satisfy litigants' compensation claims. The WP units in (15), however, are employed by litigants to demonstrate the improper handling or violation of obligations of the opposing party.

Sometimes, in order to emphasize the unlawful acts of the opposing party in his nonperformance of legal obligations, litigants may repeat the mishandling or misprocessing of the opposing party with more than one WP unit, which may be in complex relations.

(16)

[原告]: <3,6,4,1,WT,C>原告去XX快餐公司购买快餐食品，<3,6,4,2,WF^{1},A>被告服务员在收款时将一个纸杯子碰掉在地上。<3,6,4,3,WF^{2},A>服务员去捡纸杯子时用于取食物的夹子掉到地上，<3,6,4,4,WP^{1},A>后服务员在未经消毒情况下用夹子给原告拿食品。<3,6,4,5,WF^{3},A>其与该服务员进行交涉，<3,6,4,6,WF^{4},A>要求给予更换食品，<3,6,4,7,WP^{2},A>但服务员不予更换。

[P]: During the plaintiff's purchase of food in XX Fast Food Restaurant, the defendant accidentally clashed the thongs down on the floor when she tried to pick up the paper cup which was dropped by her at the cash desk. **Without being sterilized, the thongs were used by the defendant to pick food for the plaintiff.** Despite the plaintiff's negotiation and request, **the defendant refused to replace the food.**

The plaintiff exposes the defendant's violation of his legal obligation by pointing out his improper handling in the sale of food, which eventually results in the plaintiff's health problem.

In the context model constructed by the plaintiff, the defendant's non-performance of legal obligations is highlighted by two WP units (WP^{1} and WP^{2}), which are the nucleus information units of the discourse. The WP units are supported by four WF units, which help to reveal the logical relation of the defendant's behaviors. The relation between information units in this extract can be interpreted as a functional-semantic one that make up the logic of language.

According to Halliday & Matthiessen (2004), the functional-semantic relation in the context model can be analyzed into "Head" or "Modifier", represented by Greek alphabet " α " and " β " respectively. Unit WP^{1} is the presupposition and is the modifier, while unit WP^{2} reveals the defendant's improper solution of the dispute and is therefore the head. Each of these WP units are either supported or modified by information units of other types. For example, unit WP^{1} is modified by one WT unit and two WF units (WF^{1} and WF^{2}), with unit WT introducing the background of the incident and the two WF units the negligent acts of the defendant. Unit WP^{2} is modified by units WF^{3} and WF^{4}, which are employed to describe the plaintiff's dissatisfaction and requirement for the defendant to replace the food.

As is illustrated by Figure 4-6, all the information units in this extract constitute a logical presentation of information and can help to increase the reliability of the plaintiff's demonstration of the defendant's non-performance of obligations.

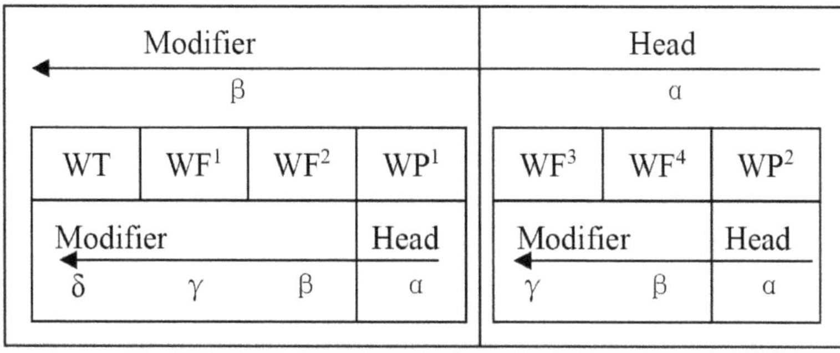

Figure 4-6. Modification Relation of Information Units.

It can be seen that when litigants assert unlawful acts of the opposing party, WJ and WP units are usually used as the nucleus information of the discourse. When proving the performance of unlawful acts, WJ units tend to be combined with WF, or WB units to form such information patterns as "WF-WJ" or "WB-WJ". When demonstrating the nonperformance of legal obligations, WP units are usually the nucleus information and inclined to make combinations with WF units to form "WF-WP" patterns.

To sum up, subjective discourse information is the major means employed by litigants to make claims or counterclaims in interest appeal. This is illustrated by the nucleus position of such subjective information units as WA, WI, WJ and WP in discourse. During litigants' claiming for damage compensation, WP and WA units are the most frequently used information units. In the attribution of intentional fault, WI units usually take the nucleus position of the discourse. When asserting unlawful acts of the opposing party, litigants tend to rely on WJ and WP units to demonstrate the violation of legal obligations.

Moreover, when claims or counterclaims are made, these subjective information units usually do not appear alone. Instead, they tend to be combined with other information types to form more complex information patterns. In most cases, the information sharing category of these units is category A. In some cases, WF units are deliberately engaged by litigants to form pseudo-WF units to convey their personal position or attitude towards certain issues. These features conform to the subjective nature of the process of making claims or counterclaims.

4.3 Objective Information: Providing Basis

According to Article 7 of the Civil Procedure Law of the PRC, "the people's courts must take the facts as the basis and take the law as the criterion when adjudicating civil cases." Therefore, in court hearings, apart from making claims or declaring attitudes during interest appeal, litigants would also try to provide objective basis for the litigation so as to make their claims or requests persuasive and well grounded.

This can be realized by objective discourse information, which, according to Du (2014), by verifying, illustrating or elaborating, can provide objective basis for subjective discourse information. Objective information types such as WB, WF and WE units may work as nucleus information and form various combinations to serve as the basis for interest appeal.

4.3.1 Background of Litigation

Articles 3 and 108 of the Civil Procedure Law of the PRC prescribe the conditions litigants have to meet for litigation. According to the prescription, the litigant must be a citizen, legal person, or an organization that has a direct interest with the case so as to be qualified for the lawsuit. Therefore, before the start of the substantial procedure for litigants to claim for damage compensation, information concerning their identity and their legal relationship is usually provided.

4.3.1.1 Participants Involved in Litigation

According to Article 123 of the Civil Procedure Law of the PRC, at the beginning of a trial, the presiding judge shall check the identities of parties who appear in court, announce the cause of action and the names of the adjudicating personnel and court clerks. This prescription can help to define the relationship between the plaintiff, defendant and the judge. Objective discourse information such as WT, WO and WR may be the most frequently used units for that purpose, as in the following extracts.

(17)

01[法官]：<WT^1， A>现在核实当事人身份。 <WO^1,O>原告任XX，男，<WN,O>1980年9月6日出生，<WR^1,O>XX市XX区XX镇XX村农民，住XX市XX区。 <WO^2,O>被告XX财产保险股份有限公司，<WR^2,O>住所地XX市XX区。<WO^3,O>法定代表人刘XX，经理。	01[J]: Now the identities of the litigants shall be checked. The plaintiff, male, born on September 6th, 1980, is a farmer of XX village, XX town, XX district of XX city and now lives in XX district of XX city. The defendant, XX Property Insurance Company, is located in XX district of XX city, with Liu XX, who is the manager, being its legal representative.
02[法官]：<WT^2, A>现在开庭。<WT^3， A>XX市XX区人民法院依法公开开庭审理原告任XX与被告XX财产保险股份有限公司（以下简称XX保险公司）保险合同纠纷一案。<WT^4, A>本案依法适用普通程序审理，<WO^4,A>由本院孙X审判长与人民陪审员刘XX、人民陪审员吕XX依法组成合议庭，<WO^5,A>由书记员张X担任法庭记录。	02[J]: The court is now in session. The XX district court of XX city is now in session to hear the case of contract dispute involving the plaintiff Ren XX and the defendant XX Property Insurance Company (hereinafter referred to as XX Insurance Company). The case will be heard in summary procedures. Sun XX, the chief judge, and Liu XX and Lv XX, the people's jurors, constitute the collegiate panel. Zhang X, the court clerk, will take recordings of the trial.

In the first fragment, the judge conceptualizes the identity of the two opposing litigants involved in the lawsuit. In the second, the judge intends to form a conceptualization in litigants the cause of action and names of the people's assessors and court clerk.

The above two conceptualizations are formed mainly on the basis of the participant component in the context model schema. Participants are divided into two types by Kress & van Leeuwen (2006): interactive participants and represented participants. The former refers to the participants in the act of communication or in a vector relation with each other, whereas the latter are participants about whom we are speaking or writing and thus are in a zero vector relation.

In the first fragment of the extract, the relationship of the participants is clearly defined and therefore in vector relation. For example, units WO^1, WN and WR^1 present the name, specific date of birth and place of residence of the plaintiff; units WO^2 and WR^2 present the name and location of the defendant; unit WO^3 presents the name and post of the legal person of the defendant. The vector relation manifests itself in the adversary relationship between the plaintiff (WO^1) and the defendant (WO^2) and the reciprocal relationship between the defendant and his legal person (WO^3), as is illustrated by the Figure 4-7.

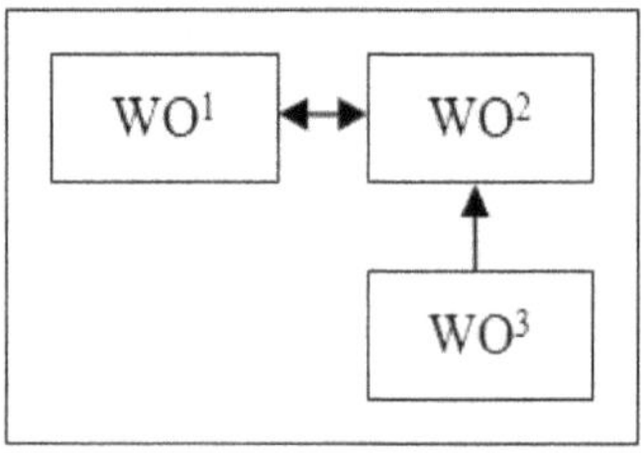

Figure 4-7. The Vector Relation of Participants.

Note: The double arrow line refers to the bidirectional adversary relation. The single arrow line refers to the unidirectional relation.

Two participants are introduced in the second fragment: unit WO^4 presents the collegial panel of the court, including the presiding judge and two people's assessors; unit WO^5 introduces the court clerk, who is responsible for court recording. However, no clear relationship is defined between these participants. Therefore, the participants involved in the second fragment are represented participants and presented separately with zero vectors, as is shown by the following figure.

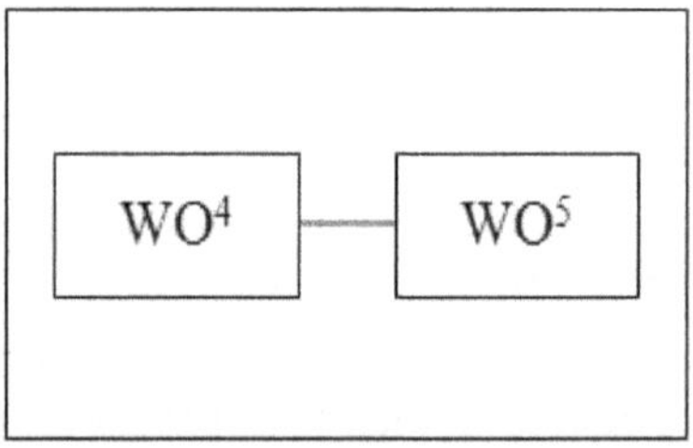

Figure 4-8. The Zero Vector Relation of Participants.

Note: The line without arrows indicates a zero vector, i.e, a relation with uncertain directions.

Altogether, the participants in the extract form the objective background of the lawsuit, on the basis of which the trial proceeds. Moreover, WO unit is the major information unit employed by the judge to introduce participants of litigation. Other information units such as WR and WN are also used to present information relevant to the identity of litigants. WT units are used to introduce cause of action, in which names of litigants may be incorporated as information elements.

4.3.1.2 Legal Relationship between Litigants

Legal relationship refers to the relation established between parties based on and protected by the law. It is legal relationship that attributes duties and obligations, the violation of which may lead to consequent disputes or even lawsuit. Therefore, the interpretation of the legal relationship between the two opposing parties lays a primary basis for their further claims in interest appeal. In court hearings, legal relationship is usually defined by objective discourse information, as is shown in the following extract.

(18)

[原告]：<1,2,2,1,WN(-),C> 2009年12月2日，<1,2,2,2,WF^{1},C>原告与被告签订了广告播出合同一份，<2,2,3,1,WF^{2},C>约定原告为被告提供2009年12月11日期间17时22分00秒至17时42分00秒左右的XX卫视片尾插广告，<2,2,3,2,WF^{3},C>广告长度为每天20分钟，<2,2,3,3,WF^{4},C>价格为1,750元/分钟，<2,2,3,4,WF^{5},C>合同总价175,000元。	[P]: On December 2nd, 2009, the plaintiff and the defendant signed a broadcasting contract, according to which the plaintiff should broadcast commercials at the end of TV series on XX TV Station from 17:22:00 to 17:42:00, 20 minutes a day till 11th December, 2009, with the price of 1,750 yuan per minute. The total price of the contract is 175,000 yuan.

Note: "(-)" in "WN(-)" refers to the retrospective discourse space.

One of the plaintiff's conceptual content about the dispute is that the defendant has failed to pay for the commercials. This conceptual content is based on the contractual relationship between the two parties which is prominent in the context model. Six information units (one WN unit and five WF units), which are distributed on two discourse information levels, are employed to elaborate the relation.

The WN unit presents the temporal setting in the context model, the exact date of the signing of the contract (2nd December, 2009). The "(-)" symbol indicates that the whole extract is a retrospective space that concerns incidents that took placed in the past. Then unit WF^1 activates the space of commercial contract, which is further developed by its constituent information units (WF^2, WF^3, WF^4 and WF^5) on the third level.

When presenting these constituent units, the plaintiff has assumed great specificity in his construal of the details of the contract. To be specific, unit WF^2 states the exact date (*from 2nd December, 2009 to 11th December, 2009*), time (*from 17:22:00 to 17:42:00*) and place (*at the end of TV series*) of the broadcasting of the commercials. Unit WF^3 reemphasizes the time element (*from 17:22:00 to 17:42:00*) in WF^2 by presenting the time duration of the broadcasting (*20 minutes*). Units WF^4 and WF^5 introduce the price per minute (*1,750 yuan per minute*) and total price of the contract (*175,000 yuan*). The elaboration of the provisions of the contract not only demonstrates the legal relationship entered into between the plaintiff and the defendant but also reveals the duties the defendant has to assume to make the payment.

Moreover, the information sharing category of all the information units in the extract is category C, which means they are shared information between the plaintiff and the defendant. This guarantees the objectivity of the legal relationship between the two opposing parties and thus lays an objective basis for the plaintiff's further claims.

The discourse exhibits a simple "WF(C)" information pattern. In this pattern, WF units are the major information units employed by litigants to introduce their legal relationship and prescribed duties. But different from the situation in (17), where participants of litigation are introduced in the *present* space, the introduction of the legal relationship between litigants usually activates a *retrospective* space. Another feature of this pattern is that all the WF units in the discourse are category C, which can help increase the acceptability of the WF units and make the litigants' claims better grounded.

Sometimes, however, more than one legal relationship is involved in a lawsuit. Apart from the contractual relationship between the plaintiff and the defendant, the legal relationship between litigants of the lawsuit and a third party may also function as an important basis for litigants' interest appeal. In such a case, the discourse may show a more complex information pattern, as in the following.

(19)

[原告]：<1,2,2,1,WN(-),A>2008年12月12日，<1,2,2,2,WF^{1},A>原告从案外人王XX处购买小客车一辆（车牌号：G****），<1,2,2,3,WF^{2},A>该车过户后车牌号为L****。<1,2,2,4,WF^{3},C>车牌号为G****的小客车在被告XX财产保险股份有限公司处投保的交通事故强制保险和商业保险，<1,2,2,5,WF^{4},C>保险期间为2008年1月28日至2009年1月27日。

[P]: On December 12th, 2008, the plaintiff bought a minibus (license plate number G****) from the third party Wang XX. The present license plate number after the transfer of ownership is L****. The minibus with the license plate number of G**** was covered by the compulsory and commercial insurance of XX Property Insurance Company from January 28th, 2008 to January 27th, 2009.

The lawsuit is based on the plaintiff's conceptualization of the defendant's failure to meet his insurance claims. The dispute in the conceptual content is whether the insurance relationship entered into between the defendant and the third party before the transfer of the ownership of the bus is still valid.

The conceptualization draws on three legal relationships in the context model: the first is between the plaintiff and the third party (the former owner of the bus), the second is between the defendant and the third party, and the third is between the plaintiff and the defendant.

The first legal relationship concerns the transfer of the ownership of the bus. Unit WN(-) activates the discourse space about the exact date of the purchase (12th December, 2008). The space is further developed by its constituent units WF^{1} and WF^{2}, which provide specific information about the identity of the former owner *王XX (Wang XX)* and former license plate number *G***** (WF^{1}), and the present license plate number *L***** after the transfer of ownership (WF^{2}).

The second relationship constitutes the second space, namely, the insurance relationship between the defendant and the former owner of the bus *王XX (Wang XX)*. The time designated in this space is much earlier than that in the former one, since it introduces the specific insurance types (*compulsory insurance and commercial insurance*) and the period of time covered by the insurance (WF^3 and WF^4).

The two discourse spaces reflect the retrospective perspective in the plaintiff's construal of the legal relations. By clarifying the two contractual relationships, the plaintiff intends to demonstrate that the transfer of the ownership of the bus brings out the transfer of insurance covered by the former owner, thus validating the third legal relationship: the insurance relationship between the plaintiff and the defendant, thus laying a solid foundation for his insurance claims.

Another aspect that needs to be noted is the different information sharing categories of the units in the discourse. It can be seen that those units (WN, WF^1 and WF^2) that concern the legal relationship between the plaintiff and the third party are category A. It shows this relationship, although closely related to the present dispute, is not known to the defendant and yet to be challenged. Those units (WF^3 and WF^4) that clarify the insurance relationship between the defendant and the third party are category C, which indicates a higher rate of acceptability for the interest appeals of plaintiff.

The analysis reveals that WF units are still the major information units employed to introduce legal relationships between litigants. But since more than one relationship is involved, these WF units demonstrate more complicated features. One is that they activate different retrospective spaces as a result of the different time of formation of these relationships. The other is that they assume different information sharing categories (category A and C), which can influence the acceptability of litigants' interest appeals.

To summarize, when clarifying background of litigation, WO and WF are the most frequently used objective discourse information. WO units usually concern the introduction of participants of the lawsuit, with WR, WN units frequently used to present information relevant to the identity of litigants. WF units are mainly used to clarify legal relationships between litigants. They usually activate retrospective spaces and assume such information sharing categories as category A or C.

4.3.2 *Cause of Litigation*

In support of their claims or counterclaims made at the beginning of the court hearings, litigants would present facts about the course of incident and facts of harm that have been incurred thereof. These facts are usually presented to back up the fault attribution and assertion of unlawful act that have been discussed in section 4.2.

Different from the subjective features of the processes of fault attribution and assertion of unlawful act, which are realized mainly by such subjective discourse information units as WI, WJ and WP, cause of litigation is usually presented by objective information.

4.3.2.1 *Course of Infringement*

In court investigation or court debate, litigants would make statements about the course of infringement or incident. Although not all of the statements can be taken as legal facts on the basis of which the final judgment is entered, litigants would try to make their account objective. Therefore, objective discourse information may still be the major discourse information employed by litigants to fulfill that purpose.

(20)

[原代]：<4,1,5,11,WO^{1},A>被告XX汽车客运有限公司驾驶员唐XX，<4,1,5,12,WN,A>于2009年5月17日下午1时40分许，<4,1,5,13,WF,A>驾驶本单位的牌号为D****的轿车，<4,1,5,14,WR,A>沿本市海宁路由东向西行驶至康乐路路口时，<4,1,5,15,WE,A>撞倒正在人行横道内由南向北过马路的被害人，<4,1,5,16,WO^{2},A>也就是本案的原告李X。

[PA]: At 1: 40 PM of May 17th, 2009, Tang XX, driver of XX Automobile Transportation Company, when driving the taxi with the license plate number of D**** from east to west on Haining Street to the crossroad of Kangle Street, knocked down the victim, plaintiff of the lawsuit, Li X, who was walking across the street on the pavement.

In this extract, in support of the conceptual content that the defendant is responsible for the damage compensation, the plaintiff makes an account of the course of infringement, which is based on his detailed construal of the course of the accident.

The context model is mainly constructed around the participant component, which in turn centers on the behaviors of the defendant. The defendant's behaviors are arranged in a particular construal perspective to form a typical "situational script" of traffic accident. According to Schank & Abelson (1977: 41), "scripts are structures that describe appropriate sequences of events in a particular context [...] a predetermined, stereotyped sequence of actions that defines a well-known situation".

In the situational script of extract (20), the identity of the defendant is first introduced with unit WO^1. Then the plaintiff moves on to present other information which concerns the happening of the accident: the exact date and time of the accident (WN), the car the defendant drove (WF), the exact place where the traffic accident occurred (WR), the result of the accident (WE), and the identity of the plaintiff (WO^2).

It can be seen that, despite the information sharing category (category A) of the units, the plaintiff tries to assume a neutral and impartial account of the traffic accident by avoiding obvious incorporation of personal attitude. Although no such subjective information units as WA, WI or WJ are employed to reveal the position or attitude of the plaintiff, the discourse provides a good basis for his compensation claims in the subsequent discourse.

In lawsuits involving breach of contract, the course of infringement is usually presented in a different way. In contrast to the detailed account of the environment of the incident, attention is usually focused on the fulfillment or non-fulfillment of the duties laid down by the contract.

But different from the asserting of unlawful act, where such subjective discourse information as WJ and WP units are employed to point out the unlawfulness of the behavior of the opposing party, in most cases, in order to increase the acceptability of their claims, litigants tend to make neutral account of the fulfillment or non-fulfillment of their duties with WF units only, as is in the following extract.

(21)

[原告]：<5,10,6,1,WF^1,A>合同签订后，我方当即向被告支付了合同定金2万元，<5,10,6,2,WF^2,A>并向第三人支付了居间服务费8,000元，及权证费等其他各项杂费人民币19,180元。<5,10,6,3,WF^3,A>2009年9月15日，我方又向被告支付了购买房屋首付款240,000元。<4,8,5,10,WF^4,A>至此，我方为履行合同已经支付了近28万元人民币。<4,8,5,11,WF^5,A>上述资金交付后，被告屡次向我方提出要在原合同的基础上涨价。<5,11,6,4,WF^6,A>先是提出涨价4万元，<5,11,6,5,WF^7,A>后又向第三人提出要涨价6万元才答应履行合同。

[P]: After the contract was signed, I **paid** immediately the defendant 20 thousand yuan as deposit, the third party 8,000 yuan for the intermediary services and 19,180 yuan for property right certificate and other relevant expenses. On September 15th, 2009, I **made another payment**, namely, the first **payment** of 240,000 yuan for the purchase of the apartment. Up till now, I have already **paid** about 280 thousand yuan for the performance of the contract. However, after the **payment** was made, the defendant asked for an **increase** of the price agreed on in the contract. After asking for an **increase** of 40 thousand yuan, the defendant requests for an **increase** of 60 thousand before the fulfillment of the contract.

In the plaintiff's conceptualization of the dispute, the defendant failed to execute the sales contract at the stipulated price and therefore should be responsible for the breach of contract. The conceptual content is based on seven WF units, which present two events of litigants' fulfillment and non-fulfillment of the duties.

In the context model, litigants' fulfillment and non-fulfillment of the duties have formed two "Event-domain Cognitive Model (ECM)". According to Wang (2007), ECM regards EVENT as the basic unit through which human beings experience and recognize the world around. One basic EVENT is composed of two fundamental elements: Action (A) and Being (B), with the former consisting of dynamic and static actions and the latter, such entities as participants and tools.

In the extract, the plaintiff's fulfillment and the defendant's non-fulfillment of duties have formed two ECMs based on the two EVENTs. In EVENT^1 the plaintiff is the "Being" component, whose action consists of four WF units (WF^1, WF^2, WF^3 and WF^4). All the WF units highlight the same component behavior of the plaintiff: *支付(payment)*, namely, the fulfillment of duties. On the contrary, in EVENT^2 where the defendant is the "Being" component, the action consists of three WF units (WF^5, WF^6 and WF^7), all of which highlight *涨价(increase of price)*, namely, the non-fulfillment of duties. The ECMs of litigant's fulfillment and non-fulfillment of duties can be shown by Figure 4-9.

The figure shows that the ECMs reflect a contractive perspective in the plaintiff's construal of the dispute. Apart from the ECMs, the contrast construal is also reflected on the micro level of the discourse. For example, when stating information units concerning his fulfillment of duties, the plaintiff employs such environment elements as *当即 (immediately)* in WF^1, *又 (another)* in WF^3, and *为履行合同 (for the performance of the contract)* and *已经 (already)* in WF^4 to show his determination and efficiency. When stating the nonperformance of the defendant, the plaintiff employs an information reporting structure *被告屡次向我方提出(the defendant repeatedly asked)* in WF^5 and a conditional structure *要……才答应履行合同(only if..., can the contract be fulfilled)* in WF^7 to reveal the defendant's unwillingness and violation of duties.

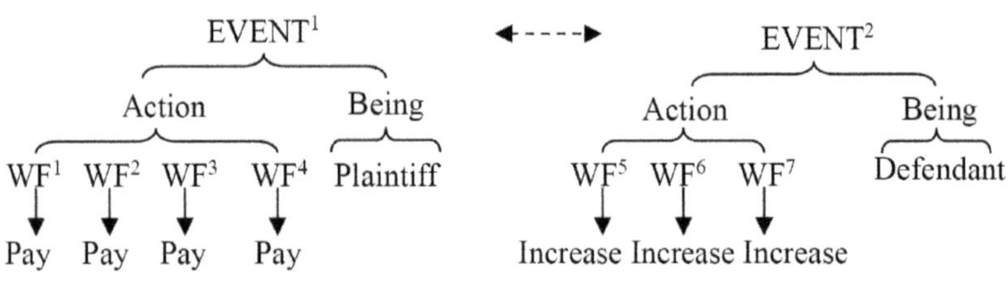

Figure 4-9. The ECMs of Litigant's Fulfillment and Non-fulfillment of Duties.

With the ECMs formed in the context model, in which litigants' acts are put in contrast, the plaintiff intends to show that it is the defendant who breaches the contract and incurs infringement.

4.3.2.2 Facts of Harm

Facts of harm is one of the integral elements in attribution of civil liability. It refers to the consequence caused by the infringement acts of litigants, which usually exists in the form of physical or mental injury or the loss of economic interest of victims (Yang 2005).

In court hearings, due to its close relationship with course of infringement, facts of harm are usually presented immediately after the infringement acts of litigants. WE units may be the most frequently used discourse information during the presentation of facts of harm, as in the following.

(22)

[原告]：<WF^{1},A>原告花费大笔医疗费用，<WE^{1},A>却毫无疗效，<WE^{2},A>越发严重，<WE^{3},A>最后不得不接受手术治疗。<WF^{2},A>现被告又利用合影留念虚假宣传，<WF^{3},A>利用原告夫妇的身份名望大作商业广告，<WE^{4},A>加深了原告的身心痛楚，<WE^{5},A>且继续误导股骨头患者，<WE^{6},A>赚取不诚信的钱财。

[P]: The plaintiff has spent a large amount of medical expenses **but got no therapeutic effect. The illness became increasingly severe so that the plaintiff had to undergo a surgical treatment.** Now the defendant is engaged in false propaganda with the photo, hoping to achieve more commercial effects with the plaintiff's fame. **The defendant's behavior has deepened the plaintiff's mental agony, continued to mislead the patients and earned dishonest money.**

The plaintiff has formed a conceptual content of three kinds of facts of harm caused by the defendant: 1) the deterioration of his health; 2) his mental agony; and 3) the potential social harm. The conceptualization is composed of nine information units, among which the three WF units present the infringement acts of the defendant, and the six WE units introduce the specific facts of harm.

Three discourse spaces are activated in the context model, developing in a chronological order according to the facts of harm. Unit WF^{1} activates the retrospective space where three constituent WE units (WE^{1}, WE^{2} and WE^{3}) are employed to present the facts of harm incurred to the plaintiff in the past.

The three WE units are carefully arranged in a successive perspective in the plaintiff's construal to indicate the deterioration of his health condition, namely, from *毫无疗效(no therapeutic effect)* to *越发严重(becoming increasingly severe)* to *手术治疗(the final surgical treatment)*.

The environment element *现在 (now)* in unit WF^{2} activates the present discourse space where units WF^{3} and WE^{4} are used to describe the plaintiff's mental agony taking place for the time being. The environment element *继续 (continued)* in unit WE^{5} activates the future space where the potential social harm is predicted (WE^{5} and WE^{6}): misleading patients and earning dishonest money.

It can be seen that the discourse spaces have exhibited a "WF-WE" information pattern, with WE units being the nucleus information of the discourse. In this pattern, WF units present litigants' infringement acts and WE units, the consequent facts of harm. The discourse spaces of facts of harm in the extract can be illustrated by Figure 4-10.

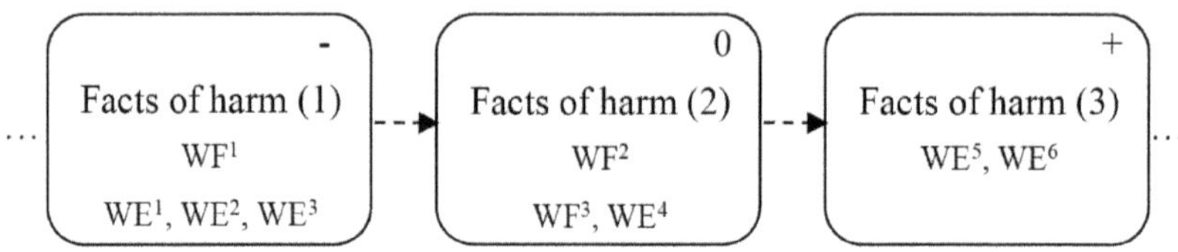

Figure 4-10. Discourse Spaces of Facts of Harm.

The distribution of information units in the extract is very helpful for the plaintiff's interest appeal since the discourse spaces activated have incorporated a successive display of facts of harm not only on the plaintiff himself but also potential for the whole society.

On some occasions, in order to make their account of facts of harm more acceptable, litigants may cite evidence to support their statements.

(23)

[原告]：<WF^{1},A>原告刚刚从楼门走出，<WF^{2},A>被告所有房屋的一页窗户突然从6楼落下，<WF^{3},A>砸在原告身上，<WE^{1},A>导致原告当场昏厥，<WE^{2},A>严重受伤，<WB,A>经解放军XXX医院诊断为"头部外伤、胸外伤、肋骨骨折"等。

[P]: The plaintiff was walking out of the door of the building when one of the windows of the defendant fell off from the 6th floor onto the plaintiff, who lost his consciousness on the spot. The plaintiff was severely injured. According to the diagnosis of the XXX Hospital of PLA, the plaintiff has suffered from head trauma, chest trauma and rib fractures.

The plaintiff claims for damage compensation for his injury caused by the defendant. The conceptualization consists of six information units, including three WF units, two WE units and one WB unit.

The WF units (WF^1, WF^2 and WF^3) present the physical setting in the context model, which mainly concerns the happening of the incident. In the physical setting, the item that led to the injury of the plaintiff, namely, the falling of the window, is profiled and foregrounded in the plaintiff's construal. Besides, the participant relation is also demonstrated in the context model with unit WF^2. The plaintiff makes it clear that the fallen window is from the apartment of the defendant, thus attributing negligent fault to the defendant and establishing the cause-effect relationship between the WF and WE units.

The WE units present the facts of harm thereby, with unit WE^1 describing the immediate symptom of the injury *当场昏厥 (lost his consciousness on the spot)*, and unit WE^2, how severe the injury is *严重受伤 (severely injured)*. The following WB unit, which provides an injury assessment as supporting information to unit WE^2, constitutes evidential setting for the plaintiff's conceptualization. According to unit WB, the plaintiff has suffered from *头部外伤 (head trauma)*, *胸外伤 (chest trauma)* and *肋骨骨折 (rib fractures)*.

When presenting the WB unit, the plaintiff takes the trouble to point out the name of the hospital *解放军 XXX 医院 (XXX Hospital of PLA)* where the injury assessment was made, thus ensuring the objectivity of the evidence. Consequently, the whole discourse is managed by the plaintiff to guarantee the objectivity of the severity of the plaintiff's injury and increase the acceptability of his corresponding interest appeals.

To sum up, when introducing cause of litigation, WF and WE units are the most frequently used objective discourse information. They can be combined with other objective information units to fulfill different purposes. When introducing course of infringement, WF units are usually combined with WO, WN and WR units to reveal other essential factors of infringement. Sometimes, WF units are distributed in such a way to form contrastive structures where litigants' performance and non-performance of duties are contrasted. When introducing facts of harm, WE units are the nucleus information and are always combined with WF or WB units to form a "WF-WE" pattern, where facts of harm are introduced successively or the cause-effect relation is clarified by revealing the sources of information.

4.3.3 Ground for Claims

Article 71 of the Civil Procedure Law of PRC prescribes that the court shall examine the statements of the parties in connection with other evidence of the case to decide whether such statements can be taken as a basis for finding the facts. Therefore, in court hearings, the statements made by litigants are supposed to be based on solid grounds before they are accepted as legal facts by the court.

Apart from providing background of litigation and course of infringement, objective discourse information can also help to provide solid grounds for litigants' claims. This is usually realized by citing specific provisions of the law or submitting evidence to court.

4.3.3.1 Legal Ground

According to Article 7 of the Civil Procedure Law of PRC, when adjudicating civil cases, the court must take the law as the criterion. Therefore, when making statements about facts of infringement or attributing civil liability, litigants would cite provisions of the law to validate their claims. Among the different types of objective discourse information units, WB is usually the most frequently used units for that purpose.

(24)

[被告二]：<WA>不同意原告的赔偿请求。<WB>根据《道路交通安全法》76条之规定，原告请求赔偿的相关费用应当由保险公司在交强险范围内予以赔付。	[D2]: I object to the compensation claims of the plaintiff. According to Article 76 of Road Traffic Safety Law of PRC, the compensation should be made by the first defendant within the scope of compulsory insurance.

(25)

[原告]：<WI>被告的行为侵犯了原告的注册商标专用权。<WB>属于《商标法》第五十二条第（五）项和《商标法实施条例》第五十条第（一）项规定所禁止的商标侵权行为。	[P]: The defendant has infringed the trademark rights of the plaintiff, which is prohibited by Paragraph 5 in Article 52 of the Trademark Law and Paragraph 1 in Article 50 of Regulation for the Implementation of the Trademark Law.

(26)

[被告]：<WB>《民法通则》规定"保护民事权利的诉讼时效为2年"。<WJ[1]>所以即便原告有继承的权利，那也超过了法律规定的诉讼时效。<WJ[2]>因此原告的各项请求都是不合法的。

[D]: According to the General Principles of the Civil Law of the PRC, "the limitation of action regarding applications to a people's court for protection of civil rights shall be two years". Therefore, even if the plaintiff has the right of inheritance, his claim has already exceeded the limitation of action and is therefore unlawful.

In these extracts, specific provisions of the law are cited by litigants as legal grounds for the support of their declared attitudes or conclusions. This is realized mainly by WB units.

In extract (24), the defendant forms a conceptualization with the WA unit about the plaintiff's compensation request *不同意原告的赔偿请求 (object to the compensation claims of the plaintiff)*. The conceptual content is supported by a WB unit, which constitutes the evidential setting in the context model. The WB unit manifests the defendant's detailed construal of the context model. In his construal, the defendant not only presents the information source of the provision, namely, Article 76 of Road Traffic Safety Law of the People's Republic of China, but also reveals the content of the provision. It states clearly that the requested compensation should be made by the first defendant within the scope of compulsory insurance. By shifting the compensation liability to the first defendant, the WB unit validates the defendant's attitude in the conceptual content that he will not accept the compensation request made by the plaintiff.

Extract (25) assumes the same discourse structure as (24). Based on the evidential setting constructed by the WB unit, the WI unit forms the conceptual content about the defendant's infringement of trademark rights. But different from the WB unit in (24), where the defendant presents the specific content of the provision, the plaintiff has taken a general perspective in his construal of the evidence by making a general introduction of the provisions, namely, *《商标法》第五十二条第（五）项和《商标法实施条例》第五十条第（一）项 (Paragraph 5 in Article 52 of the Trademark Law and Paragraph 1 in Article 50 of*

Regulation for the Implementation of the Trademark Law). Nevertheless, it provides a solid basis for the inference made in the WI unit.

Similarly, in Extract (26), the WB unit offers a legal ground for the following conclusion (WJ) that the plaintiff's claim has already exceeded the limitation of action and is therefore unreasonable.

These extracts have exhibited a consistent "WA/WI/WJ-WB" information pattern. In this pattern, WA, WI or WJ unit is subjective discourse information unit employed by litigants to activate discourse spaces to declare attitudes or make conclusions. The WB unit is objective discourse information that provides legal ground for those attitudes or conclusions.

In cases concerning breach of contract, in order to emphasize the lawfulness of their acts, litigants would cite as the basis the particular terms of contract which were agreed upon previously by the two opposing parties.

(27)

[被告]：<WF,A>原告车辆虽已办理过户手续，但……未告知XX保险公司车辆过户的事宜。<WB,C>故依据机动车商业保险单（正本）明示告知第4条，"保险车辆转卖、转让、赠送他人、变更用途等，应立即书面通知本公司并办理批改手续"，以及保险条款第一章的第3条责任免除条款中第5款规定，<WJ,A>由于原告任XX未办理批改手续，XX保险公司的责任被免除，<WA,A>不同意给付原告的经济损失4,128元。

[D]: The plaintiff has transferred the ownership of the bus but failed to inform the insurance company of the transfer of the ownership. According to Article 4 of the Commercial Vehicle Insurance (original), "the sale, transfer, giving or the change of uses of the insured vehicle should be reported to and approved in written form by the insurance company", and Paragraph 5 of the escape clause (Article 3) in Chapter 1, the XX Insurance Company is exempted from making compensation due to the plaintiff's failure to report the transfer for approval. Therefore, we object to paying 4,128 yuan to the plaintiff as economic compensation.

In this extract the defendant declares, by citing the escape clauses of the contract, that the insurance company should be exempted from the compensation liability and therefore will not make the payment.

The defendant's conceptualization is mainly expressed by the WA unit, which is also the nucleus information unit of the whole discourse. With the WA unit, the defendant expresses his disagreement to make the economic compensation. The conceptualization is first supported by the participant component in the context model, realized by the WF unit, with which the defendant shows that the plaintiff did not inform the insurance company of the transfer of the ownership of the bus, and therefore the contractual relationship between the plaintiff and the defendant has not been established.

Apart from that, the defendant also introduces the stipulations of the two escape clauses in the contract with unit WB, which formulates the evidential setting in the context model. In the evidential setting, the defendant's construal has profiled the content of the WB unit. It points out that the plaintiff's responsibility to report the transfer of ownership is clearly stipulated in the terms of contract, the violation of which will lead to the defendant's exemption from making compensation.

The WB unit offers indispensible intermediate background information to support the legal ground for the conclusion *保险公司的责任被免除 (the Insurance Company is exempted from making compensation)* in the WJ unit and attitude *不同意给付原告的经济损失 4,128 元 (object to paying 4,128 yuan to the plaintiff as economic compensation)* in the WA unit. The relation between the information units can be illustrated by Figure 4-11.

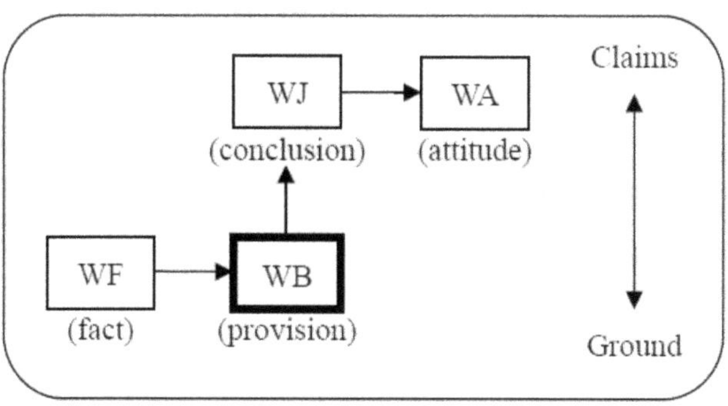

Figure 4-11. Legal Ground in Discourse Space.

In this figure, the four information units have formed a chain relation, with the WJ and WA units being subjective claims and the WF and WB units objective ground. As indicated by the thickness of the lines, the WB unit is the key element in the whole structure, since without it the whole structure would collapse and the reasonableness of the claims in the WJ and WA units would be harmed.

4.3.3.2 Evidential Ground

Article 64 of the Civil Procedure Law of PRC prescribes that litigants have the responsibility to provide evidence in support of their own propositions. It means that in civil lawsuit, the facts proposed by litigants should be demonstrated by evidence before they are accepted by the court as legal facts. Because of its importance, litigants usually employ objective discourse information to present their evidence.

(28)

01[法官]：<WA^{1},B>原告是什么态度？	01[J]: What's the opinion of the plaintiff?
02[原告]：<WA^{2},A>医疗费62,318.15元需要被告支付，<WB^{1},A>这个有XX县医院和XX第一人民医院的诊断书、医疗费收据及住院结算单等证实；<WA^{3},A>伤残鉴定费800元也应该由被告承担，<WB^{2},A>有XX司法鉴定所的鉴定费发票可查；<WB^{3},A>原告的收入证明可以证明其收入的合法性，<WB^{4},A>按照国家有关规定，<WA^{4},A>被告应赔偿原告误工费30,805元。	02[P]: The medical expenses (62,318.15 yuan) should be paid by the defendant, which can be verified by the medical records and receipt of the medical expenses and hospitalization of XX County Hospital and The First People's Hospital of XX. The appraisal fees (800 yuan) should also be paid by the defendant, which can be verified by the invoice from XX Appraisal Organ. The letter of reference can prove the lawfulness of the plaintiff's income. As stipulated by the relevant provisions, the defendant should make a payment of 30,805 yuan for his loss in income incurred from the missed working time.

The extract is from a court conciliation in which the plaintiff makes claims for three types of compensation. Each claim is based on evidence that has been examined during court debate.

Unit WA^1 produced by the judge activates a subjective discourse space, which asks directly for the plaintiff's conceptualization of the compensations. The subjective nature of the discourse space imposes constraint on the information type of its constituent units. As a response, in 02 the plaintiff provides three subjective information units (WA^2, WA^3 and WA^4) to expose his claims for compensation: medical expenses (WA^2), appraisal fees (WA^3) and loss in income (WA^4).

In order to make the claims more reasonable, each of the above WA units is assigned with several WB units, which in turn generate evidential settings for the claims. To be specific, unit WA^2 is supported by WB^1, which, by providing the medical records and receipt of the medical expenses and hospitalization, elaborates how the claimed medical expenses are calculated. Unit WA^3 is developed by WB^2, which provides evidence of invoice from the appraisal organ *XX 司法鉴定所 (XX Appraisal Organ)*. Unit WA^4 is evidenced by WB^3 and WB^4, which provide proof of the plaintiff's income and relevant provisions as the basis, since according to Article 119 of General Principles of the Civil Law of PRC anyone who infringes upon a citizen's person and causes him physical injury shall pay his loss in income due to missed working time.

It can be seen that the plaintiff has assumed an analogical construal of the claims, which in turn leads to the parallel information structure of "WA-WB". In the structure, the WB unit provides a solid ground on which the claims in the WA unit are based. Different from Extracts (24), (25) and (26), where specific provisions of the law are provided, the WB unit in this extract is evidence provided by litigants themselves and can be challenged by the opposing party in the subsequent discourse.

Sometimes the evidence provided by litigants to support their subjective claims is testimony from witnesses. Testimony can also be used as evidential ground, but in different forms, as in the following extract.

(29)

01[法官]：<WF^{1},b>出事以后，原告是否找过有关部门对种子进行鉴定？	01[J]: After the incident, did the plaintiff ask for appraisal of the quality of the seeds?
02[原告]：<WF^{2},a>开始找过种子公司，他们让我找种子监督站。	02[P]: I first went to the Seed Company, who asked me to go to the seed supervision station.
03[法官]：<WF^{3},b>监督站是怎么说的？	03[J]: What did the seed supervision station say?
04[原告]：<WF^{4},a>他们说这种情况不是种子原因，<WO, a>当时有站长、副站长到场，<WF^{5},a>他们说是因为化肥和种子没有分离造成的，所以把种子烧坏了。	04[P]: They said it was not caused by the quality of the seeds. The head and deputy head of the station were there. They said the seeds were burned because the seeds were not kept apart from the fertilizer.
05[法官]：<WF^{6},b>监督站是否出正式报告了？	05[J]: Did the station produce a formal report?
06[原告]：<WF^{7},a>没有。	[P]: No.

The plaintiff and the defendant have formed conflicting conceptualizations about the poor seedling emergence. The plaintiff claims that the poor seedling emergence is caused by the defendant's operational errors, while the defendant insists that the disqualified seeds the plaintiff bought be the main reason.

The judge's question in 01 activates the evidential setting in the context model. The judge indicates that the plaintiff should produce evidence to support his proposition on the poor seedling emergence. After getting an affirmative answer from the plaintiff (WF^{2}), the judge questioned closely about the result of the appraisal, which reveals the negligent fault of the defendant with unit WF^{5} *化肥和种子没有分离造成的 (the seeds were not kept apart from the fertilizer)*.

Another aspect that needs to be noted is that several information sources are exposed in the context model. For example, when presenting the result of the appraisal, the plaintiff makes it clear that it is produced by *种子监督站 (the seed supervision station)*, which is an organization responsible for the supervision of the quality of seeds. When attributing fault to the defendant with units WF^{4} and WF^{5}, the plaintiff takes the trouble to highlight the identities of the witnesses with a WO unit.

However, although the information sources of the units of evidence are revealed, they are not directly from the witnesses themselves but reported by the plaintiff, thus lowering its credibility. As is indicated by the questioning in 05, compared with the reported testimony, the written appraisal report is more profiled in the judge's construal of the evidential setting.

We can see that WB units are the most frequently used objective discourse information units to provide ground for claims. When introducing legal ground, WB units are combined with such subjective discourse information units as WA, WI and WJ to form a "WA/WI/WJ-WB" pattern. The WB units as legal ground are either legal provisions of the law or terms from contract. When introducing evidential ground, WB usually takes the form of written documents or oral testimony, with the former more acceptable than the latter.

To sum up, objective discourse information is often employed by litigants to provide basis for their subjective claims. Among the various types of objective information units, WF, WE and WB units often play major roles in introducing background of litigation, course of infringement and ground for claims. In most cases, they are combined with each other to form complicated information patterns to fulfill those purposes.

4.4 Explanatory Information: Ensuring Reasonableness

According to Article 8 of the Civil Procedure Law of PRC, "the people's courts shall, when adjudicating civil cases, guarantee and facilitate all parties to exercise their litigation rights, and apply the law equally to all parties." It means that, as one of the important subjects in the civil litigation relationship, the court is obliged to take corresponding responsibilities during civil litigation (Xiong 2008).

One of the responsibilities, besides conducting the trial, is the court's interpretation right. The court's interpretation refers to the practice of court to ascertain the facts of cases by questioning, reminding or inspiring the litigants to supplement insufficient statements, clarify vagueness, or eliminate inconsistencies that have existed in their claims, propositions or evidences (Tang 2003).

Although there is no specific provision in the Law of PRC to prescribe the interpretation right of court, it is commonly practiced by most judges in court hearings. On the discourse information level, the interpretation right of court can be realized by explanatory discourse information since, according to Du (2009b), the major functions of explanatory discourse information is, by defining, interpreting or clarifying, to establish connections or ensure reasonableness of the propositions of litigants.

Since the objectivity degree of explanatory discourse information lies between subjective and objective discourse information (Du 2009: 364), the information types that are employed to realize the functions of explanatory discourse information may be widely ranged.

4.4.1 Making Interpretations

In court hearings, litigants are entitled to declare their propositions or requests in the form of statements. But in some cases, these statements are not as sufficient as to make their propositions or attitudes understood by the other participants of the lawsuit. Or due to their difference in shared information, the other participants have problems in understanding their positions or requests. Under these circumstances, the judge is obliged to instruct the litigants to make further interpretations.

4.4.1.1 Defining Legal Terms or Relations

In order to ensure that litigants provide proper information in their statements, the judge may, after giving instructions about procedures of trial, define the legal terms thereof to tell the litigants what they should or should not do.

(30)

[法官]：<0,1,1,2,WT^1,A>下面进行法庭调查。<1,2,2,1,WT^2,A>首先由原告方陈述起诉的事实、理由以及诉讼请求。<2,1,3,1,WT^3,A>原告方在进行陈述时应当围绕案件事实、争议焦点、诉讼请求等与本案有直接关系的内容进行，<2,1,3,2,WT^4,A>避免陈述与本案无关的内容，<2,1,3,3,WT^5,A>一方陈述时，对方不得打断发言。

[J]: Now proceed to court investigation. The plaintiff shall first make statement about the facts, reasons and compensation requests. The plaintiff shall center his statement on the facts, focus of disputes, compensation requests and other content relevant to the lawsuit. Content irrelevant to the present lawsuit is prohibited. When one party makes statement, the other can not interrupt his or her speaking.

This extract is the beginning part of a court hearing in which the judge, after giving instructions about procedures of the trial, tries to form a conceptualization in the two parties about what they should or should not do when making statements.

The first WT unit is the nucleus information unit that activates the discourse space of court investigation. But it is too general for the participants to form any specific construal result to act upon. Therefore, it is further explained by unit WT^2 which entitles the plaintiff to make the statement first and defines the scope of the content of his statement: facts, reasons and requests of the litigation. Compared with unit WT^1, unit WT^2 assumes more specificity in its content and therefore is more prominent.

However, unit WT^2 is actually an order given by the judge to authorize the plaintiff to make opening statement in the trial and is still too general to make reference to for his statement. Therefore, immediately following it, the judge assigns more specificity to his construal by employing three other WT units (WT^3, WT^4 and WT^5). These WT units aim to give more detailed instructions, which concern the content of the statement (WT^3 and WT^4) and the behavior of the opposing party (WT^5). Compared with unit WT^2, units WT^3, WT^4 and WT^5 are of more specificity and attract more attention, as is illustrated by the following figure.

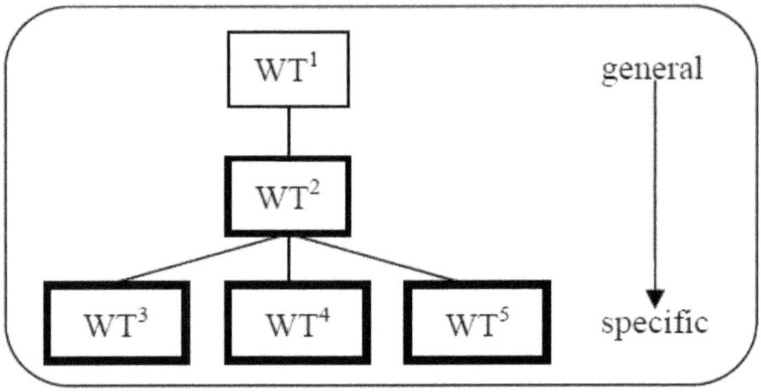

Figure 4-12. Legal Terms Elaborated in Discourse Space.

The figure also shows that the flow of the discourse information is managed by the judge to have both a vertical and horizontal development. As the core information unit, unit WT^1 (level 1) is first developed vertically by unit WT^2 on the second level, which in turn is further interpreted horizontally by three other WT units (WT^3, WT^4 and WT^5) on the third level.

These information units are assigned with different communicative functions. Unit WT^1 is procedural in declaring the start of court investigation; unit WT^2 is authoritative to entitle the plaintiff to perform his rights; units WT^3, WT^4 and WT^5 are instructive to impose either requirements or constraints on the behaviors of the two parties.

Apart from defining legal terms in instructions, explanatory discourse information also plays an important role in ascertaining legal relationships among the different parties involved in the lawsuit. This may happen when litigants make insufficient statements about the relations of participants involved in the lawsuit, as in the following extract.

(31)

01[法官]：<WT^{1},b>再陈述一下，王XX，毛XX和你之间的关系。	01[J]: Can you explain again the relation between you, Wang XX and Mao XX?
02[原告]：<WF^{1},a>王XX，……在七浦路里面它很多间这个店面都是它的，<WF^{2},a>包括我这个福建北路229号这间也是它的，<WF^{3},a>王XX，我跟它就是房东。……<WO,a>毛XX是我前任的营业员……<WF^{4},a>当时我…后面的为了缴费呢…也是按照毛XX缴费。<WF^{5},a>……它要拆迁，<WF^{6},a>毛XX就不做服装了，<WF^{7},a>我原来是在里面做服装的……。	02[P]: Wang XX, …is the owner of several stores on the Qipu Road, including my restaurant on 229 of Fujian Bei Road. Wang XX is my landlord. … Mao XX was the former tenant of my restaurant. …For the convenience of tax payment, I've been paying taxes in the name of Mao XX. …The store is going to be demolished, and therefore Mao XX stopped her clothes business. The store was used for clothes business…
03[法官]：|<WT^{2},a>是这样子的，你听我讲，<WF^{8},c>福建北路229号这个店铺是王XX公司的，<WF^{9},c>那么王XX将该店铺租赁给毛XX了。<WF^{10},c>毛XX是有营业执照的。<WF^{11},c>之后呢，毛XX不做了，所以该店铺是由你来实际经营，<WF^{12},c>所以你后来缴税是以毛XX的名义缴税的。	03[J]: |All right. Now listen to me. Wang XX has the property right to the store on 229 of Fujian Bei Road, which was first rented by Mao XX who has a business license. After Mao XX stopped her business, you've taken over the store and paid taxes in the name of Mao XX.
04[原告]：<WF^{13},c>对。	04[P]: Right.

In this case, the judge tries to form a correct conceptualization of the plaintiff's payment of taxes. The conceptualization activates the participant component in the context model. As a result, the relationship between the plaintiff, Wang XX company and Mao XX has become the focus of dispute.

In 01 the judge instructs the plaintiff with unit WT^{1} to make further explanations about the legal relationship. The word *再 (again)* in the judge's instruction indicates that it is a reactivation of the previous discourse space. It also indicates that more specificity is preferred in the judge's construal of the participant relations.

As a response, the plaintiff in 02 provides eight units as space components, which reflect great specificity of his construal. The first three components (WF^{1}, WF^{2} and WF^{3}) define the relation between the plaintiff and Wang XX Company as a lease relation. The following five components (WO, WF^4, WF^5, WF^6 and WF^7) try to define the relation between the plaintiff and Mao XX but fail to do so because, although they indicate that Mao XX and the plaintiff are closely related, no information is provided about the relation between Mao XX and Wang XX Company.

In view of this, the judge in 03 interrupts the statements of the plaintiff with a discourse marker WT^2 *是这样子的，你听我讲 (All right. Now listen to me)*, which, according to Ge (2013), usually works as a speech management strategy to maintain the same discourse topic. With unit WT^2, the judge intends to make her own contribution to the development of the discourse space.

In the following, the judge provides five units as additional components of the discourse space, which in turn help to clarify the disputed legal relationships. Units WF^8 and WF^9 define the relation between Wang XX company and Mao XX; units WF^{10}, WF^{11} and WF^{12} define the relation between the plaintiff and Mao XX. By clarifying these legal relationships, the judge concludes that Mao XX has a business license and that is why the plaintiff has been paying taxes in the name of Mao XX, which is confirmed by the plaintiff in Turn 4 with unit WF^{13}.

Unlike the monologue where only the judge is involved in the interpretation of legal terms, this extract takes an interaction form where the judge and participants of lawsuit both make contributions to the clarification of legal relationships. Especially in 03, as indicated by the information sharing category (category c), the judge summarizes the major points of the statement of the plaintiff and defines the relationships in a clearer and more logical way.

It can be seen that the judge takes a leading role in the whole process. This can be reflected not only by the question-answer form of the interaction, but also by the judge's interruption of the plaintiff's speech in 03 with unit WT^2 when the plaintiff diverges from the ongoing topic the plaintiff is elaborating with unit WF^7.

4.4.1.2 Specifying Details

In court hearings, in order to make their claims clear, litigants need to make detailed interpretations of the essential points of their arguments. This is also realized by explanatory information units under the instructions of the judge.

(32)

01[法官]：<WT^{1}>下面由原被告分别进行举证质证，<WT^{2}>证据应分组出示，并阐述证据所证明的内容。

02[原告]：<WB>第一项证据，房屋租赁协议书，<WF^{1}>证明双方自愿签定协议。<WF^{2}>原告从2006年11月起就开始承租2,000平方米的场库，<WF^{3}>协议中的第一条第三项对如遇到拆迁进行了明确的约定，<WF^{4}>该证据还说明了原告是经营使用租赁地。

01[J]: Now the plaintiff and defendant shall proceed to proof cross-examination. The evidence shall be produced in groups. The facts that the evidence aims to prove shall be elaborated.

02[P]: Evidence one, the lease contract, is used to prove that the contract was signed at the free wills of the two parties. The plaintiff has been renting the 2,000-square-meter store since November 2006. Paragraph 3 in Article 1 of the contract has made clear stipulations on demolition. The evidence also shows that the store is rented for business use.

In this case, the plaintiff sues the defendant for not paying demolition subsidy as stipulated by the lease contract. The plaintiff's conceptualization is based on the evidential setting in the context model, which mainly concerns the lease contract.

With units WT^1 and WT^2, the judge lays down requirements for the construction of the context model. They instruct the participants to highlight specificity in their construal of the evidences. For example, according to unit WT^2, evidences should be produced in groups and the facts that evidences aim to prove should be elaborated.

As a result, the information produced by the plaintiff in 02 conforms to the expectation imposed by the judge. For example, the plaintiff first announces the type of the first evidence *房屋租赁协议书 (the lease contract)* with unit WB, and then specifies the details of its content with four WF units (WF^1, WF^2, WF^3 and WF^4).

When specifying the details of the evidence, the plaintiff also exposes their specific functions. For example, with unit WF^1, the plaintiff specifies that the lease contract is to prove the voluntariness in its signing; by defining the leased area as land for business use with unit WF^4, the plaintiff indicates that his rights are protected by relevant provisions of Law of the People's Republic of China on the Contracting of Rural Land. The exposure of the functions of the evidence makes the plaintiff's statement more relevant and can contribute to the efficient cross-examination on its validity and acceptability.

In some cases litigants may express their claims or make their statements too generally to be understood by other participants. Under such circumstances, litigants are usually instructed by the judge to specify the details of their claims or account of facts.

(33)

01[法官]：<WT^{1},a>请陈述你的诉讼请求以及你所依据的事实。	01[J]: Now the plaintiff shall make statement about the compensation claims and the relevant facts.
02[原告]：<WP^{1},a>诉讼请求，请求法院判令被告赔偿人民币230,822元。	02[P]: Compensation claims: request the defendant to pay 230,822 yuan to the plaintiff.
03[法官]：<WT^{2},a>主要陈述一下赔偿的款项，数额及依据。	03[J]: Explain the item, amount and basis for your compensation.
04[原告]：<WP^{2},a>第一项是医药费，是859元。<WP^{3},a>第二项是误工费，是9万元。<WB^{1},a>那么计算的依据是按照原告每月1.5万元的收入，乘上六个月的这个误工期进行计算。<WP^{4},a>第三项是护理费，<WO, a>护理人员是原告的爱人，<WB^{2},a>其每月收入是1万元，那么护理期限是3个月，共计3万元。	04[P]: Firstly, medical costs, which are 859 yuan. Secondly, loss in income from missed working time, which is calculated by the plaintiff's salary (15 thousand yuan per month) multiplied by six months' missed working time. Thirdly, nursery cost. The plaintiff was looked after by his wife, whose income is 10 thousand yuan per month, multiplied by 3 months, totaling 30 thousand yuan.

This extract is from the beginning part of court investigation, in which the plaintiff specifies the details of his conceptualization about damage compensation under the instruction of the judge.

Unit WT^{1} activates the discourse space of opening statement about damage compensation claims. In the discourse space two aspects of contents are expected: the compensation claims and the relevant facts. As a response, in 02 the plaintiff provides unit WP^{1} as the space constituent, which gives an account of the total amount of money claimed as compensation *赔偿人民币 230,822 元 (request the defendant to pay 230,822 yuan to the plaintiff)*. But the plaintiff has taken too general a perspective in his conceptualization of the compensation to meet the judge's requirement about the discourse space. Therefore, in 03 the judge gives another instruction with unit WT^2 to elaborate his expectation on the space constituents, namely, the item, amount and basis of damages.

As a result, the plaintiff specifies in his construal the details of his claims in 04 with six units. Unit WP^2 introduces the first item of damages (medical costs) and its amount. Unit WP^3, besides introducing the cost incurred from loss of working time, explains who the calculation is made, namely, the monthly income of the plaintiff multiplied by six months' loss of working time. In the same vein, unit WP^4 introduces the nursery cost and explains how it is calculated.

On the level of speech management, it can be seen that the information units in this extract display a different mechanism of information flow, first a slow flow and then a torrent flow (Du 2009a). Units in the first three turns have a slow development, with unit WP^1 trying to fill up the information vacancy created by unit WT^1. However, there is an undercurrent underlying the slow flow caused by the insufficiency of the information in unit WP^1. The undercurrent is then disclosed by the judge with unit WT^2, which creates a larger vacancy for more information. This time the vacancy is filled up by a torrent flow of information with six units in 04, resulting in a sufficient explanation of the plaintiff's interest appeal.

To sum up, explanatory discourse information can help litigants to make detailed interpretations of legal relations, evidence or compensation requests. Court interpretations are usually first initiated by the judge with WT units in the form of instructions and then realized by litigants with explanatory information units, thus forming a general information pattern of "(J)WT-(L)WX"[2]. The judge usually takes a leading role in the interpretation and controls the information flow of the whole discourse.

2 "(J)" and "L" refer to the judge and litigant (either plaintiff or defendant) respectively. "WX" is a collection name for all the 15 types of information units except Kernel unit.

4.4.2 Elaborating Connections

Another important function of explanatory discourse information is to help elaborate the connections between different things (Du 2009b: 364). In court hearings, the claims, propositions, requests and supporting evidence are usually closely related with each other to ensure the reasonableness of the viewpoints of litigants. However, in some cases these connections are not interpreted clearly enough, therefore the judge has to ask litigants to elaborate them.

4.4.2.1 Establishing Relevance

In court hearings, one way for litigants to elaborate connections is to establish relevance between different things. In most cases, after producing facts to support their propositions, litigants are usually questioned by the judge to explain how these facts are related to each other.

(34)

01[法官]：<WF[1], b>原告、被告什么关系？	01[J]: What's the relationship between the plaintiff and the defendant?
02[原告]：<WF[2], a>男女朋友。	02[P]: We were lovers.
03[法官]：<WF[3], b>"被告借钱说干活"是干什么活？	03[J]: What work do you refer to when you said "the defendant borrowed money to do some work"?
04[原告]：<WF[4], a>承包电信工程周转，<WF[5], a>还有还一些欠的外债。	04[P]: Capital turnover for contracting a communication project and other debts.
05[法官]：<WF[6], b>有书面约定吗？	05[J]: Do you have a written agreement?
06[原告]：<WF[7], a>每次都承诺六月一日前还清，<WF[8], a>有些写了约定，有些没写。	06[P]: Every time the defendant promised to pay back before June 1st. Some have written agreements, while others do not.

In this extract, by asking a series of questions, the judge tries to form conceptual content about the relevance between the major facts concerning the process of debt-creation. According to van Dijk (2008), participants are at the center of context model schema, and their identities and relations with each other can help to expose important facts in lawsuit.

In this extract, the two opposing parties are involved in two kinds of relations: the adversary legal relation (debt relation) and the romantic one. Of the two, the debt relation becomes the more prominent in the judge's construal, which is reflected in his successive questioning; established by units WF^1 and WF^2, the romantic relation is less profiled and is employed to constitute a reasonable premise for the debt relation.

Prominent in the context model, the debt relation between the two parties entails more construal effort of the participants. For example, it is further explained by three WF units (WF^3, WF^4 and WF^5), which help to expose the reasons why the defendant borrowed money from the plaintiff and the specific job the defendant was engaged in.

However, since these are only the plaintiff's oral testimony about the debt relation, which lacks objectivity, evidence in the written form is asked to be produced, on the demand of which the plaintiff makes further explanations about the deadline of the payment (WF^6, WF^7 and WF^8).

As a result of the judge's questioning, the relevance has been established between the integral factors of debt-creation: the premise (the romantic relationship between the litigants), the reason (why the money is borrowed) and the evidence (to prove the existence of the debt).

The discourse displays a "(J)WF(b)-(L)WF(a)" information pattern. In this pattern, the judge helps to establish relevance between important facts by asking litigants questions with (J)WF(b) units, to which litigants respond with (L)WF(a) units. Different from the preceding patterns in which the judge's instructions are given in imperative forms with WT units, the instructions in this extract are realized in WH-question form. Instructions in this form can impose constraint on litigants' answering and help to make it more focused and targeted.

In some cases, litigants may have different understandings about the relevance established between facts of case, which can result in different or even opposite interpretations.

(35)

01[法官]：<3,9,4,10,WF^{1},O>这是一组合同，一共分为两类，共七份，<3,9,4,11,WF^{2}, b>这一组合同之间的关系是什么？	01[J]: This is a group of seven contracts, with two categories. How are they related with each other?
02[原告]：<4,11,5,7,WF^{3}, a>相互之间是展期。<5,7,6,3,WF^{4}, a>下一份是上一份合同的展期。	02[P]: They are contract extensions, with the one at a later time being extension of the one at an earlier time.
03[被告]：<4,11,5,8,WF^{5}, a>这一组合同是相互独立的，<5,8,6,4,WF^{6}, a>前几份是合作协议，后几份是代理协议。<5,8,6,5,WF^{7}, a>合同之间也有空白期，有的长达几个月，<5,8,6,6,WF^{8}, a>因此说都是延续的是没有依据的。	03[D]: They are separate contracts, with the first few being cooperation contracts and the others, agency contracts. There are also gap periods between contracts, with some being as long as several months. Therefore to define them as contract extensions is not well-grounded.
04[原告]：<4,11,5,9,WF^{9}, a>合同的法律关系是代理。	04[P]: The contracts are in agency relationship.
05[被告]：<4,11,5,10,WF^{10}, a>不认可，每一份都是独立的，有合作，也有代理。	05[D]: We disagree. Every contract is separate, with some in cooperation relation and some in agency relation.

The plaintiff sued the defendant for not paying agency fees that are regulated and protected by the agency contracts they have signed. In the previous discourse, the plaintiff produced seven contracts to prove the agency relationship. In this extract, the two opposing parties have formed contradictory conceptualizations about how these contracts are related to each other.

In 01 after defining the category of the contracts (WF^{1}), the judge activates the discourse space of contract relevance (WF^{2}). Both parties make contributions to the development of the discourse space. The plaintiff defines the contracts as contract extensions (WF^{3}), while the defendant regards them as unrelated or separate contracts (WF^{5}). There propositions are further elaborated by WF units at the lower information levels in 02 and 03 and reemphasized by units WF^{9} and WF^{10} in 04 and 05.

The difference between litigants' conceptualizations of the contract relation results from their conflicting intentions in interest appeal. By defining the contracts as contract extensions, the plaintiff intends to prove that the agency relationship still exists and therefore the defendant should pay the claimed agency fees. On the contrary, the defendant tries to show that the agency relationship has already come to an end and therefore he is not liable for any compensation.

Moreover, as can be illustrated by the following figure, the information units in this extract are distributed to form a contrastive structure as a result of the different interpretations of the contract relation.

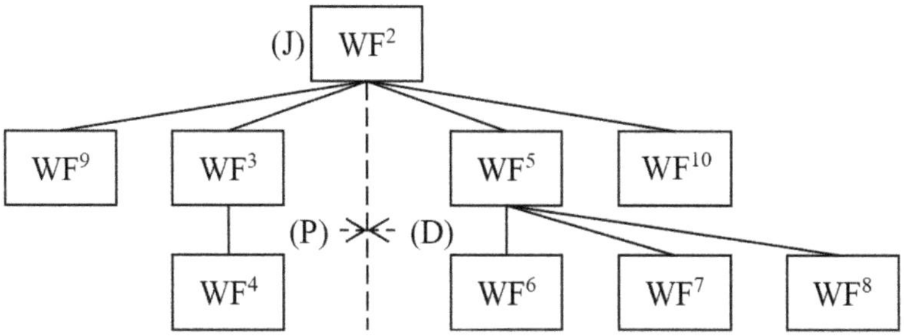

Figure 4-13. Contract Relations Defined by Opposing Parties.

The information pattern can be concluded as "(J)WF-(P)WF-(D)WF". In this pattern, unit (J)WF is initiated by the judge in question form to ask litigants to define a certain relation. Units (P)WF and (D)WF, which are contradictory in content, are two groups of information units employed by the plaintiff and defendant respectively to establish the relevance.

4.4.2.2 Questioning Relevance

Besides establishing relevance, litigants are also entitled to question the relevance established by the opposing parties. This can also be realized by explanatory discourse information since litigants would have to provide the reasons or basis for their opposition.

(36)

01[法官]：<2,4,3,7,WA^1，b>被告对上述证据的关联性有无异议？	01[J]: Does the defendant object to the relevance of the evidence?
02[被告]：<2,4,3,8,WA^2， a>对该证据的真实性没有异议，<2,4,3,9,WA^3， a>对其关联性有异议。<6,1,7,2,WF^1， c>这个文件是XX镇人民政府以拆迁人的名义发布的，<6,1,7,1,WF^2，a>这个是一个民事主体的身份。<5,1,6,2,WF^3， a>这个文件不是立法性、行政性的文件，<5,1,6,1,WF^4，a>只是民事主体单方性的。<4,1,5,2,WF^5，o>人民法院在审理案件中只能根据法律法规审理案件，<4,1,5,1,WF^6，a>这种文件只能作为参考，是不能适用的。<3,9,4,1,WJ， a>用这个证明文件证明不应该把补偿费发给被告是一个逻辑错误。	02[D]: We have no objection to the authenticity of the evidence but have objection to its relevance. This document was issued in the name of the demolition office of the XX Town government which is a civil subject, and therefore is not a legislative or administrative regulation but actually a contract between civil subjects. When adjudicating cases, the people's court can only base its judgment on laws or regulations. Therefore this document can only be used for reference but not as legal basis. It is logically wrong to use the document to demonstrate that the demolition subsidy should not be granted to the defendant.

The plaintiff produces a document issued by the demolition office of the local government as evidence to support his claims for demolition subsidy. However, the defendant forms a conflicting conceptual content about the relevance of the evidence and proposes that the demolition subsidy should be granted to him.

In the context model, the discourse space of evidence relevance is first activated by the judge with a question to ask whether the defendant has any opposition to the evidence produced by the plaintiff. In 02 the defendant declares clearly with unit WA^3 that he questions the relevance of the evidence. Then the defendant employs seven units to elaborate his opposition. Units WF^1 and WF^2 define the identity of the issuer of the document (the demolition office of the local government) as a civil subject; the documents it issues are not legislative or administrative but actually an agreement or contract between civil subjects (WF^3 and WF^4); and therefore they should not be used as the basis for final judgment (WF^5, WF^6 and WJ).

Moreover, the information units in the discourse of the defendant display a particular way of construal which reveals a logical relation of causality, with each information unit on the higher levels further explained or demonstrated by those on the lower levels, thus leading the information to have a deeper development, as is shown by the following figure.

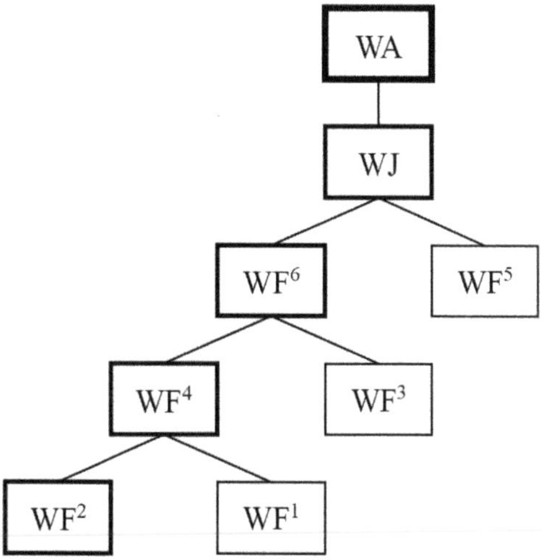

Figure 4-14. Logical Relation of Causality in the Defendant's Discourse.

In this figure, as indicated by the thickness of lines, unit WA^3 is the core information unit which declares the defendant's basic attitude towards demolition subsidy. It is first developed by another subjective unit (WJ) on a lower level. The WJ unit is then supported by six WF units, among which unit WF^2 that defines the demolition office as civil subject is the key or most fundamental unit, since it is based on this unit that the whole reasoning of the defendant is constructed. Based on unit WF^2, the civil relation between the plaintiff and the demolition office is established (WF^4) and the appropriateness of using the documents to support the plaintiff's compensation requests is questioned and opposed.

In some cases, the judge plays more important roles in questioning relevance. Apart from giving instructions or asking questions, the judge can directly challenge the relevance between the evidence and the propositions of litigants.

(37)

01[法官]：<WF^{1}, C>原告主张违约金是千分之三，<WB, b>合同依据是什么？	01[J]: The plaintiff asks for three thousandths as damages for breach of contract. What is the contract basis?
02[原告]：<WF^{2}, a>在2000年的合同第六条第八款，约定了千分之五。<WF^{3}, a>欠代理费是发生在2002年之前，之后就不欠了。<WF^{4}, a>2002年的合同约定的是千分之三，<WF^{5}, a>我们选择的是千分之三。	02[P]: We agreed upon five thousandths in Paragraph 8 of Article 6 in the contract of 2000. The defendant failed to pay the agency fees generated before 2002, but paid the fees generated after 2002. According to the contract of 2002, the damages for breach of contract are three thousandths, which is what we claim in the lawsuit.
03[法官]：<WT, A>向双方释明一下，<WF^{6}, A>最高院下发了通知，<WF^{7}, A>在当前金融危机情况下，企业经营比较困难，<WP^{1}, A>违约金应该以补偿损失为主，惩罚为辅，<WP^{2}, A>法院必须对此进行审查。	03[J]: I shall make some clarifications. As required by the Supreme Court, considering the difficulties private business face due to the financial crisis, damages for breach of contract shall be paid mainly for compensation purposes, with punishment being supplemented purposes. Therefore the plaintiff's request will be reconsidered for further examination.

The plaintiff asks for three thousandths as damages for breach of contract and provides specific terms of contract as its basis. However, his conceptualization is challenged by the judge, who explains that the calculation of damages for breach of contract should follow the instructions of the Supreme Court.

With unit WB, the judge first activates in the context model the discourse space of contract basis, which requires the plaintiff to justify his compensation claims in unit WF^{1}. As a response, the plaintiff provides four WF units in 02, which introduce two contract bases, one being five thousandths (WF^{2}), and the other, three thousandths (WF^{4}). Then with unit WF^{5}, the plaintiff declares clearly that he chooses the former as damages for breach of contract.

However, the plaintiff's contribution to the development of the discourse space is first challenged by the judge in 03, who makes it clear that, as required by the Supreme Court, damages for breach of contract will be paid mainly for compensation purposes, and therefore the plaintiff's request will be reconsidered for further examination.

The challenge of the judge in 03 reflects a different perspective in the construal of damages for breach of contract. This results from their different goals in the litigation. On the part of the plaintiff, although by choosing three thousandths over five thousandths as damages request he intends to show a posture of compromise, his only goal of litigation is to maximize his interest pursuit. On the part of the judge, his construal concerns more with balancing litigants' private interest pursuit with social equality and justice (Chen & Feng 2008). Therefore, the judge makes it clear that due to the hardship the corporations meet with during the financial crisis, penalty for breach of contract will only be considered for complementary purposes.

To sum up, explanatory discourse information plays an important role in establishing or questioning connections between facts of cases, thus helping litigants to make their claims or counterclaims more reasonable and persuasive. But different from court interpretations which are usually initiated by the judge with WT units, connections between facts of cases are usually first initiated by the judge in question forms with such units, and then elaborated by one or both litigants. In some cases, the judge can take a more active role by questioning in person the relevance established by litigants.

4.4.3 Eliminating Uncertainties

Another important function of explanatory discourse information is to eliminate uncertainties that exist in the statements or answers of litigants (Du 2009b). Due to the inadequacy of litigants' statements, the vagueness and inconsistencies that are resulted in may prevent the efficient and fair resolution of the dispute. In this case, the judge can, either by giving instructions or asking questions, help clarify the vagueness or eliminate inconsistencies that exist in litigants' statements.

4.4.3.1 *Clarifying Vagueness*

The vagueness that exists in the statements of litigants is usually caused by the indefinite reference of certain items involved in the lawsuit. In most cases, the vagueness is usually pointed out by the judge and clarified by litigants themselves. Since such clarification of vagueness involves facts of cases, WF information is usually the most frequently used information units.

(38)

01[法官]：<WF^1， C>"诉讼请求第二项，认为被告构成了抄袭"，<WF^2, b>抄袭的部分指的是哪一稿？	01[J]: "The second compensation request: the defendant's behavior has constituted plagiarism". What part do you refer to as being plagiarized?
02[原告]：<WF^3， a>修订稿的第一章。<WF^4， a>我方所陈述的事实部分，关于诉讼请求第二项，指我方作品修订稿的第一章，实际出版图书的第一章。<WF^5， a>在网上被被告抄袭，以自己的名义发表。	02[P]: The first chapter of the revised version. In our statement about the facts of the case, the second compensation request refers to the first chapter of the revised version, which is also the first chapter of the published version. It was plagiarized by the defendant on the internet and published in his own name.

In this case, the plaintiff sues the defendant for plagiarism. In the previous statement, the plaintiff mentioned that the first chapter of his book was plagiarized but did not result in a clear conceptualization in the judge about which version of the book was involved. At the request of the judge, the plaintiff clarifies the vagueness by specifying the plagiarized part.

The judge reactivates with unit WF^1 the discourse space of the second compensation request and contributes unit WF^2 as its component, which asks the plaintiff to clarify which version is involved in the plagiarism. In response to the judge's request, the plaintiff contributes to the development of the discourse space with three more WF units (WF^3, WF^4 and WF^5), which make it clear that it is the first chapter of the revised version, which is also the first chapter of the published version of the book that is plagiarized.

On the level of speech management, the strategies of quotation and repetition are employed by both parties in clarification of the vagueness. For example, before asking for clarification, the judge first uses unit

WF^{1} to report the claim of the plaintiff. The reported information not only conveys the attitude of the plaintiff but also locates the position where vagueness has occurred. The same information is also quoted by the plaintiff himself in the following discourse with unit WF^{4}, which constitutes repetition for clarification. Moreover, the expression of *第一章 (the first chapter)* is used three times in the plaintiff's discourse. *第一章 (the first chapter)* in unit WF^{3} provides a brief and direct answer to the question asked by the judge in Turn 1. Then it is mentioned twice in unit WF^{4} to establish relation between the first chapter in the revised version of the plaintiff and that in the published version.

The quotations and repetitions in the discourse not only clarify the vagueness in the statement of the plaintiff, but also help to show that it is the identical content between the two chapters that proves the plagiarism.

Sometimes, the vagueness is caused by the insufficient statements or answers given by litigants. Under such circumstances, the judge usually question them closely to clarify the vagueness and ascertain facts of the case.

(39)

01[法官]：<WF^{1}, C>你说工头带你们到工地签的字。<WY^{1}, b>为什么签字？	01[J]: You said that the foreman took you to the construction site to sign the name. Why did you sign your name?
02[证人]：<WY^{2}, a>工头领着去就签字了。	02[W]: The foreman took me there and then I signed the name.
03[法官]：<WY^{3}, b>为什么工头领着去就签了？	03[J]: Why did you do that?
04[证人]：<WY^{4}, a>他们让签就签字了。	04[W]: They asked me to sign the name and I did what they asked me to do.
05[法官]：<WF^{2}, b>你认识字吗？	05[J]: Can you read?
06[证人]：<WF^{3}, a>认识但是不多。	06[W]: Yes. But not very good at it.
07[法官]：<WF^{4}, b>你看到上边写了什么吗？	07[J]: Did you notice what was written on the paper?
08[证人]：<WF^{5}, a>没有看见。	08[W]: No.
09[法官]：<WY^{5}, b>为什么没有看见就签字了？	09[J]: Why did you sign the name without knowing what was there?
10[证人]：<WY^{6}, a>因为是工头领着去的，让签字就签字了。	10[W]: Because we were taken there by the foreman. We just did what he asked.

In this case, the plaintiff conceptualizes that the written proof produced by the witnesses for the defendant is invalid because it was signed under threat. In this extract, one of the witnesses is questioned by the judge about the credibility of the proof.

With unit WF^1, the judge first reactivates a past discourse space of the witness's signing of names. Although its information sharing category (category C) indicates that the judge accepts the testimony of the witness, it is too vague to reveal any information about whether the witnesses were under any threat or not. Therefore, the judge intends the witness to make more contributions to the discourse space by asking why they signed their names (WY^1). The discourse space component (WY^2) provided by the witness indicates that the foreman had played a role in the signing of the name but does not reveal what specific role it was.

Unsatisfied with the answer, in 03 the judge goes back to the discourse space with a question initiated by unit WY^3, to which the witness testifies that they signed their names at the foreman's request (WY^4). But the answer does not convey any information about whether the proof was signed under threat.

Therefore, in the following the judge shifts his focus of construal to the content of the written proof. The judge first affirms the inadequate literacy of the witness in 05 and 06, and then asks directly whether the witness knows anything about the content of the proof. The negative answer by the witness in 08 reveals that the witness has no idea about the content. It indicates that the signing of the names is not the true expression of the will of the witnesses.

Like Extract (38), strategies of quotation and repetition are also employed by the judge to clarify the vagueness in the statements of the witness. For example, the same expression *为什么签字 (Why did you sign your name)* appear three times in the judge's questioning to highlight its importance. Due to the inadequacy of the information provided by the witness, from 05 to 08, another strategy is employed by the judge to solicit desired information, namely, the strategy of shift of discourse topics (Ge 2013). In 05 the judge shifts the topic from the questioning of why the witness signed his name to that of his education background. The shift of topic helps to prove the illiteracy of the witness and clarify the vagueness by revealing his unwillingness in the proof signing.

4.4.3.2 Removing Inconsistencies

Apart from vagueness, inconsistency is another kind of uncertainty that exists in the statements of litigants. Here inconsistency does not mean the conflict of opinions between two opposing parties, but refers to the situation in which the content of one information unit contradicts with that of a preceding one. Inconsistency can also be removed with explanatory information by judge's questionings.

(40)

01[法官]：<WF^{1}, b>签合同当时你交了多少钱？	01[J]: How much money did you pay when you signed the contract?
02[原告]：<WF^{2}, a>签合同时交付的3万元。	02[P]: I paid 30 thousand yuan when the contract was signed.
03[法官]：<WY^{1}, b>那合同怎么写的5.2万元？	03[J]: Why is there 52 thousand yuan in the contract?
04[原告]：<WY^{2}, a>因为被告欠我2万余元，<WY^{3}, a>我们商定用这2万元顶账。<WF^{3}, a>我交了3万元，<WF^{4}, a>我先给的钱，后签的合同。	04[P]: The defendant owed me over 20 thousand yuan. We agreed to offset the payment with the 20 thousand yuan. Therefore I paid 30 thousand yuan. The contract was signed after I made the payment.

An inconsistency exists in the plaintiff's conceptualization about the amount of money he paid to the defendant. In 01 the judge activates the discourse space of the money paid by the plaintiff when the contract was signed. However, the constituent component provided by the plaintiff in 02 contradicts with that in the contract. As a result, the inconsistency activates a second discourse space which concerns the content of the contract (WY^{1}).

As a response, in 04 the plaintiff employs four information units as constituent components of the space to remove the inconsistency. Units WY^{2} and WY^{3} reveal the reason that has caused the inconsistency. The plaintiff points out that the defendant owed more than 20 thousand yuan to him before the signing of the contract and agreed to offset the debt by the contract. Units WF^{3} and WF^{4} provide further explanations about the signing of the contract, with which the plaintiff intends to show that the defendant knew and agreed to the debt offsetting plan.

It can be seen that the judge and plaintiff take different roles in the interaction. It is the judge who points out the inconsistency and the plaintiff who removes it by offering further explanations.

In some cases, however, the two opposing parties have different explanations or attitudes towards the inconsistency. In that case, the judge may allow both parties to make their own interpretations. But as for which interpretation will be accepted, it is left to the judge to make the final decision.

(41)

01[法官]：<WF[1], b>李XX所说的股权比例在工商局是否有登记？	01[J]: Has the equity ratio proposed by Li XX been registered in the local Trade and Industry Bureau?
02[原代]：<WF[2], a>没有。	02[PA]: No.
03[被代]：<WF[3], a>没有。	03[DA]: No.
04[法官]：<WY[1], b>既然股权比例在工商局没有登记，那么股权转让协议上为什么说XX印刷厂的股份白XX和李XX各占50%呢？	04[J]: Such being the case, why does the equity transfer agreement say that Bai XX and Li XX each hold 50% of the stock shares of the XX Printing Factory?
05[原代]：<WF[4], a>实际上，双方约定的股份和股权在法律上讲是合伙协议，<WY[2], a>因为当事人当时不懂法。	05[PA]: Actually, due to their lack of legal knowledge, in a legal sense the equity transfer agreement entered into by the two parties is a partnership agreement.
06[被代]：<WA[1], a>我们并不认可这件事。<WA[2], a>我们首先对股权转让协议不认可，<WA[3], a>更谈不上其他的。<WF[5], a>且股权转让协议是在白XX晚期病重期间没有第三人证明的情况下写的。	06[DA]: We don't agree. We first don't accept the validity of the equity transfer agreement, let alone other claims. The equity transfer agreement was signed when Bai XX was seriously ill and without being witnessed by a third party.
07[法官]：<WF[6], b>原告按照你所讲，白XX与李XX间的约定是两人内部约定吗？	07[J]: According to the plaintiff's explanation, is the agreement between Bai XX and Li XX a private agreement?
08[原代]：<WF[7], a>对。	08[PA]: Yes.

In this extract, the plaintiff and defendant have formed quite different conceptual contents about the equity ratio. In Turn 1 the judge activates the discourse space of the registration of equity ratio. After getting a negative answer as space components from both parties, the judge questions with unit WY[1] the inconsistency that, according to the equity transfer agreement, Bai XX and Li XX each hold 50% of the stock shares of the printing factory.

In 05 and 06 both parties contribute conflicting explanations as space components. The plaintiff first defines the equity transfer agreement as a partnership agreement with unit WF[4], and then explains with unit WY[2] why the equity ratio was not registered. However, the plaintiff's explanation is challenged by the defendant in Turn 6 with three WA and one WF units. After declaring with three WA units that he does not accept the equity transfer agreement, the defendant further explains the reason for his opposition.

However, except for unit WF[5], the other three units (WA[1], WA[2] and WA[3]) in the defendant's discourse are subjective information units that are employed to reveal attitudes of litigants and contribute little to the explanation of the inconsistency. Therefore, in 07 the judge makes another effort to define the nature of the equity transfer. The positive answer given by the plaintiff in 08 finally removes the inconsistency by defining the equity transfer as a private agreement, which further explains why it is not registered in the local Trade and Industry Bureau.

We can see that, like in Extract (40), the inconsistency of equity transfer in this extract is also initiated by the judge's questioning. But what is different is that the two opposing parties in this extract provide different explanations about the inconsistency, which, although being contradictory, contribute to its final removal.

To sum up, explanatory discourse information can help litigants to eliminate uncertainties in their statements and therefore make their interest appeals more precise and accurate. This is also usually first initiated by the judge either by quoting the utterances of litigants or asking questions which lead to inconsistencies. Then the vagueness or inconsistencies are removed by the joint effort of the judge and litigants.

Explanatory discourse information plays a very important part in ensuring reasonableness of court hearings by helping litigants to make interpretations, elaborate connections and eliminate uncertainties. But different from subjective and objective discourse information, which adopts comparatively fixed information types as their core information units (for example, WA, WI, WJ, WP and pseudo-WF for subjective discourse information; WF, WE and WB for objective discourse information), explanatory discourse information has a wider range in that it can provide explanations not only for subjective discourse information but objective information as well.

Moreover, in court hearings although litigants are the common information source of explanatory discourse information, it is usually first initiated by the judge either in his instructions or with questions.

4.5 Summary

This chapter has explored the features of discourse information in interest appeal in Chinese civil court hearings. Through data analysis, it has been found that subjective discourse information is frequently used by litigants when they make claims or counterclaims. Such information types as WA, WI, WJ, WP and pseudo-WF usually function as the core information units which are combined with other information types to form different information patterns to help litigants claim damage compensation, attribute fault and assert unlawful acts.

Moreover, objective discourse information is usually used by litigants to provide basis for their subjective claims. Such information types as WF, WE and WB are frequently combined with each other to form different information patterns to introduce background, course of infringement, facts of harm and legal or evidential ground for lawsuits.

It has also been found that explanatory discourse information can help participants in lawsuits to make interpretations, elaborate connections and eliminate uncertainties about facts of cases, thus ensuring the reasonableness of court hearings.

Last but not least, it has been found that judges play an important role in ensuring the reasonableness of court hearings in that explanatory discourse information is usually first initiated by judges and then realized by litigants.

5 Factors Influencing Interest Negotiation

5.1 Introduction

In Chapter 4, features of discourse information have been analyzed, offering a detailed description of the distribution and combination of discourse information in interest appeal in Chinese civil court hearings. As was discussed previously, apart from interest appeal, resolution of COI in court hearings also involves negotiation of interest between different parties of lawsuit, which is conducted either between the judge and litigants on the vertical level or between litigants themselves on the horizontal level.

Interest negotiation is mainly a cognitive process that concerns the processing of discourse information. Therefore, in this chapter I will explore the major factors that influence the cognitive process of interest negotiation in Chinese court hearings. Following the analytical framework constructed in Chapter 3, I will analyze the sociological, psychological and discursive factors that are involved in the processing of discourse information during interest negotiation.

5.2 Sociological Factors

According to van Dijk (2008: 56), contexts are a socially based mental model dynamically constructed by participants about "the for-them-relevant properties" of communicative situation. Therefore, the construction of context model can be understood as a sociological process which involves "the definition, interpretation, representation or construction of participants of their social situation" (van Dijk 2008:

19), which influences the distribution of discourse information and the final production and understanding of discourse.

As for the sociological factors that work as the integral components of context models, van Dijk (2008) mainly recognizes two elements: settings and participants. In the following section, I will have a discussion of how these two factors influence negotiation of interest between different parties of lawsuit in court hearings.

5.2.1 Settings

According to van Dijk (2008), settings have two major dimensions, one being temporal settings, and the other, spatial settings. The primary function of settings is to "provide the scene of action, sets temporal and spatial constraints that allow social coordination of social interaction" (van Dijk 2009: 64), and consequently, organize the information about the temporal and spatial properties of interaction (van Dijk 2009: 45).

In court hearings, temporal and spatial settings delineate the time and place of the past or ongoing interactions and may have a direct impact on the negotiation of interest between different parties.

5.2.1.1 Temporal Settings

Time is relevant in the construction of social interaction and discourse, since time is not just chronometric or categorical but a social and interactional construct associated with many different meanings (Collett 1989). Therefore, time is socially meaningful or significant, particularly in such institutional interactions as court hearings in that such interactions are usually temporally monitored to control the production of discourse (van Dijk 2009: 129).

(42)

01[法官]：<WF,C>上次开庭时被告说原告主张的被告欠原告代理费18,202.45元被告方对此不清楚，<WA^1,b>现在还不清楚吗？	01[J]: **In the last court hearing**, the defendant said that he was unclear about the plaintiff's request of the agency fee of 18,202.45 yuan. Is the defendant still unclear **now**?
02[被告]：<WA^2,a>还要继续核实。	02[D]: We still need to check the request.
03[法官]：<WT,A>向被告释明，<WP,A>如果你方对是否欠原告代理费做不置可否的答复，法院可能做出对对方有利的判决。	03[J]: The court has to make it clear that **if** the defendant still gives a vague answer to the plaintiff's request for the agency fee the court **may** enter into a judgment favorable to the plaintiff.
04[被告]：<WA^3,A>我们明白。	04[D]: We understand.

In this extract, the judge tries to form conceptualization about whether the defendant has made payment to the plaintiff for the agency fee. The conceptualization is mainly based on the construction of the temporal setting realized by two deictic expressions *上次开庭时 (in the last trial)* and *现在 (now)* and a conditional structure *如果 ...可能 (if...may)*. The temporal setting is constructed by the judge to impose temporal constraint on the response of the defendant.

In 01 the judge first quotes with a reporting structure *被告说 (the defendant said)* the defendant's attitude towards the agency fees. In the reporting structure, the deictic expression *上次开庭时 (in the last trial)* in the WF unit assigns a temporal feature to the information *被告方对此不清楚 (he was unclear)* provided by the defendant and defines it as a "past" event. It also indicates that the information is still legally effective in that it was made *when the court was in session (开庭时)*.

In unit WA^2, the judge switches the temporal settings from the "past" to the "present" with another temporal deixis *现在 (now)* and asks whether the defendant still holds the same attitude towards the agency fees. The deixis highlights the contrast between the two temporal spaces, with which the judge intends to constrain the defendant's response to a clear answer in the present setting.

Unsatisfied with the defendant's vague answer in 02, in 03 the judge shifts to the "future" setting with a WP unit. Different from the "past" and "present" settings which are activated by temporal deixis, the "future" setting is activated by a conditional structure *如果... 可能 (if...may)* to generate construal of the potential risks the defendant may face for not providing definite answers. The judge's construal of the temporal settings can be illustrated by Figure 5-1.

It can be seen that the judge has an efficient management of the temporal settings of the discourse, which ranges through three spaces: past, present and future. The past setting, by describing the insufficient information the defendant provides, points to the present setting, which asks for his clear attitude. The future setting also offers strong support for the present one by predicting the potential consequence of the vague answers. The judge's management of temporal settings can contribute to the final resolution of the dispute by imposing constraints on the information provided by the defendant and ensuring the smooth operation of the trial.

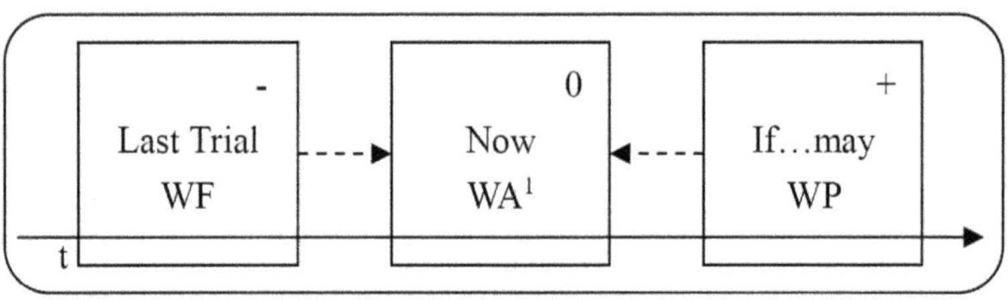

Figure 5-1. The Judge's Construal of the Temporal Settings.

Apart from designating temporal constraints on actions of participants, time can also help to organize the order of discourse or communicative events by assigning beginnings and endings or sequential organizations (van Dijk 2009: 61). This function of temporal setting is of significant importance in the negotiation of the attitudes of opposing litigants.

(43)

01[法官]：<1,2,2,21,WT^1,A>法庭调查结束。<0,1,1,3,WT^2,A>现在开始法庭辩论。<1,3,2,22,WT^3,A>首先由上诉人发表辩论意见。	01[J]: That's the **end** of court investigation. **Now** proceed to court debate. **First** the appellant shall give out his opinions.
02[上诉人]：<2,22,3,35,WF^1,O>被上诉人给杨X交了一年社保，<2,22,3,36,WJ,A>证明了双方的劳动关系……	02[AT]: The appellee has paid social security for Yang X for one year, which can prove the labor relation between them.
03[法官]：<1,3,2,23,WT^4,A>下面由被上诉人发表辩论意见。	03[J]: **Next** the appellee shall give out his opinions.
04[被上诉人]：<2,23,3,37,WA,A>我们认为两被上诉人没有录用杨X的约定和法定义务，<2,23,3,38,WF^2,A>实际上也没有录用过杨X。	04[AE]: We think that the two appellees do not have the legal obligations to hire Yang X. Actually, we didn't ever hire Yang X.

In this extract, the two litigants negotiate over the validity of their labor relations, which constitute an important component of the context model. In the instructions the judge employs such temporal deixis as *结束(the end of court investigation)*, *现在开始 (now proceed to)*, *首先(first)* and *下面(now)* to organize the sequence of the communicative events of the litigants.

The first deictic expression *结束(the end of court investigation)* signals the closing of the discourse space of court investigation and the end of evidence production and examination. The following expression *现在开始(now proceed to)* activates the discourse space of court debate and constrains the litigants' speech to the negotiation of the disputed issues. Similarly, the deictic pair *首先(first)* and *下面(next)* assign a procedural sequence to the communicative events of the two opposing parties.

On the level of speech management, the temporal deixis can also help to control the flow of discourse information. For example, the expressions *结束(the end of court investigation)* and *开始(now proceed to)* in 01 make a perfect pair in regulating the flow of discourse information on the first level (<0,1,1,2> and <0,1,1,3>), by which the information flowing to the information knot of <0,1,1,2> is switched off while that to <0,1,1,3> is switched on. In the same vein, the judge's instruction with *首先(fist)* and *下面(next)* impose constraint on the direction of information flow on the second level, especially on such units as WF^{1}, WJ, WA, and WF^{2}. The management helps the litigants to have an intensive discussion of the validity of the labor relation between the two opposing parties.

From here we can see that temporal deixis can help to assign beginnings and closings to trial procedures or organize the sequence of communicative actions and thus impose constraints on the interest negotiation between the opposing parties.

5.2.1.2 Spatial Settings

Like temporal settings, spatial settings or places are also socially relevant to the production and interpretation of discourse, in that they are not merely locations where communicative events take place but are closely associated with socially shared knowledge, attitudes and ideologies as well (van Dijk 2009: 46). Accordingly, van Dijk (2009: 47) divides spatial settings into three basic types: personal and interpersonal places/spaces, geographical places/spaces, and social places/spaces.

Personal and interpersonal space "deals with spatial aspects of communicative situations, such as the location of the participants and the distances between each of them" (van Dijk 2009: 48) and is relevant for the interpretation of spatial deixis in discourse. In court hearings, expressions of spatial deixis are employed to highlight the interpersonal space between the opposing parties and thus may exert influence on the outcome of interest negotiation.

(44)

[被告]：<WF^{1},A>针对原告在本次交通事故中受到的伤害，<WA,A>本代理人代表XXX运输公司在此对原告表示同情和歉意。<WF^{2},O>在事故发生后，我们在第一时间赶赴现场参与伤员救治，<WF^{3},O>在医院积极垫付医疗费3万2千余元。<WP,A>上述情况提请法庭在裁判时予以注意。

[D]: As for the injury the plaintiff suffered in the traffic accident, on behalf of XXX Transportation Company the attorney **here** expresses our sincere sympathy and apology. After the accident, we arrived at **the scene of the accident** immediately and took part in the rescue of the injured. We also made an advance payment of 3.2 thousand yuan **in the hospital**, which we hope should be noticed by the court when entering into the final judgment.

The extract is part of the closing argument of the defendant in a traffic accident lawsuit. The defendant negotiates with the plaintiff over the amount of compensatory damages. The defendant's conceptualization is mainly based on the participant component in the context model.

To be specific, the defendant employs such deictic expressions as *在此 (here)*, *现场 (scene of the accident)* and *在医院(in the hospital)* to shorten the interpersonal distance between him and the plaintiff.

Units WF^1 and WA are used to express the defendant's sympathy and apology for the hurt the plaintiff suffers from the accident. In unit WA, the spatial setting (the court) is highlighted by a deictic expression *在此 (here)* to make the court occasion prominent. In the following discourse, two other spatial deixis, *现场 (scene of the accident)* in unit WF^2 and *在医院 (in the hospital)* in unit WF^3, are used to indicate that the defendant was with the plaintiff all along and tried his every effort to offer help.

Cognitively, the spatial deixis in the extract reflect the successive way of construal of the defendant in the construction of the context model. Moreover, the spatial deixis are associated not only with the facts concerning the accident but also with such context model elements as the defendant's attitudes towards these facts. For example, in the two spaces (the scene of the accident and hospital) activated by units WF^2 and WF^3, the defendant highlights his effort in saving the injured: *参与伤员救治(took part in the rescue of the injured)* and *积极垫付医疗费(made an advance payment)*. Their information sharing category (Category O) indicates that these two WF units are common knowledge shared by the litigants and the judge as well. Moreover, in the space of courtroom activated by unit WA, the defendant highlights *在此(here)* to emphasize the formality and sincerity of his sympathy and apology.

The employment of the spatial deixis can help to shorten the interpersonal space between the defendant and the plaintiff, which lays a foundation for the following court conciliation.

According to van Dijk (2009: 52), the notion of geographical place is mainly used to outline boundaries between ingroups and outgroups, which set up obstacles for such outsiders as strangers, foreigners, etc. Therefore, geographical places are often taken as "markers for exclusion, ethnocentrism, racism and nationalism" (van Dijk (2009:

52). Consequently, geographical places may work as a constraint on the speaking manners of conversation participants. This can be illustrated by the institutional features of the discourse produced by litigants in court hearings.

(45)

01[法官]：<WT,A>下面法庭向双方当事人进行发问。<WF^{1}，b>原告，事故发生后在医院有没有动手术？	01[J]: Now the **court** shall ask questions to the two parties. Did the plaintiff ever undertake any surgical operations in the hospital after the accident?
02[原告]：<WF^{2}, a>动过两次手术。	02[P]: I have undergone two operations.
03[法官]：<WF^{3}, b>哪个部位？	03[J]: On which part of the body?
04[原告]：<WF^{4}，a>右边这个…这个脑部…那个颅脑。	04[P]: The right, well…the right **brain**, well…the right **craniocerebrum**.
05[法官]：<WF^{5}，b>你受伤之后你所经营的餐饮（店）有没有停业？	05[J]: Was your restaurant closed down after you were injured?
06[原告]：<WF^{6}，a>当时我根本就不知道，<WY, a>都在里面躺着。	06[P]: I didn't know because I was in the hospital.
07[法官]：<WF^{7}, b>有没有停业？	07[J]: Was it closed down?
08[原告]：<WF^{8}, a>我老婆…我自己…我夫人都在医院里面。	08[P]: My missus…and I myself… my **wife** were both in hospital.

The judge here negotiates with the plaintiff over two important conceptual contents: 1) the part of the body that was operated on and 2) whether the restaurant was closed down. The plaintiff's answer is obviously influenced by the institutional setting of the context model.

In 01 the judge initiates the questioning and answering process with a WT unit, in which the word *法庭 (the court)* highlights the geographical setting of the following conversation. At the same time, it also activates the relevant institutional features that exert influence on the discourse of the litigants. One of the important features of court discourse is its legal professionality (Ge 2011), which is mainly manifested in the diction of discourse.

The feature of professionality associated with the geographical setting of court has greatly influenced the plaintiff's construal of the situation, which is finally reflected in his word choice. For example, in 03 when the judge asks the plaintiff which part of the body was operated on, the plaintiff first uses *脑部 (brain)* and then changes it to a very professional medical term *颅脑 (craniocerebrum)*. It shows that the plaintiff is obviously unsatisfied with the first term *脑部 (brain),* which is mainly used in everyday conversations and does not conform to his construal of the formality of the court setting. Thus the plaintiff changes it to a more formal one which he believes is preferred by the court.

The constraint is also indicated on the level of speech management, which is demonstrated by the hesitation that exists in the process of the plaintiff's word selection, marked by the discourse markers *这个 (well)* and *那个 (well)*. Before *脑部 (brain)* is produced, discourse marker*这个(well)* is used twice. The hesitation shows that the plaintiff is trying to search in his vocabulary for the right word to answer the question of the judge. When he finds that*脑部(brain)*is not professional enough, the plaintiff makes a second try, indicated by discourse marker*那个(well)*, and finally finds the professional one *颅脑 (craniocerebrum)*.

Similarly, hesitation also happens in the judge's negotiation with the plaintiff over the second fact. In 07 when the judge asks him for the second time whether the restaurant was closed down, the plaintiff, instead of giving a definite answer, describes the fact that he and his wife were both in the hospital. In this answer, the plaintiff first uses a very colloquial deictic expression *我老婆 (my missus)* to refer to his wife. After realizing the inappropriateness of the expression, the plaintiff goes back to make a repair and changes it to *我夫人 (my wife)*, which conforms to the solemnity of the geographical setting.

What can be seen from the above is that geographical setting exerts great influence on the word choice of the participants during interest negotiation by activating the constraint of the institutional features of court hearings.

Apart from interpersonal and geographical settings, social settings are also important factors in spatial settings that may affect the process of interest negotiation. Social settings are defined by van Dijk (2009: 48) in terms of people's joint and collective activities in everyday life. They are concerned with norms, rules and constraints that influence or even control the discourses that take place there (van Dijk 2009: 50). As a typical institutional setting, the verbal exchanges between participants in court hearings are strictly constrained by the court rules.

(46)

01[法官]：<WT,A>第二被告保险公司对该组证据发表质证意见。	01[J]: The second defendant, the insurance company shall give out his opinions on the evidence.
02[二被代]：<WP^{1},A>法官请允许我加一下，<WY,A>因为复印件不清楚。	02[DA2]: Please allow me to make the calculation, because the copy is not clear enough.
03[法官]：<WA^{1},A>好的。	03[J]: OK.
04（*[一被代]：<WF^{1},A>这个我已经加过了。*	04*([DA1]: I've made the calculation about this one.*
05*[二被代]：<WF^{2}, b>加过了？*	05*[DA2]: Have you?*
06*[一被代]：<WF^{3}, a>加过了。*	06*[DA1]: Yes. I have.*
07*[二被代]：<WP^{2},A>去掉那个…去掉那个…*	07*[DA2]: Take out that one…take out that one.*
08*[一被代]：<WA^{2},A>对。<WF^{4},A>他把那个躺椅费加在里面了。）*	08*[DA1]: Yes. He has included the expenses of the deck chair.)*
09[二被代]：<WP^{3},A>我们要求扣除躺椅的费用。	09[DA2]: We request that the expenses of the deck chair be excluded.

Note: The italicized exchanges in brackets are conducted in a very low voice.

The two defendants negotiate with each other over their attitudes towards the evidence produced by the plaintiff. Due to the constraint of the court rules, which form the social setting of the context model, the conversation between the defendants and the judge displays quite different features from that between the defendants themselves.

In 01 the judge instructs the second defendant with a WT unit to cross-examine the evidence produced by the plaintiff. However, feeling that he cannot form an immediate attitude, the second defendant proposes with a WP unit to calculate the amount of the compensatory damages.

This proposition reflects the second defendant's construal of the court rules which in turn impose constraint on the participants' behaviors in that, according to Article 7 of the court Rules of the PRC, the speaking and arguing of litigants cannot be performed without the permission of judges. The constraint is also shown by the defendant's polite expression *请允许我 (please allow me)* and the revealing of the reason with the WY unit.

From 04 to 08, the two defendants engage a negotiation of the amount of compensatory damages. Although being permitted by the judge in 03 with unit WA[1], the conversation is still conducted in a very low voice, which is indicated by the italicization of the interaction in brackets. It shows that the two defendants' construal of the social space still constrains their behaviors, because they recognize that how the calculation is made is not the focus of the court.

In contrast, in 09, as a response to the judge's instruction in 01, the second defendant resumes the normal speaking voice and reports to the court with unit WP[3] the result of their negotiation. The different features manifested in the conversation between the two defendants and in that between the judge and the defendant show that court rules can exert great impact on interest negotiation.

To sum up, temporal and spatial settings play important roles in the negotiation of interest in court hearings. Temporal settings are usually activated by temporal deixis to organize or impose constraint on the sequence of communicative actions of litigants. As for spatial settings, spatial deixis can be emphasized to shorten the interpersonal space between litigants; geographical settings can influence the word choice of litigants; and social settings can exert constraint on the speaking manners of participants of lawsuits.

5.2.2 Participants

Van Dijk (2009: 65) defines participants as social actors that occupy the central position of communication, since "it is quite likely that in general gender, ethnicity, age, occupation (profession), position or status of social actors have a systematic impact on activities, text and talk". Therefore, the properties of social actors define the appropriateness of activities and discourse (van Dijk 2009: 65–66). Of the various properties of social actors, social identities and social relations will be analyzed in the following to see how they influence the negotiation of interest in court hearings.

5.2.2.1 *Social Identities*

People participate in social situations not only as individuals with personal experiences but also as members of social groups with shared beliefs, evaluations and emotions, etc. (van Dijk, 2009: 70–71). Social identity is usually used as opposed to personal identity and defined by Tajfel & Turner (1986) as the individual identification with a group, which has a causal relationship to the actions and behaviors of participants.

In court hearings, social identity may function as one of the important factors that influence the outcome of interest negotiation. For example, in the following extract, the identity of the information source of the testimony has increased the acceptability of the plaintiff's claims.

(47)

01[法官]：<WR^{1}，a>种子是从哪进的？	01[J]: Where did you buy the seeds?
02[原告]：<WR^{2}，b>平X种子公司。<WF, a>该单位是国营单位。	02[P]: Ping X Seed Company. It's a **state-run company**.
03[原告]：<WI^{1}，A>我的庄稼出现问题和种子无关。<WY, A>我的种子是从正规企业购买，<WI^{2},A>不存在质量问题。	03[P]: The poor seedling emergence has nothing to do with the seeds because I bought them from a **formal enterprise**. They had no quality problems.

In this case, the issue whether the poor seedling emergence was caused by the defendant's mishandling in the wheat-sowing process or by the disqualified seeds the plaintiff bought becomes the focus in the conceptualizations of participants of the lawsuit. In the extract, the quality of seeds is the subject of negotiation between the judge and the plaintiff.

The plaintiff's conceptualization is mainly supported by the "identity" element in the context model, which is initiated by the judge's questioning with a WR unit (WR^{1}). The judge indicates that since the quality of the seeds cannot be detected directly, the business entity that sells seeds can be used as a reference for seed quality. Therefore, in 02 the plaintiff provides two information units (WR^{2} and WF) as an answer to the judge's question. Unit WR^{2} provides the name of the seed company *平X种子公司 (Ping X Seed Company)*. Unit WF reveals the identity of the company: *国营单位(a state-run company)*.

Among the various features associated with the seed company, its identity as a state-run company becomes prominent in the construal of the plaintiff in that it activates such hidden evaluations and shared beliefs as good reputation and honest business. The shared evaluations are then made explicit by the plaintiff with unit WY in 03, with *正规企业 (formal enterprise)* being emphasized. It indicates that as a formal enterprise, *平X种子公司(Ping X Seed Company)* is believed to comply with laws and regulations. The plaintiff makes it clear that it is impossible for them to sell disqualified seeds (WI^2), and therefore the poor seedling emergence has nothing to do with the quality of the seeds the plaintiff bought (WI^1).

We can see that during interest negotiation the plaintiff has based his inference on his construal of the social identity of the seed company. Social identity can help to increase the acceptability of the claims of participants by activating its shared evaluations or beliefs.

In some cases, in order to emphasize the different social responsibilities that litigants take, more than one social identity can be introduced. Together with these social identities, different social values and beliefs are activated as well, as is in the following extract.

(48)

[原告]：<WF^1,A>在我父亲病重的时候汪某作为妻子没有尽到照顾的责任，<WF^2,A>我父亲被迫无奈要求在我哥哥家养老。<WF^3,A>作为继承人都没有履行抚养义务，<WJ,A>我相信继承法也有这条规定，她不应该享有继承的权利。	[P]: When my father was seriously ill, Wang X did't fulfill her responsibility **as a wife**. Having no choice, my father had to ask my brother to take care of him. **As an inheritor**, she didn't fulfill her legal obligations to look after her husband. I'm sure it is prescribed in the inheritance law that she has no right of inheritance.

The two opposing parties negotiate over the inheritance rights to a real estate. In the conceptualization of the plaintiff, the defendant's inheritance right is strongly opposed.

The opposition is based on his construal of the defendant's identities from two different perspectives: the construal of the defendant as a wife and as an heir. In unit WF^1, the plaintiff introduces the defendant's first social identity *妻子(wife)*. It activates the shared beliefs related to the identity of a wife, one of which is, according to Chinese traditional culture, to take care of her husband. Therefore, when the plaintiff states with unit WF^1 that the defendant did not look after his father when he was seriously ill, he indicates that she has failed to perform her responsibilities associated with the identity of wife and thus should not get the inheritance.

In unit WF^3, the defendant's second social identity *继承人 (heir)* is introduced. Different from the identity of wife, which defines responsibilities from the perspective of traditional culture, the identity of heir activates the relevant provisions on the legal obligations the defendant has to fulfill. According to Law of Succession of the PRC, although spouse is first in order when getting inheritance, Article 13 makes it clear that "successors who had the ability and were in a position to maintain the decedent but failed to fulfill their duties shall be given no share or a smaller share of the estate". With units WF^3 and WJ, the plaintiff declares that the defendant has failed to fulfill her duty to look after her sick spouse, and therefore has no right to get the inheritance.

The defendant's different social identities have activated different evaluations or beliefs about the duties the defendant should fulfill, which can function as the premise of the propositions of litigants in interest negotiation.

5.2.2.2 Social Relations

Social relations refer to the interpersonal relationships between individuals, which have impacts on the motivation, production, comprehension and evaluation of human social life (Fiske 1992). The actual discursive performance of such relationships usually depends on "socially shared and culturally variable knowledge about social relations" (van Dijk 2009: 78).

In court hearings, apart from the power or deputy relations, participants of lawsuits may be involved in other kinds of social relations, which may have influence on the production, comprehension or acceptance of their discourses.

(49)

01[证人]：<WF^{1},A>我要证明的内容是：被告曾承诺如果原告第一个在拆迁协议书上签字，将获得5,000元额外奖励。	01[W]: What I want to prove is that the defendant once promised that if the plaintiff was the first who signed his name of the demolition agreement he would get 5,000 yuan as extra award.
02[法官]：<WT, b>双方当事人有无向证人发问的？	02[J]: Do the two parties have any questions to ask the witness?
03[被告]：<WF^{2}, b>你与原告是什么关系？	03[D]: What social relation are you in with the plaintiff?
04[证人]：<WF^{3}, a>原告是我叔公。<WF^{4}, a>但我说的都是事实。	04[W]: The plaintiff is my great uncle. But what I said is true.
05[被告]：<WY, A>证人与原告有利害关系，<WA, A>其证言我们不认可。	05[D]: The witness and the plaintiff have interest involvement. Therefore we do not accept his testimony.

The defendant negotiates with the witness over the acceptability of the testimony. The social relation between the witness and the defendant becomes prominent in both parties' conceptualizations.

In 01 with a WF unit the witness activates a past discourse space, where the defendant has promised to pay 5,000 yuan to the plaintiff as a reward if the plaintiff is the first to sign on the demolition contract. In the discourse space, the focus of the witness's construal is on the content of the defendant's promise, which would put the defendant in an unfavorable position if the court accepts the testimony.

However, on the part of the defendant, the witness's testimony is construed differently, with the focus shifted to the social relation between the witness and the plaintiff. With unit WF^{2}, the defendant intends to challenge the credibility of the testimony by proving the kinship relation between the witness and the plaintiff, since, according to Article 77 of Some Provisions of the Supreme People's Court on Evidence in Civil Procedures, the evidence provided by witnesses who are in kinship or other close relations with litigants has a weaker probative force compared with that of other witnesses.

Recognizing the defendant's intention, the witness, after admitting the kinship (great-uncle) between him and the plaintiff (WF^{3}), promises with unit WF^{4} that what he testifies is sound facts. However, this promise is not convincing enough compared with the defendant's challenge in 05. The defendant declares clearly that he will not accept the witness's testimony because of the kinship relation between the witness and the plaintiff.

It shows that social relation is a very important factor that influences the acceptability of the witness's testimony. Sometimes, however, social relation is employed by litigants to support their propositions in interest negotiation.

(50)

01[原告]：<WF^{1},A>我父亲去世2005年12月15日到现在，这个房屋贷款都是我偿还的。<WF^{2},A>我对我父亲尽到了主要的赡养义务，<WF^{3},A>一直和我父亲居住在一起，<WF^{4},A>我一直在老人身边照顾，<WJ,A>所以我应该多分。	01[P]: I've been making the mortgage payment ever since the death of my father on December 15th, 2005. I have fulfilled my obligation of maintenance of my father by living with him, and taking care of him. Therefore I should get more inheritance right.
02[被告]：<WF^{5},C>我们是1982年8月登记结婚。<WF^{6},C>当时原告2岁，<WF^{7},C>原告母亲在原告8个月的时候就去世了。<WF^{8}, A>我和马X结婚后真心实意对她（原告）好，<WF^{9},A>照顾原告，<WF^{10},A>非常喜欢原告。	02[D]: We got married in August, 1982, when the plaintiff was two years old, whose mother passed away when she was only eight months old. After I got married with Ma X, I've been sincerely kind to her (the plaintiff). I've been taking care of her and like her all the time.

The plaintiff and the defendant (the plaintiff's stepmother) negotiate over the inheritance right to an apartment. In their conceptualizations, they resort to different social relations in the context model to back up their claims for the right to inherit the apartment.

In 01 the relationship between the plaintiff and her father becomes prominent in the plaintiff's construal of all the social relations. The relation is elaborated from two respects: the plaintiff's repayment of mortgage (WF^{1}) and her fulfillment of the obligation of maintenance (WF^{2}, WF^{3} and WF^{4}). The plaintiff's construal of the relation helps to back up her claim that she should get more inheritance right (WJ).

In contrast, in 02 the relationship between the defendant and the plaintiff is made prominent in the defendant's construal. Units WF^{6} and WF^{7} describe the miserable situation of the plaintiff when they entered into the social relation of mother and daughter. The defendant indicates that there was a good basis for them to foster a close relationship since the relation of mother and daughter was established at her early age (at the age of two). Units WF^{8}, WF^{9} and WF^{10} describe the defendant's care and fondness of the plaintiff.

On the level of speech management, the two opposing parties have employed different strategies in interpreting the social relations involved in the lawsuit. The plaintiff focuses more on the legal aspects of the social relation when she talks about the kinship. For example, with the legal expression *赡养义务(maintenance obligation)*, unit WF^{2} activates the legal features of the social relation between the plaintiff and her father. Units WF^{3} and WF^{4} describe the details of how the plaintiff fulfilled the legal obligations required by that social relation: living with her father (WF^{3}) and looking after him (WF^{4}).

In contrast, the defendant focuses more on the emotional aspects when talking about her relation with the plaintiff. The defendant indicates that she has fulfilled the duty of a mother and used to be in good terms with the plaintiff. The defendant's emotional appeal in her argument expresses her regret for the ongoing lawsuit with the plaintiff and lays a foundation for the final conciliation.

It shows that the definition of social relations in interest negotiation is a dynamic selection by litigants themselves. Social relations can activate either legal or emotional features, which function as the basis for the propositions of litigants.

In short, the identities and relations of participants in lawsuits can exert great influence on interest negotiation in court hearings. By activating the social values or beliefs associated with them, social identities and relations can help to increase the acceptability and reliability of the testimony or evidence produced.

5.3 Psychological Factors

According to van Dijk's (2008) definition, context is participants' mental or psychological construct of social situations. Therefore, apart from the sociological factors analyzed in the previous section that affect the process of communication, psychological factors also have influence on the information distribution and final production and interpretation of participants' discourses.

Among the various kinds of psychological factors, van Dijk (2008, 2009) highlights intentions and goals and knowledge. Focusing more on the cognitive aspects of social communication, Langacker (2008) regards construal phenomena as one of the essential psychological factors that influence discourse production and interpretation. Therefore, in this section, I will have a discussion of how participants' intentions and goals, information sharing and construal phenomena influence the process of interest negotiation in Chinese civil court hearings.

5.3.1 Intentions and Goals

Intentions and goals play important roles in the production and interpretation of discourse (Zwaan & Radvansky 1998), since it is the understanding of intentions or goals that help language speakers infer what the others are doing, thus making their discourse meaningful (van Dijk 2009). Van Dijk (2008: 81) distinguishes between intentions and goals by defining the former as the starting point of participants' actions and the latter as the wanted consequences of their actions.

According to Xu (2013), goals mainly influence the layout of discourse information as a whole and are thus more general, while intentions facilitate the attainment of goals by driving the local development of discourse information and are thus more concrete. Therefore, in the following analysis, I will mainly focus on the discussion of how the intentions of litigants influence the local development of discourse information, which in turn helps to facilitate their attainment of goals during interest negotiation.

5.3.1.1 Expression of Intentions and Goals

In court hearings, participants' precise expression and recognition of the intentions and goals of their own or the opposing party may have a direct influence on the result of interest negotiation. Therefore, in most cases, participants of lawsuits tend to express their intentions and goals in a direct and explicit way, on the basis of which their different attitudes or positions are negotiated.

(51)

01[原告]：<WF^{1},A>第四组证据，【2009】0800号批复，<WF^{2},A>证明丰台环境保护局审批仅同意原告经营中餐服务项目，碳烧烤加工食品被禁止经营。<WF^{3},A>在合同第二条中有约定。
02[被告]：<WA^{1},A>真实性无异议，<WA^{2},A>对证明目的有异议。<WF^{4},A>对方应该知道有该规定，但仍进行经营，<WI,A>不足以导致原告所诉事实。<WF^{5},A>补充一点，该批复日期是09年12月，<WF^{6},A>但开业时间09年6月9日，<WJ,A>所以原告的损失与我们无关。

01[P]: The fourth evidence, the No. 0800 approval of 2009, to **prove that the Environmental Protection Bureau of Fengtai has only approved the plaintiff's business of food service, with the barbecue being prohibited.** This is also made clear in Article 2 of the contract.
02[D]: No objection to the authenticity of the evidence. We object to the purpose of the evidence. The opposing party should have known of the prohibition but has still been engaged in the business, **which should not lead to the facts described by the plaintiff.** One more thing, the approval was made in December 2009. However, the restaurant opened on June 9th, 2009. **Therefore, the plaintiff's losses have nothing to do with the defendant.**

In this case, the plaintiff signed a contract with the defendant to run a franchised outlet and later sued him for not fulfilling the duty of disclosure which led to the plaintiff's economic losses. During the negotiation over the evidence in the extract, both parties have given an explicit expression of their intentions and goals.

The discourse in 01 is composed of three WF units, among which unit WF^{2} becomes prominent in the construal since it reveals the intention of the plaintiff. With unit WF^{2}, the plaintiff intends to prove two facts, one being the approval for the plaintiff to deal in Chinese food, and the other, the prohibition to deal in barbecue food. The intention is supported by units WF^{1} and WF^{3}, which reveal the fact that the two parties have reached an agreement on dealing in barbecue food. By exposing the intentions underlying the WF information, the plaintiff aims to achieve the goal to blame the defendant for his non-performance of duties to disclose the potential policy risks.

The discourse of the defendant in 02 is based on a different construal of the event: to contrast and rebut that of the plaintiff. Although the defendant first affirms the credibility of the evidence with unit WA^1, he immediately challenges its proving intention with unit WA^2. In the following, the defendant makes further explanations of his challenge with units WF^4, WF^5 and WF^6. On the basis of the challenge, with unit WI, the defendant denies his responsibility to disclose the potential risks. Units WF^5 and WF^6 make a further description of the inconsistency between the approval date of Environmental Protection Bureau and the opening date of the restaurant, based on which a WJ unit is employed to reveal the ultimate goal of the defendant: *原告的损失与我们无关 (the plaintiff's losses have nothing to do with the defendant)*. The construal and revelation of the two opposing parties' intentions and goals can be illustrated by Figure 5-2.

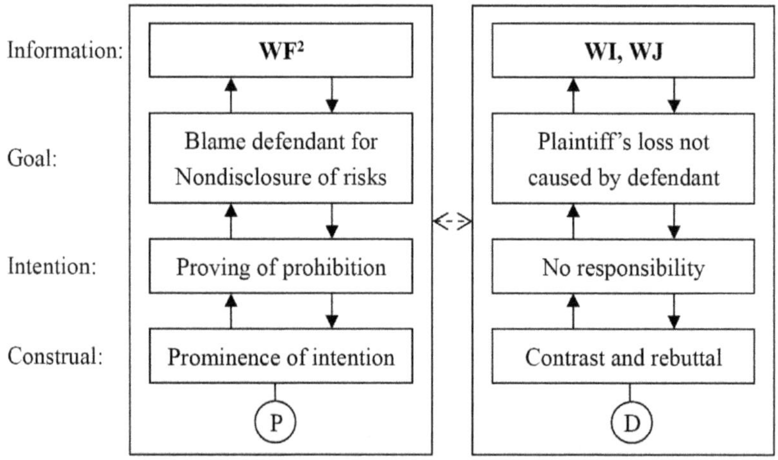

Figure 5-2. Revelation of Participants' Intentions and Goals.

It shows that the two litigants have exposed their intentions and goals in a clear and straightforward way. This can facilitate the negotiation of different positions of the opposing parties. However, sometimes the expression of litigants' intentions or goals is not as clear as required. Under such circumstances, the judge may have an active interference with the negotiation process to help reveal their intentions.

(52)

01[法官]：<WA^1, a>原告，你的意思就是说拆迁补偿款中有一部分是你们应该拿到的，<WP, a>因此主张按评估报告来计算出你们应得的补偿款？	01[J]: **Does the plaintiff mean that you are entitled to part of the demolition compensation** and therefore you propose to allocate the compensation based on the appraisal report?
02[原告]：<WA^2, b>是这样的。	02[P]: Yes.
03[法官]：<WF^1, a>被告的意思是根本就没有拆迁，**<WF^2, a>**也没有得到赔偿款？	03[J]: **Does the defendant mean that there was no demolition and therefore no demolition compensation?**
04[被告]：<WF^3, b>是的。	04[D]: Yes.

In this case, the plaintiff rented the defendant's vegetable greenhouses for vegetable growing, which were demolished later. The plaintiff claimed that he should get the compensation for his economic losses caused by the demolition. However, during the court investigation, both parties focus on the negotiation of details of facts, with their intentions undisclosed. Therefore, the judge interferes actively with the negotiation and asks questions about their intentions.

In 01 the judge asks about the intentions of the plaintiff with units WA^1 and WP. Unit WA^1 reveals the plaintiff's intention to get part of the demolition compensation: *拆迁补偿款中有一部分是你们应该拿到的(you are entitled to part of the demolition compensation)*. Unit WP reveals the plaintiff's intention to allocate the compensation based on the appraisal report. These intentions conform to the ultimate goal of the plaintiff in the lawsuit, namely, to require the defendant to pay for his economic losses caused by the demolition.

In 03 the judge asks about the defendant's intentions underlying his account of facts about the demolition. Unit WF^1 reveals his intention to prove that the demolition did not happen; unit WF^2 reveals his intention to prove that there was not compensation for demolition at all. These intentions are consistent with the goal of the defendant that he will not make any payment for the so claimed economic losses of the plaintiff.

In the extract, in order to reveal the litigants' intentions, the judge has imposed an effective management on the way the questions are asked. For example, the judge starts both his questions with interrogative structures *你的意思就是说 (Do you mean)* and *被告的意思是 (Does the defendant mean)*, which are usually employed to disclose the communicative aims of participants (see Figure 5-3).

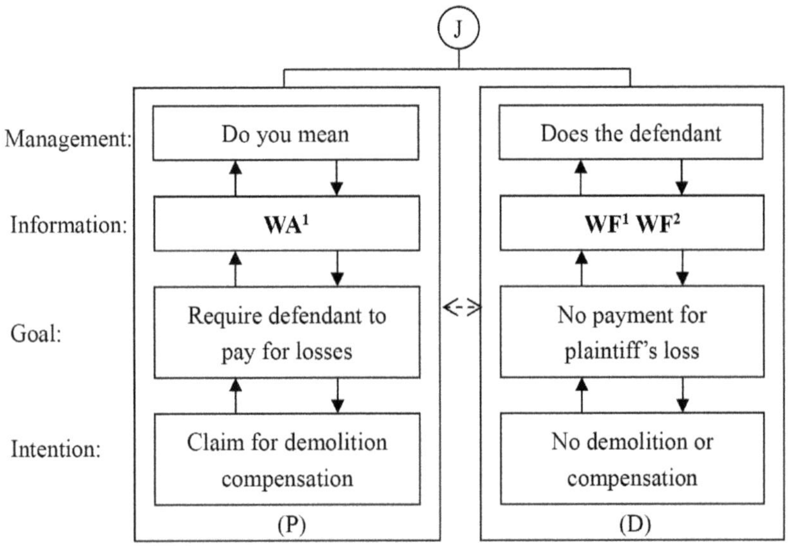

Figure 5-3. Judge's Effort to Reveal Participants' Intentions.

By revealing the intentions of the litigants, the judge's questioning can facilitate the understanding of their basic goals in the lawsuit, thus making preparations for the employment of effective measures to resolve the dispute.

5.3.1.2 Modification of Intentions and Goals

According to Du (2010), litigants' communicative intentions and goals are modified with the progress of court hearings. Xu (2013) investigates the adjustment of the communicative goals of litigants in court conciliation and has found that opposing parties adjust their goals through rounds of offers and counter-offers. Apart from the adjustment of communicative goals through negotiation between opposing parties, their goals can also be completely modified through the conciliation of judges, as is in the following extract.

(53)

01[法官]：<WA^1,A>被告认可事实，<WA^2,A>也认可协议。<WF^1,A>本院和被告做了调解工作，**<WA^3,A>**被告同意返还你两幅画。<WF^2,C>你们两个人又是网友，<WF^3,C>也认识这么长时间了。<WF^4,O>但是（被告）今天未到庭，<WA^3,b>你陈述一下最后意见？	01[J]: The defendant accepts the facts and the agreement. The court has conciliated with the defendant. **He agreed to return the two pictures.** You are net friends and have known each other for quite a long time. But the defendant is not here today. Can you make a closing argument?
02[原告]：<WF^5,O>既然被告同意返还两幅画……，<WF^6,A>我们俩还涉及一个借款，<WB,A>并给我打了欠条，<WY,A>因为那个借款没有还给我，<WP^1,C>我就想要回我送给被告的两幅画。**<WP^2,A>**画我就不要了，**<WP^3,A>**我今天就撤诉吧。	02[P]: Since the defendant agrees to return the two pictures.... We've been also involved in a loan and he's written an IOU to me. It is because he failed to pay back the loan that I wanted to get the pictures back. **I surrender my right to the pictures and withdraw the lawsuit now.**

In the extract, the plaintiff claims for the return of the two paintings given to the defendant as gifts. As a result of the judge's conciliation, the plaintiff modifies his communicative goals and decides to withdraw the lawsuit.

In 01 the judge first conveys with two WA units (WA^1 and WA^2) the defendant's positive attitude towards the facts and evidence of the case, which lays a foundation for the following negotiation. After introducing the conciliation effort the court has exerted on the defendant (WF^1), the judge presents with unit WA^3 the modification of the defendant's goal of litigation: *被告同意返还你两幅画(He agreed to return the two pictures)*. By conveying the attitudes and modification of the goal of the defendant, the judge implicitly expresses the intention to ask the plaintiff to modify his litigation goals. For that purpose, the judge recounts the social relation between the two parties with two WF units (WF^2 and WF^3), which highlight the good terms they have been in.

The judge's introduction of defendant's modification of goal of litigation and the emphasis of the social relation between the two parties has positively affected the plaintiff's construal of the litigation. As a result, in 02 the modification of the litigation goals of the defendant is reemphasized (WF^5) by the plaintiff. After introducing the debt dispute and his original intention of the litigation (WP^1), the plaintiff decides to modify his litigation goal and withdraw the lawsuit (WP^2 and WP^3).

It can be seen that the judge can exert great impact on the modification of the intentions and goals of participants, which in turn influences the process and result of interest negotiation.

To sum up, intentions and goals are important psychological factors that influence both the process and the outcome of interest negotiation. In order to gain the support of the court for their compensation claims, litigants tend to make explicit expressions of their intentions and ultimate goals of litigation. Sometimes, judges can have an active interference with the negotiation process by helping to reveal the intentions and goals of litigants. Moreover, litigants would make frequent modifications of their intentions and goals, which in turn can promote conciliation in interest negotiation.

5.3.2 Information Sharing

Court hearing is a process of information transfer, during which the information sharing category of litigants is modified and transformed frequently (Du 2007, 2010). During negotiation of interest, information provided by one litigant can be accepted, rejected, ignored or dropped deliberately by the opposing party. Therefore, information sharing category is also an important factor that may influence the process of interest negotiation.

According to Du (2010: 365), the analysis of information sharing between participants of court hearings can be conducted from two aspects: degree of information sharing and acceptability of shared information. Apart from that, in court hearings the transformation of information sharing category is also an important factor that may influence the result of interest negotiation. Therefore, in the following analysis, I will have a discussion of how these aspects of information sharing influence the process of interest negotiation.

5.3.2.1 Information Sharing Category

As is illustrated by Table 2-3, discourse information is classified into six information sharing categories: A, B, C, E, O and D. These categories are different both in mutual manifestness and acceptability. Among these categories, category E, which refers to information that is unknown to both parties, has the lowest degree of information sharing. Therefore, in court hearings, E-category information may block the natural flow of discourse information, which in turn may hinder the interest negotiation between litigants.

In the following case, Li X (an insurance agent) introduces the plaintiff to have his car repaired by Xie X (the first defendant) in the auto repair plant (the second defendant). Later the plaintiff sued the two defendants for failing to mend his car and asked for repayment of the repair cost.

(54)

01[法官]：<WF^1, b, P>原告，你当时修车知道具体谁修车，<WF^2, b, P>以及汽修厂是几级资质？	01[J]: Did the plaintiff know the name of the mechanic and the qualification of the auto repair plant?
02[原告]：<WF^3, a, P>我们信任李X，<WF^4, e, N>所以其他的不知道，<WF^5, a, P>只知道是谢X的修理厂，也就是第一被告。	02[P]: We trusted Li X and knew nothing else. We only knew that Xie X owned the repair plant, who is the first defendant in the lawsuit.
03[法官]：<WF^6, b, P>被告，你们汽修厂什么资质？	03[J]: Defendant, what is the qualification of your repair plant?
04[被告一]：<WF^7, e, N>我不知道。	04[D1]: I don't know.

Note: Letters "P" and "N" in "<>" indicate the value of information. "P" means that the information unit is in favor of the development of discourse information, while "N" means it is not.

In this extract, the judge tries to form conceptualizations about the repair plant, which is based on the discourse spaces of mechanic and qualification of the auto repair plant activated by units WF^1 and WF^2 respectively. The value of these two information units "P" shows that these two units are in favor of the development of the information of the whole discourse in that they can help to define responsibilities for the failure to repair the car.

As a response, the plaintiff contributes to the construction of context model by providing three WF units in 02 as space components, among which unit WF^5 satisfactorily answers the first question and closes the first discourse space. In contrast, units WF^3 and WF^4 make no satisfactory contribution to the second one. With unit WF^3, the plaintiff indicates that he has confidence in the qualification of the repair plant. But the following WF^4 unit (category E) reveals that he knows nothing about the rank of its qualification. The value of this E unit "N" shows that WF^4 blocks the discourse information which flows to the discourse space of qualification of the auto repair plant and hinders the interest negotiation conducted by the judge.

Unsatisfied with the plaintiff's answer, with unit WF^6 in 04 the judge intends the defendant to contribute to the development of the discourse space. But the defendant also provides an E-category unit (WF^7) as his answer. This time, the judge has no choice but to drop the question and closes the discourse space. It indicates that the COI between the two opposing parties cannot be negotiated by the judge based on the qualification of the auto repair plant.

Among the six information sharing categories, category A/B concerns personal specific knowledge (Xu 2013) and therefore also has a low degree of information sharing (Du 2010). However, it plays very important roles in court hearings, one of which is to work as the start point of interest negotiation, since it is usually through category A/B that litigants make their attitudes or facts of cases known to the other participants of lawsuit. On the other hand, A/B information is usually low in acceptability in that it is open to challenge by the opposing party.

(55)

01[法官]：<WT, B, P>原告方明确一下经济损失的计算过程。 02[原告]：<WF^1, A, P>地里总共能产出1,000公斤核桃，<WF^2, A, P>是扒完皮之后的重量，<WF^3, A, P>市场价每公斤是10元。	01[J]: Can the plaintiff explain how are your economic losses calculated? 02[P]: We've got 1,000kgs of walnuts from the land, which are the net weight with the market price of 20 yuan per kg.

In this extract, the judge intends to arrive at a conceptualization about how the plaintiff calculates his economic losses. The information sharing category of the WT unit employed by the judge is B. It indicates that the calculation of the economic losses is the plaintiff's personal knowledge, which is still not in the construal of other participants.

In 02 the plaintiff provides three WF units (WF^1, WF^2 and WF^3) to explain the calculation process, which reflects the specificity in his way of construal. Units WF^1 and WF^2 introduce the net weight of walnuts and unit WF^3, their market price. The information sharing category of the three WF units is A, which conforms to the judge's expectation with unit WT (category B).

As indicated by the information value "P" of the WF units, their non-construal by the other participants make them in favor of the information development of the whole discourse, since these WF units are open to challenge by the defendant in the following interest negotiation. In this sense, A/B information can promote the negotiation of interest between opposing parties of lawsuit.

Different from categories E and A/B, category C refers to the information accepted by two parties of litigation and therefore has a higher degree of mutual manifestness (Xu 2013). Category C is very important in court hearings because it is preliminary agreement reached between two parties as a result of negotiation and can function as the basis for further negotiation of interest. Therefore, C information may have very positive effects on the final resolution of conflict, as is shown in the following extract.

(56)

01[原告]：<WF^{1}, a>2009年春节，我向被告索要车辆，<WF^{2}, a>被告说要开车回老家，<WN, a>让我正月初五去找她要。<WF^{3}, a>正月初六左右我再向被告打电话要车，<WF^{4}, a>被告说她母亲来北京治病，<WF^{5}, a>她哥哥要用车接送母亲，<WF^{6}, a>后来再给她打电话她就不接了。	01[P]: On the Spring Festival of 2009, I asked the defendant to give the car back. But she said that she would drive the car home and promised to give it back on lunar January 5th. On lunar January 6th, I called the defendant, but she said that her mother would come to Beijing for cure of a disease and her elder brother would use the car to pick her mother up. Afterwards, she didn't answer my phone any more.
02[法官]：<WA, b>被告对原告所述上述情况有无异议？	02[J]: Does the defendant object to the statement of the plaintiff?
03[被告]：<WF^{7}, a>当时的车已经过户到了我名下，<WF^{8}, c>原告确实打电话给我，<WF^{9}, c>说是要用车去串门，<WF^{10}, c>我当时的回答也属实，<WF^{11}, c>跟他解释不方便送他，<WY^{1}, c>我因为回家，<WY^{2}, c>而且母亲也在生病，<WF^{12}, c>所以我也要用车。	03[D]: At that time, the ownership of the car had already been transferred to me. The plaintiff did phone me and said he'd use the car to drop around. And I did make the reply that it was inconvenient for me to drive him around and I needed the car since I would go home and my mother was sick.

In the extract, the two opposing parties have formed conflicting conceptualizations about the ownership of a car. However, except for the disputed information, the two parties also arrive at agreements on some of the facts of the lawsuit. This is reflected by the knowledge status component in the context model.

In 01 the plaintiff tries to facilitate in participants of the lawsuit a conceptualization about how the defendant acquired an illegal possession of the car. All the information units provided are based on the plaintiff's personal construal of the event. For example, unit WF^{1} describes how the plaintiff tried to ask the car back, indicating that he is still the real owner of the car. Then the plaintiff reports with six WF units and one WN unit how the defendant refused to give the car back. The personal construal of the information units is indicated by their category A, which means that they are presented for the first time and will be either confirmed or challenged by the opposing party.

The plaintiff's contribution of information in 01 provides important basis for the defendant's construal of the dispute. With unit WF^7, the defendant rebuts the plaintiff's claim of ownership by claiming that the ownership of the car had already been transferred to him. Then in the following discourse, the defendant confirms the statement made by the plaintiff with five WF and two WY units. The information sharing category of these units (category C) shows that the two opposing parties have reached a preliminary agreement in their construal of how and why the defendant refused to give the car back to the plaintiff. This agreement can facilitate the following process of interest negotiation.

Like category C, category D also has a high degree of information sharing. But it is very low in acceptability. D information is of significant importance in court hearings because it is the initiation or cause of interest negotiation. If category A/B is called the start point of interest negotiation, category D can be regarded as the driving force of the development of discourse information and interest negotiation. This can be illustrated by the following extract, in which the two opposing parties negotiate over the disputable proposition whether the taxi company should shoulder the compensation responsibility for the harm incurred to the victim.

(57)

01[原告]：<1,2,2,7,WF,C>其所属的驾驶员在客运时段内，交通肇事并逃逸，<1,2,2,8,WI^1,D>出租车公司应当对其驾驶员的职务行为承担全部的赔偿责任。	01[P]: The driver of the company has committed a hit-and-run in his business hours. Therefore the taxi driver should shoulder all the compensation responsibilities for his official behavior.
02[被告]：<3,20,4,32,WA^1,D>唐XX的逃逸行为与我们公司没有关系。	02[D]: The hit-and-run behavior of Tang XX has nothing to do with our company.
03[原告]：<4,46,5,39,WN,C>肇事是在营运时间内，<4,46,5,40,WI^2,D>是唐XX的职务行为。	03[P]: The hit-and-run took place in business hours and therefore was the official behavior of Tang XX.
04[被告]：<1,4,2,10,WP^1,D>请法院就他的逃逸行为与我们公司之间的关系予以认定。	04[D]: We require that the court define the relation between the Tang's hit-and-run behavior and our company.

05[原告]：<1,4,2,16,WY,A>肇事司机所在单位由于对职工教育不足造成对他人的伤害，<1,4,2,17,WP^{2},D>理应承担相应的赔偿责任。	05[P]: The company the taxi driver belongs to should shoulder compensation responsibility for its inadequacy in the education of its staff members.
06[法官]：<1,5,2,21,WT,A>法庭对争议焦点归纳如下：<2,21,3,49,WP^{3},D>一、是否认定被告对事故的赔偿责任承担全责。	06[J]: The focus of the dispute can be summarized as follows: firstly, whether the defendant should shoulder all the compensation liability for the traffic accident.

In 01, the plaintiff first points out with a WF unit that the hit-and-run of the driver took place in his business hours, and then forms a conceptualization with unit WI^{1} that the taxi company should shoulder all the compensation responsibilities. As its information sharing category (D) indicates, WI^{1} is the unit that causes sharp dispute between the opposing parties. As a response, in 02 the defendant declares clearly with unit WA^{1} that the hit-and-run behavior of the driver has nothing to do with the taxi company, thus refuting the plaintiff's proposition in WI^{1}.

The information sharing category of the units in 03, 04 and 05 is also D, which shows that the dispute over the taxi company's compensation responsibilities continues to be the focus of interest negotiation. This can also be illustrated by the judge's summary of focus of controversy in 06 with unit WP^{3}.

On the level of information structure, it can be seen that the D-category units are distributed on different information levels: from level two (e.g. <1,2,2,8> and <1,5,2,21>) to level five (e.g. <4,46,5,40>). It indicates that category D is a very important information category that can affect the flow of discourse information in interest negotiation. Moreover, it also shows that D-category information is also the focus of attention of interest negotiation, in that it runs through almost all the phases of court hearings from court investigation (<1,2,2,8>) to court debate (<1,4,2,10>) and summary made by the judge (<1,5,2,21>). Therefore, the processing of D-category information in court hearings can exert influence on the final results of interest negotiation.

Among all the information sharing categories, category O enjoys the highest degree of mutual manifestness and acceptability (Du 2010: 365). It refers to the shared social or cultural knowledge or objective facts that can hardly be challenged by others. In interest negotiation, O-category information usually appears together with A/B- or D-category information to function as supportive evidence.

(58)

[被告]：<WF^1, O>医学常识，对股骨头坏死的治疗，有保守疗法及手术疗法两种，<WF^2, O>这两种疗法各有千秋，<WF^3, O>病人有权利选择这两种治疗方式。<WA^1, A>但不能因选择了手术治疗就否定保守治疗的效果，<WA^2, A>无论是哪种治疗方法都不可能加重病情。

[D]: It's basic medical knowledge, there are two kinds of treatment of the illness of ONFH: conservative therapy and surgery, with each having its own advantages. Patients are free to choose either of the two treatments, but cannot deny the positive effects of conservative treatment because of their choice of surgery. Neither of the two treatments will aggravate the illness.

In the extract, the defendant conceptualizes with two WA units (WA^1 and WA^2) that neither conservative nor surgical treatment aggravates the illness of ONFH (osteonecrosis of the femoral head), and therefore the positive effects of conservative treatment should not be denied. These WA units are category A, which, as demonstrated previously, are the defendant's personal construal, comparatively low in both mutual manifestness and acceptability.

Therefore, before presenting the two WA units, the defendant provides three WF units (WF^1, WF^2 and WF^3) as their construal basis. Units WF^1 and WF^2 introduce the two treatments for ONFH and their own advantages. Unit WF^3 points out in particular that patients are free to choose the treatment that they deem appropriate. As indicated by the phrase *医学常识 (basic medical knowledge)*, these WF units are category O. Their high degree of mutual manifestness and acceptability helps to increase the credibility of the defendant's attitudes revealed by the two WA units. Apart from that, it can also help the defendant to occupy a favorable position in the process of interest negotiation by persuading the court to accept his propositions.

5.3.2.2 Transformation of Information Sharing Category

According to Du (2010: 365), transformation of information sharing category is an inevitable result of communication, which runs through the whole process of information development and information transfer. In the process of interest negotiation, the information sharing categories of information units in the discourse of litigants would change constantly. The change of information sharing category is the preliminary result of negotiation and can also have a profound influence on the final outcome of interest negotiation.

Among the six information sharing categories, categories E and O are two extremes both in mutual manifestness and acceptability. As was shown previously, these two categories can have a significant influence on the result of interest negotiation. But they are usually stable and not easy to change. In contrast, categories A/B, D and C are more dynamic and change more constantly. In the following analysis, I will have a discussion of how the mutual transformation of these four information sharing categories influences both the process and outcome of interest negotiation.

(i) Category A/B to Category D

As was discussed previously, Category A/B concerns personal knowledge of facts or expression of attitudes and has a lower degree in both mutual manifestness and acceptability. Therefore, they are under constant challenge by the opposing party and transformed into category D. The transformation can help litigants and the court to ascertain the focus of interest negotiation, as is in the following extract.

(59)

01[法官]：<WT, a>原告，陈述过户手续没有办理的原因。	01[J]: Now the plaintiff shall explain why the ownership was not transferred.
02[原告]：<WF^{1}, a>被告屡次向我方提出要在原合同的基础上涨价，<WF^{2}, a>先是向提出涨价4万元，<WF^{3}, a>后来又说6万元才答应履行合同。<WY^{1}, a>没有协商成功，<WE, c>就没有办理过户。	02[P]: The defendant asked several times for an increase of the price agreed on in the contract. After asking for an increase of 40 thousand yuan, the defendant requests for an increase of 60 thousand before the fulfillment of the contract. Because no agreement was reached, the ownership was not transferred.
03[法官]：<WA^{1}, b>被告，对没有办理过户手续的原因有异议吗？	03[J]: Does the defendant agree with the plaintiff on the reason why the ownership was not transferred?
04[被告]：<WA^{2}, d>我方不予认可，<WY^{2}, d>原告方是因为税费涨了，<WF^{4}, d>想在12月17日以后办理过户。	04[D]: No. The ownership was not transferred because of the increase of deed tax, for which the plaintiff intended to transfer the ownership after December 17th.

In this extract, the two opposing parties have formed different conceptualizations about the reasons why the transfer of ownership of the house was not executed.

In 02 the plaintiff first states the facts with three WF units (WF^{1}, WF^{2} and WF^{3}) about the unreasonable demands of the defendant to raise the price of the house. The WF units indicate that the plaintiff construes the defendant as the party who sets up obstacles to the performance of the contract and finally leads to the failure of ownership transfer (WY^{1} and WE). The information sharing category of the WF units is A, since it is the personal construal on the part of the plaintiff, which is to be either confirmed or challenged by the opposing party in the following negotiation.

As indicated by unit WA^{2}, the defendant in 04 forms a conflicting construal of the non-transfer of ownership. With units WY^{2} and WF^{4}, the defendant elaborates his construal of the reason why the transfer of ownership was not executed, namely, the increase of deed tax. The defendant means that it is the plaintiff who should be responsible for the nonperformance of the contract.

The information sharing category of all the information units in the defendant's discourse is category D. It means that the two parties' different construal results of the non-transfer of ownership form one of the major disputes of the case. Consequently, these D-category units define the focus of interest negation in the following hearing and will have a profound impact on the development of information.

(ii) Category A/B to Category C

In some cases, as a result of interest negotiation, the personal knowledge or expression of attitude of litigants is accepted and confirmed by the opposing party. Consequently, the category A/B is transformed into category C, as is shown in the following extract, where the two parties negotiate over the plaintiff's compensation claims for traffic expenses.

(60)

01[原告]：<WF^1, A>原告进行相关治疗所产生的交通费，共计是189元，<WF^2, A>出租费和公共交通费用。	01[P]: The total amount of transportation expenses generated in the hospitalization is 189 yuan, including taxi and public transport expenses.
02[法官]：<WT, A>被告发表质证意见。	02[J]: Now the defendant shall cross-examine the plaintiff's statement.
03[被告]：<WY^1,A>就原告所提供的这些证据材料，因为原告无法说明其与就医相符合，<WF^3,A>这个可能被告无法核实，<WF^4,C>但是他所主张的这个金额189元，<WA,C>被告表示同意。	03[D]: As for the evidence produced by the defendant, we cannot verify its authenticity as the plaintiff cannot explain its conformity to his hospitalization. But we agree to the amount of 189 yuan he claims.

In 01 the plaintiff proposes with two WF units (WF^1 and WF^2) that the total amount of expenses for taxi and public transport is 189 yuan. The information sharing category of these WF units is A, which indicates that they are only personal construal on the part of the plaintiff. It also explains why in 02 the judge instructs the defendant to cross-examine the claims.

In 03 the defendant first challenges with units WY^1 and WF^3 the correlation between the evidence (invoices) and the plaintiff's hospitalization. However, the defendant drops the challenge right away and confirms the amount of traffic expenses (189 yuan) in the following with units WF^4 and WA. Consequently, the A-category units (WF^1 and WF^2) in the plaintiff's discourse have been transformed into category C.

The transformation of information sharing category puts an end to the negotiation over traffic expenses.

(iii) Category D to Category C

Another important transformation of information sharing category during interest negotiation is from category D to category C. This usually happens when the disputed information is accepted by one or both parties of the lawsuit.

The following extract is from a lawsuit about a piece of calligraphy, which was damaged during its delivery. The major disputes of the lawsuit are the value of the piece of calligraphy and the determination of responsibility for its damage.

(61)

01[法官]：<WF^1,A>原告主张所损坏字画价值2,600元，<WA^1, b>被告是否认可？	01[J]: The plaintiff claims 2,600 yuan for the damaged calligraphy. Does the defendant agree?
02[被告]：<WA^2, d>不认可。	02[D]: We don't.
……	…
03[法官]：<WF^2, b>该字画是否由你店售出？	03[J]: Was the calligraphy sold in your shop?
04[证人]：<WF^3, a>是。	04[W]: Yes.
05[法官]：<WF^4, b>当时售出价格是多少？	05[J]: What was the selling price?
06[证人]：<WF^5, a>2,600元。	06[W]: 2,600 yuan.
07[法官]：<WF^6, b>是否开具过发票？	07[J]: Did you produce the invoice?
08[证人]：<WF^7, a>当时没开发票，但有具体的流水记录可以查证。	08[W]: No invoice was produced, but the price can be demonstrated by the turnover of the store.
……	…
09[被告]：<WA^3, C>……认可原告主张的字画价值，<WA^4, D>但字画的损坏与原告要求临时变更行车路线有很大关系。<WP, A>因此，请求法院对赔偿责任依法进行认定。	09[D]: …We accept the plaintiff's claim for the price of the calligraphy. But its damage was closely related to the temporary change of the transportation route. Therefore, we request the court to define the compensation liability according to law.

This extract is composed of three segments of discourse. In the first segment, the judge first repeats with unit WF^{1} the plaintiff's proposition about the value of the damaged calligraphy, and then asks with unit WA^{1} about the defendant's attitude toward the proposition. In 02 the defendant expresses his disagreement, which turns the A-category information into category D, thus constituting one of the major disputes of the lawsuit.

In the second segment, with unit WF^{4} the judge activates the discourse space of the selling price of the calligraphy. The witness's answer in 06 provides an important space component that confirms the value (2,600 yuan) proposed by the plaintiff in the first segment. The witness further proposes with WF^{7} that, although no invoice was produced when the sale occurred, the value of the calligraphy can be demonstrated by the turnover of his store. The witness's testimony provides very strong support for the plaintiff's proposition and thus makes it possible for the defendant to accept the value of the calligraphy.

As a result, the testimony of the witness has an important impact on the defendant's construal, who expresses clearly with unit WA^{3} his willingness to accept the value of the calligraphy, thus transforming the D-category unit to category C. It shows that, as a result of the interest negotiation, the two parties have reached an agreement on one of the major disputes of the lawsuit. Although the following WA unit (WA^{4}) shows that the defendant still disagrees with the plaintiff on the responsibility of the damage of the calligraphy, the transformation of the information sharing category has terminated their negotiation over the first dispute and therefore will contribute to the final resolution of the conflict.

In short, information sharing is an important psychological factor that influences negotiation of interest between opposing parties. Different information sharing categories manifest diverse features in their mutual manifestness and acceptability, which in turn can have great influences on the process of interest negotiation. As a result of interest negotiation, information sharing categories can be transformed in court hearings. The transformation of information sharing category can either generate new disputes or promote consensus between opposing parties.

5.3.3 Construal Phenomena

According to Langacker (2008: 55), the meaning of an expression is not just related to the conceptual content it evokes but also closely related to the way how the content is construed. This is also true for the production and interpretation of discourse information. Construal phenomena have a profound impact on the development and distribution of discourse information, which in turn influence the outcome of communication.

During interest negotiation in court hearings, based on their different interest appeals, litigants would construe the same fact or event of a case in quite different ways. Therefore, in the following analysis, I will have a discussion of how construal phenomena influence the distribution of discourse information and the process of interest negotiation.

5.3.3.1 Specificity: Information Elaboration

Specificity is concerned with the level of precision and detail at which an event or situation is characterized (Langacker 2008). In court hearings, whether a situation is described specifically or schematically influences the interpretation of discourse information and the negotiation of interest between the opposing parties.

(62)

[原告]：<WF^{1}，A>原告去地里捡玉米，<WY^{1}, A>那个玉米地已经收完了，<WY^{2}, A>当时有好多人去捡，<WF^{2}, A>原告也就去了，<WF^{3}, A>之后被告与原告发生口角，<WF^{4}, A>并打了起来。	[P]: The plaintiff went to pick corns in the land of the defendant, where the corns had already been harvested. Since there were a lot of people, the plaintiff went there too. Later the defendant and the plaintiff were involved in a quarrel and fought with each other.

In this extract, the plaintiff tries to conceptualize how the physical conflict between him and the defendant broke out. Units WF^{1} and WF^{2} present the fact that the plaintiff went to pick corns in the land of the defendant. The following two WY units (WY^{1} and WY^{2}) explain the reasons for the corn picking. The last two WF units (WF^{3} and WF^{4}) describe the quarrel and fight between the plaintiff and the defendant.

On the whole, the event is presented in a very schematic way. With the six information units, the plaintiff introduces three composing incidents of the event: 1) the corn-picking; 2) the quarrel between him and the defendant; and 3) the fight between them. As for the specific details of the three incidents, the plaintiff provides no further detailed information.

The schematicity of the construal shows that the plaintiff focuses more on the general description of the whole event and the interrelation between the three composing incidents. By the schematicity, the plaintiff intends to inform the court that his behavior of corn-picking is not illegal since the defendant has already finished the collection (WY^{1}) and there are lots of others engaged in the corn-picking (WY^{2}). Moreover, although the plaintiff provides no details about the quarrel and the following fight, by putting *被告(the plaintiff)* in front of *原告(the defendant)* in unit WF^{3}, namely, *被告与原告发生口角(the defendant and the plaintiff were involved in a quarrel)*, the plaintiff indicates that the defendant should be responsibility for the quarrel and fight.

However, in the following extract, the same event is construed quite differently by the defendant, who focuses more on the specificity of the composing incidents.

(63)

[被告]：<WF^{1}, A>原告说这个地是你们家的吗？<WF^{2}, A>我说这个地是合法承包的。<WF^{3}, A>我跟原告讲道理，<WF^{4}, A>原告就骂我。<WF^{5}, A>我说这个地方就是我们家的财产，<WF^{6}, A>后原告张嘴又骂我，……<WF^{7}, A>我们之间发生很长的口角。<WF^{8}, A>我把玉米倒在地上，<WF^{9}, A>把袋子也扔给原告，<WF^{10}, A>原告捡起袋子就要走，<WF^{11}, A>之后我拦着原告不让捡。<WF^{12}, A>原告对我进行辱骂并进行推搡，<WF^{13}, A>一拳打在我的脸上，<WF^{14}, A>之后他把我推沟里去了，<WF^{15}, A>之后我们一起掉沟里去了。<WF^{16}, A>原告起来之后还想对我进行殴打。	[D]: The plaintiff asked whether it was my land. I said the land was legally contracted by me. I tried to bring out the facts and reasons, but the plaintiff shouted verbal abuses back. I explained that the land was our property and the plaintiff abused me again…We were involved in a quarrel for quite a long time. I poured the corns out and threw the bag back to the plaintiff, who picked it up and tried to leave. I prevented him from getting the bag back and he abused, pushed me, punched me in the face and finally pushed me into the ditch. We both ended up falling into the ditch. After getting up, the plaintiff attempted to beat me up again.

The discourse of the defendant is composed of 16 WF units, which conceptualize how the quarrel and fight broke out between the opposing parties. Compared with Extract (62), the incidents are construed more specifically by the defendant.

Units WF^{1} to WF^{7} are concerned with the specific content of the quarrel. Compared with unit WF^{3} in Extract (62), which is only an overall introduction of the happening of the quarrel, the seven WF units in this extract present the details of the conflicting dialogue between the plaintiff and the defendant. Particularly, with units WF^{4} and WF^{6}, the defendant indicates that during the conflict it was the plaintiff who shouted verbal abuses and therefore should assume the responsibility for the quarrel.

Units WF^{8} to WF^{11} introduce the direct cause of the fight. The description shows that the plaintiff was prevented by the defendant from taking the corn away and leaving the land, which caused the fight between them. Units WF^{12} to WF^{16} give a detailed description of the process of the fight. The description indicates that the defendant was under such attacks of the plaintiff as *推搡 (pushing)*, *一拳打在我的脸上 (punch me in the face)*, *把我推沟里 (pushed me into the ditch)* and *殴打(beat me up)*, and therefore the plaintiff is actually the person who caused harm.

It can be seen that, in contrast to the plaintiff's discourse in Extract (62), the defendant in Extract (63) has formed a more specific construal of the whole event. The specificity of the construal reveals the defendant's basic position in the interest negotiation that the plaintiff should assume the responsibility for both the quarrel and the fight.

5.3.3.2 Focusing: Information Foregrounding and Backgrounding

According to Talmy (2000: 257), linguistic expressions can place one portion of a coherent situation into the foreground of attention while placing the remainder of the situation into the background. Langacker (2008: 58) goes one step further by proposing that linguistic expressions invoke background knowledge as the basis for their understanding. This is true as well for the production and interpretation of discourse information. In court hearings, based on their different interest appeals, litigants tend to foreground or background different information units in interest negotiation.

(64)

[原告]：<4,11,5,6,WF^1, O>被告医院下属的整形科是一家专门从事激光整形美容的医疗机构，<4,11,5,7,WF^2, A>在周女士毫不知情的情况下，擅自使用周女士的照片，<3,9,4,11,WE^1, A>会使大众误认为周女士在整容中心做过整容。<4,11,5,8,WF^3, O>近年来，周女士曾多次在国内模特比赛获奖，<3,9,4,12,WE^2, A>医院的行为使社会公众对周女士的个人形象产生了误解，<2,5,3,9,WE^3, A>损害了周女士的名誉。

[P]: The plastic surgery subordinate to the hospital of the defendant is a medical institution that has been engaged in laser plastic surgery, which used Miss Zhou's photo without being authorized. It can mislead the public into believing that Miss Zhou has undergone plastic surgery in the hospital. In recent years, Miss Zhou has taken part in several domestic model contests and won awards. The defendant's behavior has infringed Miss Zhou's reputation right and brought about misunderstandings about her personal image.

In the extract, the plaintiff proposes that the hospital's unauthorized use of the photo has infringed his right of reputation. This conceptual content is foregrounded in the discourse with unit WE^3, which is a core information unit (<2,5,3,9>). On the lower information levels (<3,9,4,11>,<3,9,4,12>), units WE^1 and WE^2 are backgrounded in relation to unit WE^3, in that they offer explanations of how the plaintiff's right of reputation is infringed.

Analogously, units WF^1 and WF^2 are backgrounded in relation to unit WE^1, as is unit WF^3 in relation to WE^2. Unit WF^1, which is category O, introduces the specific profession the defendant is engaged in. Unit WF^2 states the fact that the defendant has used the plaintiff's photo without being authorized. The correlation between units WF^1 and WF^2 facilitates the emergence of the following unit WE^1. In a similar way, the O-category unit WF^3 introduces the publicity of the plaintiff, which promotes the understanding of the following unit WE^2. The foregrounding and backgrounding of the information units in the extract correspond nicely to the information levels of the discourse, as is illustrated by Figure 5-4.

We can see that both the foregrounding and backgrounding of discourse information play important roles in clarifying the plaintiff's position in interest negotiation. The foregrounding of the information helps the plaintiff to make his positions in interest negotiation well-targeted and unambiguous. The backgrounding of information provides a solid basis for the interpretation of the foregrounded information, and, more importantly, helps to increase its acceptability.

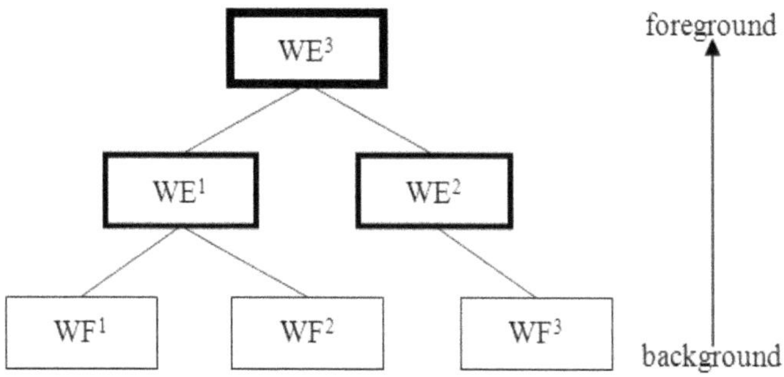

Figure 5-4. Foregrounding of Information Units.

However, due to their different positions in interest negotiation, the same discourse information may be foregrounded or backgrounded quite differently. The following extract is description of the same event with Extract (64), in which the defendant draws a conclusion contradictory to that of the plaintiff.

(65)

[被告]：<3,22,4,13,WF^1,A>原告并未证明我方使用的照片就是原告；<3,22,4,14,WF^2,A>即便照片是原告，<2,20,3,22,WI,A>我方也不构成侵权，<3,22,4,15,WF^3,A>我方使用照片是为了赞扬原告。	[D]: The plaintiff failed to prove that the photo we used is the photo of the plaintiff. Even if it is, our behavior does not constitute infringement because what we've done with the photo is to praise the plaintiff.

In this extract, the defendant claims with a WI unit that his behavior does not infringe the plaintiff's right of reputation. The WI unit is foregrounded and thus is the core information unit of the discourse. The three WF units (WF^1, WF^2 and WF^3) are backgrounded in relation to unit WI, in that these WF units provide basis for the inference the defendant makes with unit WI.

By putting the two extracts together, we can see that it is the divergence of the backgrounded information between the two opposing parties that leads to the conflicting conclusions. For example, unit WF^1 in Extract (65) contradicts unit WF^{2} in the discourse of the plaintiff by challenging the identity of the person in the photo; unit WF^{3} denies the plaintiff's accusation in unit WE^{2} by claiming that the use of the photo causes appreciation and praise instead of misunderstanding. Consequently, based on the conflicting backgrounded information, the plaintiff and defendant have arrived at opposing conclusions in the negotiation of interest.

5.3.3.3 Prominence: Information Profiling

According to Langacker (2001), when connection is established between two entities, there is always an asymmetry in the relation. In this asymmetric relation, the most prominent entity is called the trajectory (tr) and the less prominent one, the landmark (lm) (Langacker 2008: 70).

The asymmetry of a relationship has a manifestation in both language structure and discourse information. In court hearings, due to their different positions in interest negotiation, litigants tend to construe the same relationship in quite different ways. The varying degrees of prominence of the relationship are usually realized by profiling different information units.

In the following two extracts, which are from Chapter 4 and reproduced here as (66) and (67), the two opposing litigants negotiate over who should take more responsibility for the traffic accident. The profiling of information units in the two extracts has reflected the different positions of the two parties in interest negotiation.

(66)

[原代]：<WO^{1},A>被告XX汽车客运有限公司驾驶员唐XX，<WN,A>于2009年5月17日下午1时40分许，<WF^{1},A>驾驶本单位的牌号为D****的轿车，<WR,A>沿本市海宁路由东向西行驶至康乐路路口时，<WF^{2},A>撞倒正在人行横道内由南向北过马路的被害人，<WO^{2},A>也就是本案的原告李X。

[PA]: At 1: 40 PM of May 17th, 2009, Tang XX, driver of XX Automobile Transportation Company, when driving the taxi with the license plate number of D**** from east to west on Haining Street to the crossroad of Kangle Street, knocked down the victim, plaintiff of the lawsuit, Li X, who was walking across the street on the pavement.

In this extract, the attorney forms a detailed conceptual content about the course of accident. Among those information units, units WO^1, WF^1, WF^2 and WO^2 have formed a cause-effect relationship of incident happening. The two WF units (WF^1 and WF^2) describe the action involved and its consequence respectively. The two WO units present the agent (WO^1 for the defendant) and patient (WO^2 for the plaintiff) of the action.

The cause-effect relationship can be generally expressed as "WO^1 is responsible for WF^1 and WF^2, which affect WO^2". The cause-effect relationship of the four information units can be illustrated by Figure 5-5.

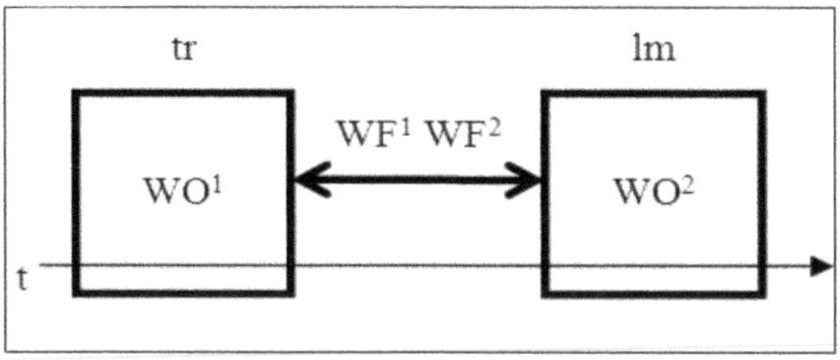

Figure 5-5. Prominence of Cause-effect Relation of WO Units.

In this relationship, unit WO^1 is the most prominent participant and therefore is the trajectory; unit WO^2 is less prominent and therefore is the landmark. Units WF^1 and WF^2 are the actions that connect these two participants. Symbol "t" (time) refers to the development or flow of discourse information. By placing unit WO^1 (defendant) into the position of trajectory and unit WO^2 (plaintiff) into the position of landmark, the plaintiff indicates that the defendant should assume responsibility for the traffic accident and the harm caused to the plaintiff.

However, for the same traffic accident, the defendant has a quite different account. This can be illustrated by the fact that the information units in Extract (67) have a different prominence in Extract (66).

(67)

[被代]：<WB,C>根据交警出具的这份事故认定书，<WJ,A>可以认定原告在事故发生的时间节点上存在违法行为，<WF^1,C>因为在一个红灯的状态，他在通行和横穿马路，<WF^2,C>而出租车则是在绿灯状态下通行。	[DA]: According to the Report of Traffic Accident, **we have good reasons to believe that the plaintiff did perform unlawful act at the time of the accident.** He was walking and crossing the street when the traffic light was red, while the taxi was going at a green light.

In this extract, the defendant conceptualizes with a WJ unit that the plaintiff should be responsible for the traffic accident since it is his unlawful acts that led to the accident. This proposition is supported by the following two WY units that report the course of the accident. Unit WY^1 points out that at the time of the accident the plaintiff was walking through a red light, while unit WY^2 makes it clear that when the defendant drove through the intersection the light was green.

Of the two WY units that are used to report the course of the accident, unit WY^1, which is concerned with the act of the plaintiff, is the more prominent. The cause-effect relation presented by the two WY units can be illustrated by Figure 5-6.

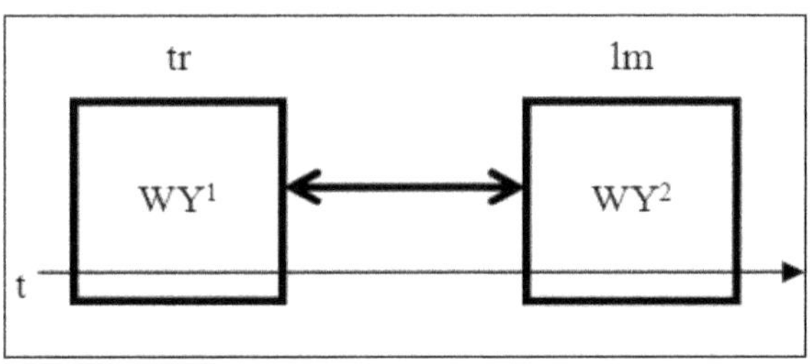

Figure 5-6. Prominence of Cause-effect Relation of WY Units.

Different from Figure 5-2, in this figure, the unit concerning the action of the plaintiff (WY^1) is the trajectory, and that concerning the defendant (WY^2) is the landmark. The prominence of unit WY^1 conforms to the defendant's conclusion with unit WJ that the unlawful acts of the plaintiff are the main cause of the accident. The prominence of information units and the corresponding conclusion impose challenge to the plaintiff's intention in Extract (66) to pass all the responsibilities on to the defendant.

5.3.3.4 Perspective: Information Selection

Perspective refers to the viewing arrangement, namely, the relation between the *viewers* and the situation being *viewed* (Langacker 2008: 73). Perspective is very important in our daily life since it not only determines how we perceive the surrounding world but also influences the results of that perception.

In court hearings, the opposing parties tend to assume different perspectives on the same event or incident involved in the lawsuit. Perspectives are determined by their different positions in interest negotiation and have an obvious manifestation on the level of discourse information. For example, in the following two extracts, the incident was construed from different perspectives by the plaintiff and the defendant, in which both of them were injured to varying degrees.

(68)

[原告]：<WF^{1}, A, 狗没拴>早上我家狗没拴着，<WF^{2}, A, 被告来串门>被告到我家来串门，<WY, A, 看见狗>可能是看到我家狗了，<WF^{3}, A, 吓得跑>吓得就跑，<WE^{1}, A, 被告撞到原告>被告在逃跑中撞到我身体上了，<WE^{2}, A, 原告受伤>造成我身体伤害。	[P]: on that morning my dog was not fastened to the post when the defendant dropped in. At the sight of the dog, he was scared to run away and knocked me down, which led to my severe injury.

In this extract, the plaintiff makes an account of the event and proposes that he was knocked down and injured by the defendant. The six information units in the conceptualization correspond to six composing incidents which are selected and arranged by the plaintiff in a chronological order.

Unit WF^{1} provides background information about the unfastening of the plaintiff's dog. Units WF^{2}, WY and WF^{3} describe how the defendant was scared to run away by the dog when he dropped in. The following two WE units (WE^{1} and WE^{2}) present the harm to the plaintiff caused by the runaway of the defendant. The presentation of the information in the above discourse can be illustrated by figure 5-7.

The figure shows that the composing incidents of the event are presented by the plaintiff with the corresponding information units in order of their occurrence. However, starting from the purpose to claim for compensation, the plaintiff has assumed a perspective that focuses more on his own injury, which in turn influences his information selection.

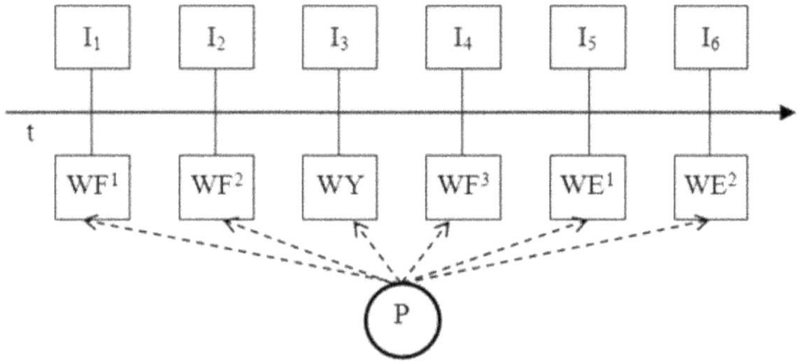

Figure 5-7. The Plaintiff's Presentation of Information Units.

Note: I: incident; P: plaintiff
I^1: dog not fastened; I^2: defendant dropped in; I^3: defendant saw the dog
I^4: defendant ran away; I^5: defendant knocked plaintiff down; I^6: plaintiff injured

For example, when the plaintiff makes account of the first four incidents (I_1 to I_4), the four information units (WF^1, WF^2, WY and WF^3) reveal nothing about the fear or harm the defendant incurred as a result of the chase of the dog. On the contrary, these incidents are presented only as evidence to demonstrate how the plaintiff was injured by the runaway of the defendant. Therefore, as a result of the information selection based on the personal perspective of the plaintiff, the information units (WE^1 and WE^2) and their corresponding incidents (I_5 and I_6) that help to reveal his own injury are selected and highlighted.

On the part of the defendant, information is also selected to demonstrate the harm he has suffered as a result of the chase of the dog, as is in the following extract.

(69)

[被告]：<WF^1, A, 被告敲门>我去原告家之前敲了原告家门，<WY, A,狗可能咬人>听到原告家的狗叫并可能咬我，<WF^2, A, 吓得跑>我就跑，<WE^1, A, 被告没撞到原告>但我没有撞到原告，<WE^2, A, 被告被狗咬>而且自身还被狗咬了，<WE^3, A, 被告身上缝针>我身上还缝了几针呢。

[D]: I knocked at the door before I entered the house of the plaintiff. I heard the barks of the dog of the plaintiff. Afraid of being bit, I tried to run away. But I didn't knock the plaintiff down. Instead I was bit by the dog and received several stitches for the wound.

In this extract, the defendant proposes that he did not knock the plaintiff down and instead he himself was bitten by the dog. The discourse is also composed of six information units, with each corresponding to a particular composing incident. The first three units (WF^1, WY and WF^2) describe how the defendant was scared by the dog and ran away from the house of the plaintiff. The last three WE units (WE^1, WE^2 and WE^3) are used to present the injury the defendant has suffered as a result of the chase of the dog. The presentation of information in the discourse can be illustrated by Figure 5-8.

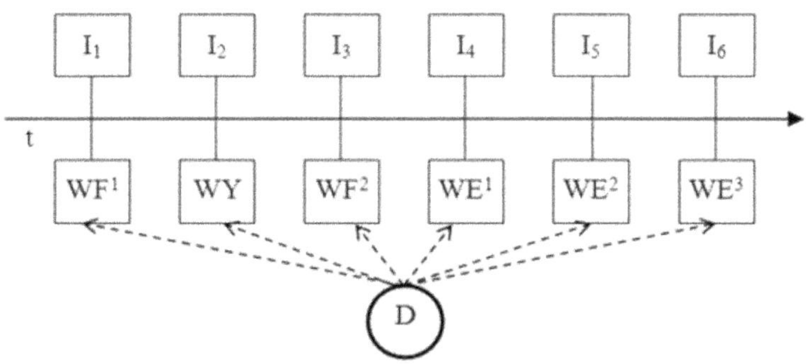

Figure 5-8. The Defendant's Presentation of Information Units.

Note: I: incident; D: defendant
I^1: defendant knocked at the door; I^2: dog might bite; I^3: defendant ran away
I^4: defendant didn't knock plaintiff down; I^5: defendant bitten by dog;
I^6: defendant received medical treatment

The figure shows that the composing incidents in the defendant's discourse are quite different from those in the discourse of the plaintiff. Unit WF[1] emphasizes the fact that the defendant had knocked at the door before he entered the house, indicating that his entry was permitted by the plaintiff. Unit WY describes the direct cause of the defendant's runaway. However, different from the WY unit in the discourse of the plaintiff in Extract (68), in which a neutral verb *看到 (saw)* is employed, the WY unit in the defendant's discourse has employed *听到原告家的狗叫(heard the barks of the dog of the plaintiff)* and *可能咬我(was afraid of being bit)* to emphasize the fear caused by the dog.

The last three WE units describe the severe consequence of the previous incidents. With unit WE[1], the defendant claims that he did not knock the plaintiff down, thus denying the correlation between his runaway and the plaintiff's injury. Units WE[2] and WE[3] emphasize that the defendant himself was seriously injured, thus establishing the relation between his injury and the dog's barks.

The divergence of the presentation of information and incidents in the discourses of the two parties is caused by their different perspectives, in that both of them have highlighted their own injuries and request the other to make compensations. Therefore, in court hearings, the negotiation of different perspectives of the opposing parties is of significant importance to the final resolution of COI.

To sum up, interest negotiation between different parties of lawsuits is under great influence of their construal phenomena. Litigants can choose to describe the course of infringement either specifically or schematically. In their descriptions, the same discourse information can be either foregrounded or backgrounded based on their different positions. When accounting for such relationship as cause and effect, litigants can choose to profile and make prominent different discourse information. Moreover, litigants tend to assume different perspectives on the same event involved in the lawsuit, which lead to the different selection and arrangement of information units.

5.4 Discursive Factors

Besides the physical, mental, social and cultural circumstances, another integral element that may influence the result of communication is "the speaker's and hearer's apprehension of the ongoing discourse itself" (Langacker 2001: 145). Previous and subsequent discourses contribute a great deal to interlocutors' understanding of the ongoing discourse. Therefore, apart from the social and psychological factors, discursive factors are another kind of elements that may influence the negotiation of interest between opposing parties of a lawsuit in that it is through language that the negotiation is conducted.

Langacker (2001: 144) defines discourse as a linguistic unit abstracted from a usage event, which consists of a comprehensive conceptualization, comprising its full contextual understanding and elaborate vocalization. Langacker (2001: 144) further proposes that conceptualization is mental spaces shared by interlocutors as a basis for communication. According to Langacker (2001: 151), the flow of discourse is usually composed of three successive frames: a minus frame, a zero frame and a plus frame. These three frames can be analyzed as corresponding to the activation and integration of discourse spaces and discourse expectations. Therefore, in this section, I will have a discussion of how the activation and integration of discourse spaces and discourse expectations influence the process of interest negotiation in Chinese civil court hearings.

5.4.1 Activation of Discourse Spaces

According to Fauconnier (1994), discourse spaces are activated by discourse producers on the basis of their different perspectives or focuses. In court hearings, the activation of discourse spaces is usually realized by judges in the form of court instructions. By imposing constraint on the discourse information that will appear as their constituents, the activation of discourse spaces can help to make preparation for the ongoing interest negotiation.

(70)

01[法官]：<WT^{1}, A>北京市XX区人民法院今天依法公开开庭审理原告张XX诉被告仉XX、李XX、XX保险公司道路交通事故人身损害赔偿纠纷一案，现在开庭……	01[J]: The People's Court of XX District of Beijing is now in session to hear the case of traffic accident compensation damages involving the plaintiff Zhang XX, the defendants Ji XX, Li XX and XX Insurance Company…
02[法官]：<WT^{2}, A>现在开始法庭调查，<WT^{3}, A>先由原告陈述起诉的事实、理由及诉讼请求……	02[J]: Now proceed to court investigation. The plaintiff shall first make statement about the facts, reasons and compensation requests…
03[法官]：<WT^{4}, A>下面由原被告分别进行举证质证，<WT^{5}, A>证据可以按照证明内容分组出示……	03[J]: Now the plaintiff and defendant shall proceed to proof cross-examination. The evidence shall be produced in groups according to the content it tries to prove…
04[法官]：<WT^{6}, A>法庭调查终结，<WT^{7}, A>下面进行法庭辩论……	04[J]: That's the end of court investigation. Now proceed to court debate…

In the four turns of the extract, the judge activates four different discourse spaces by giving court instructions. Unit WT^{1} in 01 activates the discourse space of the opening of the court session. In order to have a more accurate definition of the discourse space, the judge also provides the major dispute and the identities of litigants involved in the lawsuit.

Unit WT^{2} in 02 activates the discourse space of court investigation, which is then followed by the judge's explanation of the order and relevant content of the litigants' statements (WT^{3}). Unit WT^{4} in 03 activates the space of cross-examination, in which, the judge explains, evidence can be displayed in groups according to its content (WT^{5}). Units WT^{6} and WT^{7} in 04 close the discourse space of court investigation and activate the new space of court debate.

The activation of the discourse spaces by the judge in this extract assigns different topics to their subsequent discourses and defines the general orientation of the flow of their constituent information units.

However, during interest negotiation, litigants may also have the right to activate new discourse spaces based on their interest pursuits, as long as these discourse spaces conform to the ones activated by the judge.

(71)

01[法官]：<WN^1, b>你什么时间告诉你妻子签订居间合同的事情的？
02[被告]：<WN^2, a>签订居间合同的晚上。<WF^1, A>9月1日早晨我母亲就找到原告要求解除合同，<WF^2, A>9月1日晚上，我们又去找原告一次，<WA, A>但是原告一直不同意解除合同。
03[法官]：<WF^3, b>原告，是这样吗？
04[原告]：<WF^4, a>不是。<WN^3, A>被告是在9月3日才提出不卖房子的，<WF^5, A>9月1日下午，我们还带着2个客户去看过房子。<WF^6, A>解除合同的请求是被告的母亲提出的，<WY, A>她提出不卖房的理由是：他们已经申请两限房了，这套房子就不打算卖了。<WC, A>如果要是卖的话，<WP, A>就得把房屋售价提高到51万元……。

01[J]: When did you tell your wife about your signing of the intermediary contract?
02[D]: The night when the contract was signed. On the morning of September 1st, my mother went to the plaintiff to ask for termination of the contract. On the night of September 1st, we went to the plaintiff again but he refused to terminate the contract.
03[J]: Was it so, plaintiff?
04[P]: No. It was not until September 3rd that the defendant proposed to stop the sale of the apartment. On the afternoon of September 1st, we went to inspect the apartment with two of our customers. The request to terminate the contract was first proposed by the defendant's mother. The reason why they didn't want to sell the apartment is that they have applied for an apartment with limited price and habitable area. If the apartment is sold, they have to raise the price to 510 thousand yuan…

In this extract, the two parties negotiate over the exact date of the defendant's request to terminate the sales contract of the real estate. However, instead of being activated by the judge, the discourse space concerning the request for the termination of the contract is initiated by the defendant.

In 01 the judge activates the discourse space of the signing of the brokerage contract. Unit WN^1 confines the defendant's contribution of the space constituent to the time when the defendant told his wife about the signing of the contract. However, in 02 after providing the necessary information with unit WN^2, the defendant moves on to activate a new discourse space with unit WF^1: the request for the termination of the contract. Following the activation of the space, the defendant provides two more information units as its constituents (units WF^2 and WA). Unit WF^2 describes the effort the defendant has exerted on the termination of the contract; unit WA reveals the plaintiff's attitude towards the defendant's request.

Although the new discourse space and its constituents are in obvious divergence with the first discourse space of the signing of the brokerage contract activated by the judge at the beginning of the extract, by activating the new discourse space, the defendant intends to prove that his timely request for termination of contract is unlikely to cause any harm to the interest of the plaintiff. Moreover, since the exact date of the defendant's request for termination of the contract is one of the major disputes to be resolved by the court, the activation of the new discourse space also contributes to its final resolution through interest negotiation. Therefore, the new discourse space is accepted by the judge, who, with unit WF^3 in 03, asks the plaintiff to confirm the three information units (WF^1, WF^2 and WA) provided by the defendant as space constituents in 02.

As a response, after denying the information units given by the defendant with unit WF^4, the plaintiff provides six more information units (WN^3, WF^5, WF^6, WY, WC and WP) as new constituents of the space, which reveal the date and reason for the request for termination of the contract and the conditions for the performance of the contract. The plaintiff's contribution of the information units to the new discourse space offers a different description of the defendant's request to terminate the contract and thus helps to deepen the negotiation as for who should be responsible for the nonperformance of the contract.

We can see that the activation of new discourse space by litigants is usually conducted from their own interest pursuit, and by contributing to the final resolution of COI, the new space can be further developed in the following discourse.

5.4.2 Integration of Discourse Spaces

With the development of discourse, discourse spaces tend to be combined with each other to form larger spaces at higher levels (Langacker 2001). Therefore, the flow or development of discourse is the process of integrating different discourse spaces.

In court hearings, the successful integration of discourse spaces can promote the process or even result in interest negotiation, since it can help to determine the facts on which litigants have arrived at consensus or reveal the major disputes they are involved in.

(72)

01[法官]：<WT^1, b>请被告出示房屋产权证。	01[J]: Now the defendant shall produce the property ownership certificate.
02[被告]：<WT^2, a>(出示房屋产权证。)	02[D]: (Producing the property ownership certificate.)
03[法官]：<WR^1, b>原告，请明确涉诉房屋坐落位置。	03[J]: Plaintiff, please clarify the location of the apartment.
04[原代]：<WR^2, a>房屋位于14号楼6单元102室，<WF^1, a>建筑面积60.62平方米。<WF^2, a>据我了解，产权人是赵X，<WF^3, a>赵X在此房屋内居住。	04[PA]: Room 102, Unit 6, Building 14. The construction area is 60.62 square meters. As far as I know, the ownership of the apartment belongs to Zhao X, who lives in it.
05[法官]：<WN^1, b>房屋是什么时间，<WO^1, b>由谁出资购买的？	05[J]: When and who bought the apartment?
06[被告]：<WN^2, a>房屋是98年购买的，<WO^2, a>房款有我出资部分……<WO^3, a>由夫妇出资。<WF^4, a>08年7月25日从我名下过户到被告名下。<WA, a>我认为该房屋属于夫妻共同财产，<WF^5, a>现在被告三口在该房屋内居住。	06[D]: The apartment was bought in 1998. I invested part of the money…I mean we, when we were still in marital relation, made the investment. On July 25th, 2008, the ownership was transferred from me to the defendant. I think the apartment is our joint property. Now the defendant's three-member family all live in the apartment.

In this extract, participants of lawsuit negotiate over the property right to the disputed real estate. After the discourse space of property right to the real estate is activated, the opposing parties have made valuable contributions to its development by integrating its constituent spaces.

In 01 the judge first activates the discourse space of property right with unit WT^1. This space is then further developed from 02 to 06 with the participants' joint efforts by integrating its constituent spaces. In 02 the defendant produces the House Property Ownership Certificate as evidence for his ownership of the house. In 03 the judge activates the location of the house as the constituent space of the space of property right. As a response, the plaintiff's attorney provides units WR^2 and three WF units (WF^1, WF^2 and WF^3) as its constituents. Among these information units, unit WR^2 and WF^1 define the exact location and building area of the disputed house; the other two WF units emphasize the fact that Zhao X has undisputable ownership of the house.

Although the attorney's contribution of the last two WF units (WF^2 and WF^3) deviates from the space of the location of the house, they are in adequate conformity to the space of property right and therefore promote the development of the whole discourse.

In 05 the judge activates two other constituent spaces with units WN^1 and WO^1: the purchase time and investor of the house. Then in 06, the counsel for the defense, who is the wife of the defendant, provides three information units (WN^2, WO^2 and WO^3) as space constituents. With these information units, the counsel for the defense emphasizes that she and her husband Zhao X are the co-investors of the house (WO^2 and WO^3), and therefore, although the ownership was transformed to the defendant in the year of 2008 (WF^4), the house is still their common property (WA).

The development of the discourse spaces in this extract can be illustrated by Figure 5-9.

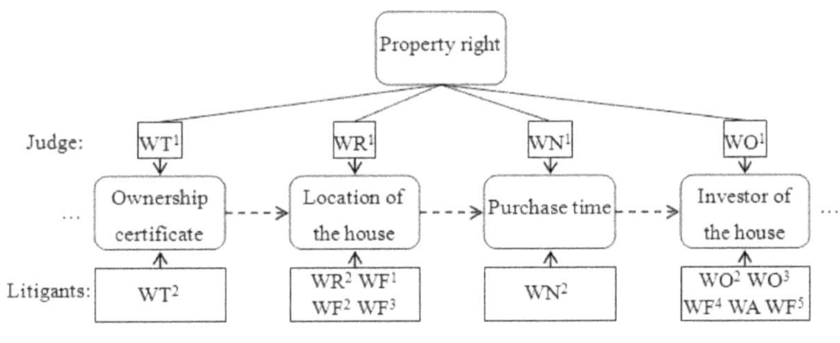

Figure 5-9. Integration of Discourse Spaces.

It can be seen that the four discourse spaces of ownership certificate, location of the house, purchase time and investor of the house are integrated to form the larger discourse space of property right. Each of these four constituent spaces is activated by the judge and then further developed by litigants on the basis of the integration of its constituent information units. The integration of the discourse spaces shows that the discourse spaces of ownership certificate and purchase time are the spaces that cause the least dispute. On the contrary, the other two spaces --location and investor of the house, which are more closely related to the discourse of property right--are the focus of negotiation and attract more attention of the litigants.

In short, the successful integration of discourse spaces can help to promote the flow of discourse information and help to define the major disputes and litigants' positions in interest negotiation.

However, in some cases, discourse spaces may not be integrated as satisfactorily as expected. This may be caused by the inadequacy of the space constituents provided by litigants. The inadequacy of the integration of discourse spaces may prevent the interest negotiation between participants from achieving any desirable result.

(73)

01[法官]：<WT^1, a>下面法庭就XX建筑工地运输车生产事故问你几个问题，<WT^2, b>你要客观公证地提供证言，听清了吗？
02[证人]：<WT^3, a>听清了。
03[法官]：<WN^1, b>你从什么时间开始在XX建筑公司干活的？
04[证人]：<WN^2, a>去年8月。
05[法官]：<WF^1, b>你认识张XX吗？
06[证人]：<WF^2, e>听说过，但不认识。
07[法官]：<WF^3, b>具体分管什么工作知道吗？
08[证人]：<WF^4, e>不知道。
09[法官]：<WF^5, b>你们工地有几辆建筑废料运输车？
10[证人]：<WF^6, a>有四五辆吧。
11[法官]：<WO^1, b>都由谁开？
12[证人]：<WO^2, e>不清楚。
13[法官]：<WO^3, b>在7月10号晚上的事故中受伤的魏X即本案的原告是你们工地的司机吗？
14[证人]：<WF^7, a>听说车是我们工地的，<WO^4, e>司机不认识。

01[J]: Now the court will ask you some questions concerning the production accident on the construction site. You shall give objective and fair testimony. Are you clear?
02[W]: Yes.
03[J]: When did you start working in XX Construction Company?
04[W]: Last August.
05[J]: Do you know Zhang XX?
06[W]: I've heard of him but don't know him.
07[J]: Do you know what work he was in charge of?
08[W]: No.
09[J]: How many muck cars were there on your site?
10[W]: Four or Five.
11[J]: Who drove them?
12[W]: I don't know.
13[J]: Is Wei X, the plaintiff of the lawsuit, who was injured in the accident on the night of July 10th, a driver of your site?
14[W]: I heard he was but I don't know him.

In this case, the plaintiff, who was injured when driving the muck car of a construction site, sued the XX Construction Company and Zhang XX, who was in charge of the construction site where the plaintiff worked, for compensation for his injury. The plaintiff claimed that, although driving the muck car is not the due obligation stipulated in the contract, the driving task on July 10th, 2010 was assigned and approved by the assistant manager Zhang XX and therefore his injury should be defined as work injury. In the extract, the judge questions the witness for the defendant for the definition of the compensation responsibility.

The question and answer between the judge and the witness in the first two turns have activated the discourse space of production accident on the construction site. The judge's question in 03 activates the constituent space of the witness's identity, and the witness's answer in 04 helps to ensure the credibility of his testimony. In 05, the judge activates the constituent space of the identity of the assistant manager Zhang XX by asking whether the witness knows him. However, as is demonstrated by the information sharing category (category e) of the information units in 06 and 08, the witness contributes no substantial constituent to the space by giving two negative answers. Then in 09, another constituent space of muck car is activated by the judge. But apart from the approximate number of the muck car on the construction site (WF^6), the witness provides no information about their drivers (WO^2). Therefore, with unit WO^3 the judge makes another effort to ask about the identity of the driver injured in the muck car accident on July 10, but still gets no adequate answer from the witness.

Because of the inadequacy of the answer provided by the witness, the information units in the discourse of the extract fail to be integrated into their relevant discourse spaces, which in turn are unable to be integrated into the lager discourse space of production accident at the higher level. The non-integration of discourse spaces, although not hindering the interest negotiation between the opposing parties, makes no contribution to the solution or even definition of the disputes involved.

5.4.3 Discourse Expectations

According to Langacker (2001, 2008), the multiple events in discourse tend to manifest certain regularities or patterns in discourse sequences. These regularities or patterns can generate discourse expectations which may impose influence or constraint on the subsequent discourse (Langacker 2001: 151).

In court hearings, discourse expectations are usually generated by judges when court instructions are given. Discourse expectations may help to increase the efficiency of interest negotiation by judges' regulation on the behaviors of litigants.

(74)

[法官]：<0,1,1,2,WT^{1},A>现在进行法庭调查。<1,2,2,1,WT^{2},A>法庭调查首先由当事人进行陈述，<1,2,2,2,WT^{3},A>当事人陈述应当依原告及其代理人，被告的顺序进行；<1,2,2,3,WT^{4},A>陈述应当围绕案件事实、争议焦点、诉讼请求等与本案有直接关系的内容进行，<1,2,2,4,WT^{5},A>避免陈述与本案无关的内容；<1,2,2,5,WT^{6},A>一方陈述时，对方不得打断发言。

[J]: Now proceed to court investigation. The court investigation begins with the opening statement of the two parties, with the plaintiff and his attorney being the first and the defendant being the second. The parties shall center their statements on the facts, focus of disputes, compensation requests and other content relevant to the lawsuit. Content irrelevant to the present lawsuit is prohibited. When one party makes statement, the other can not interrupt his speaking.

In this extract, after declaring the start of court investigation, the judge makes further elaborations on its specific procedural requirements. Unit WT^{1} on the first information level activates the discourse space of court investigation and its relevant properties. It indicates that the discourse space is now open to the litigants' contribution of its information constituents.

On the second information level in the following discourse, the judge makes further explanations of the content of its constituents and the order of their appearance in the discourse space. These explanations generate expectations for the discourse to be produced by litigants. Unit WT^{2} makes it clear that the space of court investigation is mainly composed of the statements of litigants. Unit WT^{3} defines the order that their statements appear in the space. Units WT^{4} and WT^{5} prescribe the specific topics the negotiation should concern. By preventing from being interrupted by the opposing party, the last unit (WT^6) ensures the smoothness of the information flow into the discourse space.

We can see that the discourse expectations generated by the activation of the discourse space have imposed an obvious constraint on the information flow of the subsequent discourse. By prescribing the topics of negotiation and the way that litigants make their statements, the judge ensures the efficiency of the interest negotiation between the opposing parties.

Sometimes discourse expectations can also be generated by litigants themselves, in which their aims or positions in interest negotiation are clearly expressed, as is illustrated in the following extract.

(75)

01[上诉人]：<WA^1, A>不管以前的处理方式是怎么样的，现在在法庭上，我们带着调解的诚意，<WP^1, A>希望双方能够调解解决。<WC^1, A>如果达成调解协议，<WP^2, A>我们不会拖延或不履行调解协议的内容，<WP^3, A>一周之内就可以支付。	01[AT]: Regardless of the previous resolution, now here in court we have the sincerity for conciliation. We hope the dispute will be resolved in conciliation on both sides. If conciliation is reached, we will not delay or refuse to execute the conciliation results. The payment will be made within one week.
02[被上诉人]：<WA^2, A>不同意调解。<WY^1, A>在与公司打交道的6年时间里，我已经充分认识到上诉人没有诚信。<WY^2, A>如果现在调解，社会保险个人不能补交。<WY^3, A>为了以后养老的问题，我们必须要坚持补交保险的主张。	02[AE]: We object to conciliation. In the last 6 years when we were in contact with the company, we came to fully realize the dishonesty of the appellant. If conciliation is reached, the social insurance cannot be repaid. Therefore, for the consideration of my life in age, we insist on the company's repayment of the social insurance.
03[上诉人]：<WC^2, A>如果达成调解的话，<WP^4, A>5个工作日内我们可以支付1万元。	03[AT]: If conciliation is reached, we will make a payment of 10 thousand yuan within five working days.
04[被上诉人]：<WA^3, A>不同意调解。	04[AE]: We object to conciliation.
05[法官]：<WY^4, A>双方分歧较大，<WP^5, A>法庭不再调解。	05[J]: Due to the divergence between the two parties, the court will stop the conciliation.

In this case, the two litigants try to negotiate over the amount of compensation made to the appellee. In 01, after expressing his sincerity to resolve the dispute through conciliation (WA^1), the appellant activates the discourse of court conciliation with unit WP^1. With unit WC^1, the appellant generates discourse expectations about his specific proposal for the resolution of the COI. Then in the following discourse, the appellant substantiates the discourse expectations with two information units: WP^2 and WP^3. With these units, the appellant promises that payment to the appellee will be made within one week.

In 02 the appellee first expresses his position against court conciliation with unit WA^2. This unit also generates discourse expectations about the reasons why the appellee refuses to accept the proposal put forward by the appellant in 01. In the subsequent discourse, these expectations are made concrete by the appellee with three WY units (WY^1, WY^2 and WY^3). Unit WY^1 reveals the dishonesty of the appellant; unit WY^2 predicts his disability to make payment for the social insurance; and unit WY^3 makes it clear that social insurance closely concerns his pension arrangement and therefore his propositions for the appellant to repay the social insurance will not be abandoned.

Although the appellant makes another effort in 03 to regenerate discourse expectations with unit WC^3 and promises that they will make a payment of 10,000 yuan within five working days (WP^4), the appellee confirms his position against court conciliation with unit WA^3. As a result, the judge closes the discourse space of court conciliation in 05 by declaring the irreconcilability of the divergence between the two opposing parties (WY^4 and WP^5).

It shows that discourse expectations help to reveal more directly the litigants' attitudes or positions in court hearings, based on which they can make more efficient negotiations over the final outcome of the lawsuit, whether in the form of conciliation or judgment.

To sum up, such discursive factors as the activation and integration of discourse spaces and discourse expectations tend to have a direct influence both on the process and outcome of interest negotiation between opposing parties. The activation of discourse spaces not only prepares litigants for their contribution of information units but also imposes constraint on the content and order of appearance of these units. The successful integration of discourse spaces can help the court to ascertain the major disputes or arrive at consensus between opposing parties, while the inadequacy of integration of discourse spaces prevent the negotiation from achieving any desirable results. By revealing litigants' positions or attitudes, discourse expectations can help to promote the final outcome of interest negotiation.

5.5 Summary

In this chapter, I have analyzed the factors that influence information processing in interest negotiation. The analysis has been conducted from three dimensions: sociological, psychological and discursive factors. Through data analysis, it has been found that, among the sociological factors, settings and participants are the two major factors that can influence the process of interest negotiation between opposing parties. Temporal settings impose constraint on the sequence of litigants' communicative actions while spatial settings can influence their speaking manners. Participants' social identities and relations can activate relevant social beliefs or values, which in turn can help to increase the reliability of their testimony or evidence.

Among those psychological factors, the exposure of litigants' intentions and goals can promote conciliation in interest negotiation; the transformation of information sharing can promote consensus or generate more disputes between opposing parties; moreover, litigants' construal phenomena can influence the distribution or arrangement of information units, through which both the process and outcome of interest negotiation can also be affected.

It has also been found that, among the discursive factors, the activation of discourse spaces can make preparations for or impose constraint on the topics to be discussed in the subsequent discourse; the integration of discourse spaces can help to define the major disputes of the court hearings; furthermore, discourse expectations can help to reveal litigants' positions and thus contribute to the final resolution of COI.

Still, the judge plays an important role in the construction of context model, the activation and integration of discourse spaces, modification of litigants' goals of litigation and conciliation of their construal phenomena.

6 Discourse Management for Reaching Agreement

6.1 Introduction

The last two chapters have analyzed features of discourse information in interest appeal and factors influencing interest negotiation respectively. As is illustrated by the analytical framework in Chapter 3, another important aspect in resolution of COI is for participants to reach agreements on certain facts of cases. This is usually realized through discourse management on the basis of participants' expression of interest appeals and their corresponding efforts of interest negotiation. Therefore, in this chapter I will discuss how discourse is managed by participants of litigation to reach agreements between opposing parties, which in turn promotes the final resolution of COI.

As discourse is regarded as the outer manifestation of participants' cognitive activities and information processing, the analysis of discourse management will be conducted from three aspects: information management, cognitive management and linguistic management. The agreement-reaching may take place between the judge and the plaintiff, the judge and the defendant, or the plaintiff and the defendant.

6.2 Information Management

As is demonstrated by Du (2007, 2014), the production and interpretation of discourse center on the processing of information. Discourse information develops and passes forward with the building up of the discourse surface, which constitutes the information flow (Du 2009a). However, in communicative contexts, information flow is usually at the hands of interlocutors, who may exert influence on its direction, strength or depth. Therefore, "how the speaker manages information plays a critical role in discourse production and comprehension" (Tomlin et al. 1997: 68).

In court hearings, participants tend to exert influence on the production and interpretation of discourse information so that agreement can be reached in their own favors. This can be realized by participants' manipulation of information flow and engagement of information transference.

6.2.1 Manipulation of Information Flow

In most cases, the producer of discourse may arrange in advance the direction of the flow of information. However, since in court hearings information is transferred among different participants of litigation, other parties may also try to exert their own influence on the direction of information flow. Therefore, the information flow in court hearings may put up a lot of dynamic features. One of the important features is that the direction of the flow of information can be changed or manipulated by participants. Participants' manipulation can result in three kinds of information development: the horizontal, the vertical and the cycling development of information.

6.2.1.1 The Horizontal Development of Information

The horizontal development of information refers to the information structure in which different information units flow from the same core information unit in a parallel way (Du 2009a: 38). The horizontal development of information is usually adopted by participants when they make conclusions or summaries of the major points of the case.

(76)

[法官]：<1,2,2,30,WT,A>经过法庭调查，法庭对争议焦点归纳如下：<2,30,3,45,WF, O>第一，交警队认定唐XX在本次交通事故中承担全责的依据是其肇事之后逃逸行为，<2,30,3,46,WI,D>是否可以据此认定被告XX交通公司对事故的赔偿责任也承担全责；<2,30,3,47,HW[1], D>第二，原告误工损失以及残疾赔偿金的计算方式；<2,30,3,48,HW[2],D>第三，原告护理费是否能够按照其家属对其进行护理而产生的误工损失予以计算。

[J]: After the court investigation, the focus of dispute can be summarized as follows: Firstly, the hit-and-run behavior of Tang XX is the basis on which the traffic police concluded that he should take the whole responsibility of the traffic accident. The dispute is whether the defendant, XX Transportation Company is accordingly presumed to take all the responsibility for the compensation. Secondly, how to calculate lost income due to missing work hours and disability damages of the plaintiff. Thirdly, whether the lost income incurred to the defendant's wife during his nursery should be taken as the basis for the calculation of the nursery expenses.

In the extract the judge arrives at a conceptualization of the major disputes of the case. The discourse is composed of five information units, which, under the control of the judge, assume a horizontal development.

The WT unit is the core information unit of the whole discourse, by which the judge declares that the next task of the court is to summarize the major disputes of the case. The WT unit has displayed a strong manipulation of the judge on the development of information. For example, the expression *经过法庭调查(after the court investigation)* cuts off the information flow on the deeper information levels in the previous discourse about court investigation; then with the expression *归纳如下(be summarized as follows)*, the judge sets a new direction for the flow of information in the following discourse. The expression *归纳如下(be summarized as follows)* indicates that the following information units will be distributed on a flat surface of the discourse.

Consequently, as is indicated by the tagging symbols of information levels (<2,30,3,45>, <2,30,3,46>, <2,30,3,47> and <2,30,3,48>), the following four information units all flow on the third information level, taking the WT unit as their superordinate unit. Among the four information units, the WF unit is category O, which states the police's definition of the hit-and-run behavior of the defendant. Unit WI points out the first dispute in relation to the WF unit, namely, whether the defendant's behavior can be used as evidence to support the plaintiff's claim that the transport company should take full responsibility for the injury of the plaintiff. The two HW units (HW^1 and HW^2) point out the second and third disputes over the calculation of the lost income, disability compensation and nursing cost. The horizontal development of the discourse information in this extract can be illustrated by Figure 6-1.

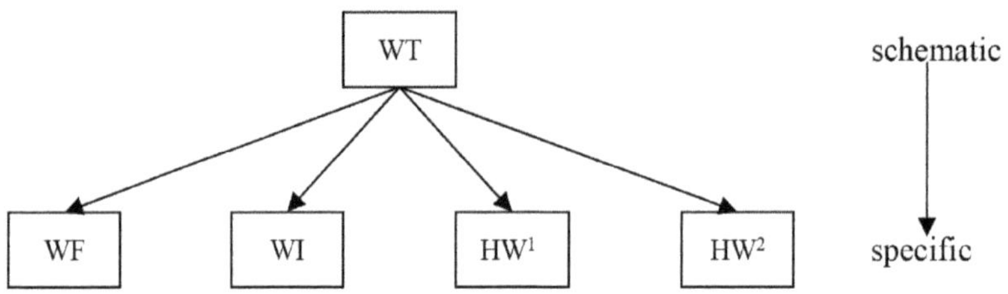

Figure 6-1. Horizontal Development of Information.

The figure shows that the four information units WF, WI, HW^1 and HW^2 develop in a parallel way from the same superordinate unit WT, which assumes a schematic-specific pattern of construal. Their development stops on the subsequent information level without going any further. The horizontal development of the discourse information can help the participants to grasp the major disputes that will be discussed or debated over in the following court hearings. It narrows down the scope of the disagreement between the opposing parties and thus helps them to concentrate their concordant attention on the major disputes of the case.

In some cases, the horizontal development of discourse information is the result of the co-effort of the participants of lawsuit. Under this circumstance, all the participants manipulate with joint effort the flow of information on the same discourse level by providing necessary information units. At the same time, they may compete with each other for the manipulation of the information flow, as is in the following extract.

(77)

01[法官]：<3,11,4,16,WF^{1}，a>最后一份合同的保证金约定和其他的合同不一样，<3,11,4,17,WF^{2}， b>原被告对这份合同的保证金的约定有什么解释？	01[J]: The security deposit in the last contract is different from others. Can both parties make explanations about the deposit in the last contract?
02[原告]：<4,17,5,5,WF^{3}， a>这里边有个前提，“本协议”是指哪个协议。<4,17,5,6,WF^{4}， a>原告认为本协议是指07年的协议，<4,17,5,7,WF^{5}，a>协议的终止是指07年的协议的终止。<4,17,5,8,WF^{6}, a>而07年没有发生任何可以抵扣的事项。	02[P]: We need to clarify one premise. What does “this contract” refer to? The plaintiff thinks it refers to the contract of 2007. The termination of the contract refers to that of 2007. However, in 2007 no violation of contract was committed.
03[被告]：<4,17,5,9,WF^{7},a>07年的时候原告并没有交纳保证金。	03[D]: The plaintiff didn’t pay security deposit in 2007.
04[原告]：<4, 17, 5, 10, WF^{8}，a>2003年之前的话费是银行托收的，<4, 17, 5, 11, WF^{9}， a>2003年之后有一部分是我们收取客户的现金，然后交给被告的。<4, 17, 5, 12, WF^{10}，a>但是话费的拖欠全部是银行托收的。	04[P]: Before 2003, the telephone charges were collected by banks. After 2003 part of the telephone charges were collected by the plaintiff and then given to the defendant. But all delinquent charges have been collected by banks.
05[被告]：<4, 17, 5, 13, WF^{11}， a>是的。	05[D]: Yes.

In this case, the plaintiff has entered into an agency relationship with the defendant and later provided agency service for him. The agency relationship finally ended up with the plaintiff suing the defendant for failing to return the security deposit. In the extract, the two litigants have formed conflicting conceptual contents about the performance of the contract.

In 01 by pointing out the inconsistency in the last contract, the judge activates the discourse space of security deposit (WF^{1}). With unit WF^{2}, the judge asks the two litigants to develop the space by offering their explanations of that inconsistency. Unit WF^{2} sets the macro-direction for the information flowing into the space and thus is the core information unit of the whole discourse.

However, different from the core information unit in Extract (76), which is developed by the information units contributed by the judge himself, unit WF^{2}, which is presented in question form, is developed by the two opposing litigants. It indicates that, although the judge sets the macro-direction for the information flow of the whole discourse, the micro-direction of information flow on the lower levels is at the hands of the litigants themselves.

From 02 to 05, the two opposing parties compete for the manipulation of the development of discourse information. In 02 the plaintiff assumes a specific way of construal and clarifies the contract the judge refers to (WF^3, WF^4 and WF^5). He further proposes that he has committed no violation of the contract (WF^6). However, he fails to provide any information about the security deposit specified in the contract. Therefore, in 03 the defendant fills out the information vacancy by proposing that the plaintiff actually did not pay the security deposit to the defendant. With unit WF^7, the defendant intends to challenge the proposition made by the plaintiff and leads the flow of information to deeper levels.

However, for the information the defendant provides in 03, the plaintiff offers no further opinion, thus preventing the information from flowing to the deeper levels on which they might dispute over whether the payment was made or not. Instead, in 04 the plaintiff continues to provide information on the same information level to prove that he has fulfilled his obligations stipulated in the contract (WF^8, WF^9 and WF^{10}). This time, the defendant gives up his attempt to exert influence on the flow of information and confirms the information units provided by the plaintiff. The development of the discourse information in the extract can be demonstrated by Figure 6-2.

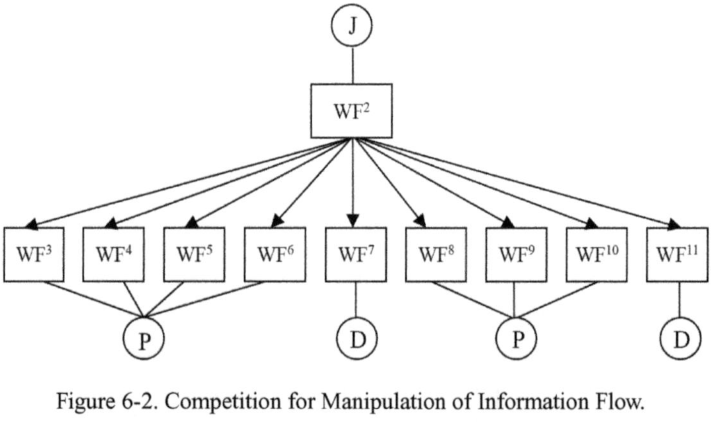

Figure 6-2. Competition for Manipulation of Information Flow.

Note: J: judge; P: plaintiff; D: defendant

The figure shows that on the top level of the discourse information, the judge is the person who activates the discourse space and sets the general direction of the flow of information. The two opposing parties compete for manipulation of the information flow on the subordinate information level. It can be seen that the plaintiff is the party that contributes more information units to the whole discourse and thus exerts more influence on the horizontal development of discourse information. The defendant's attempt to manipulate the information flow with unit WF[7] bears no fruit and finally expresses his consensus with the information units provided by the plaintiff. The manipulation of the horizontal development of the discourse information helps the plaintiff to demonstrate his fulfillment of the duties regulated by the contract, thus occupying a favorable position for the final resolution of the COI.

6.2.1.2 The Vertical Development of Information

The vertical development of information refers to the discourse structure where the information continues to flow to the deeper levels of discourse. The information units in this vertical structure are in a subordinate relationship (Du 2009a: 38), as is illustrated by the following figure.

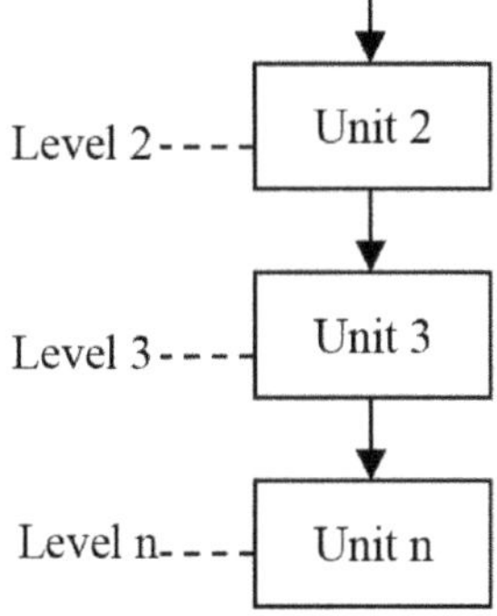

Figure 6-3. Vertical Development of Information.

In this figure, instead of being parallel with each other, the information units at the lower levels are subordinate only to the one at the upper level. This subordinate relationship constitutes a vertical development of discourse information. In court hearings, the vertical development of information can help participants to make detailed elaborations of certain disputes and thus promote their resolution in their own favor.

(78)

01[法官]：<1,4,2,35,WT,A>原告发表辩论意见。	01[J]: Now the plaintiff shall pronounce his opinion.
02[原告]：<2,35,3,30,WF,C>刚才保险公司提到有证据证明原告李X在本次交通事故中有过错。<3,30,4,21,WA,A>我们认为保险公司的这种说法是没有依据的。<4,21,5,11,WB,C>在交通事故责任认定书中已经明确表明了“没有证据证明李X有过错”，<5,11,6,9,WI,A>所以才认定唐XX的（违法）行为，<6,9,7,1,WJ,A>才认定是由唐秋君承担全部责任。	02[P]: Just now the insurance company mentioned that they had evidence to demonstrate that the plaintiff Li X had committed fault in the traffic accident. We think that this proposition is groundless. The Report of Traffic Accident has made it clear that “there is no evidence to demonstrate that Li X has committed fault”, on the basis of which Tang XX’s behavior is regarded as unlawful and therefore should assume all the responsibilities.

In this case, who should assume the main responsibility for the traffic accident becomes the focus of debate that affects the final resolution of the COI. In the previous discourse, the defendant conceptualized that the victim (also the plaintiff) should take the major responsibility for the accident. However, this position is rebutted by the plaintiff in this extract.

In expressing his opposition, the plaintiff has achieved an effective control of the discourse information, which flows vertically from the surface to the deeper levels of the discourse. On the whole, the discourse of the plaintiff is subordinate to the WT unit which instructs him to present his opinions. In the discourse of the plaintiff, the WF unit (<2,35,3,30>) is at the top level since it reactivates the discourse space of the ascertaining of responsibility of the traffic accident by quoting the remarks of the defendant. The reactivation of the space paves the way for the development of the following information units which function as its space components.

On the subordinate level, unit WA demonstrates a contrastive way of construal by rejecting the content of the WF unit by declaring that the defendant's claim is groundless. The WA unit is then supported by the following WB unit which highlights the specificity in construal by proving the plaintiff's absence of fault. Moreover, based on the WB unit, a further inference is made by the subordinate WI unit that the defendant actually committed unlawful acts in the traffic accident, and therefore should assume all the responsibilities.

The vertical development of the information in the discourse of the plaintiff not only helps him to rebut the defendant's proposition that the victim committed negligent fault in the traffic accident, but also proves that the defendant should be responsible for all the severe consequences. By highlighting the opposition between them, the plaintiff indicates his basic position will not be surrendered in the final resolution of the COI.

In some case, the vertical development of discourse information can help to make preparations for the finding of the important facts of the lawsuit, which can lead to the resolution of the disputes in the COI.

(79)

01[法官]：<2,9,3,6,WF^{1}，b>合同中对工作性质有约定吗？	01[J]: Does the contract stipulate on the job categories?
02[证人]：<2,9,3,6,WF^{2}，a>没有具体说明，只说确保找到工作。	02[W]: No specific job is stipulated. It only guarantees to find jobs for us.
03[法官]：<3,6,4,4,WA，b>对那里的工作满意吗？	03[J]: Are you satisfied with your jobs there?
04[证人]：<3,6,4,4,WF^{3}，a>就是在工地打工，收入还可以。	04[W]: Just did some temporary work on construction sites, with satisfying income.
05[法官]：<4,4,5,2,WY^{1}, b>那你们为什么放弃工作回国？<4,4,5,3,WY^{2}，b>都有哪些原因？	05[J]: Then why did you give up the job opportunity and chose to come back? What were the reasons?
06[证人]：<4,4,5,3,WY^{3}，a>我是（因为）家里的事，没办法呆下去。	06[W]: I came back for personal reasons and couldn't stay there any more.
07[法官]：<5,3,6,1,WY^{4}，b>还有没有其他原因？	07[J]: Any other reasons?
08[证人]：<5,3,6,1,WY^{5}，b>听说有些是签证问题，强制送回来了。	08[W]: I heard some were repatriated due to visa problems.

One of the major issues of the case is whether their repatriation of the workers was caused, as the plaintiffs conceptualize, by the early expiration of the visas, or, as the defendant proposes, by the Belgium employers' violation of contracts. In the extract, the judge tries to form a conceptualization about the reasons of their repatriation by questioning the witness.

The judge's questioning starts from the work the plaintiffs did and then has a vertical development to the reasons why they left Belgium. In 01 the judge takes a specific construal and questions whether the contracts have stipulated on the job categories, in that the workers' dissatisfaction with their jobs may be a possible reason for their coming back. After getting a negative answer, the judge in 03 asks directly if the plaintiffs were satisfied with their jobs. The witness's answer with *收入还可以(with satisfying income)* in unit WF^3 indicates that their dissatisfaction with the jobs is not the cause of their coming back.

Therefore, the judge goes deeper to lower information levels to question directly why they quit their jobs (WY^1 and WY^2). These WY units try to reveal the witnesses' real intention of quitting the jobs. In 06 the witness testifies that he came back for private business. Unsatisfied with the answer, in 07 the judge asks if there are any other reasons that caused their repatriation. This time, the witness testifies that some of the workers were repatriated because of visa problems. This answer supports the plaintiffs' claim that the defendant should be responsible for the undesirable visas, thus solving the dispute over the visa problem.

It shows that the judge's manipulation of the vertical flow of discourse information is very effective in the resolution of the dispute by controlling the witness's answer. For example, on the first two levels of the discourse information (<2,9,3,6> and <3,6,4,4>), the judge's questioning about the work category has excluded their dissatisfaction as one of the possible reasons for their coming back, thus narrowing down the witness's choices in the following questioning. On the lower levels (<4,4,5,3> and <5,3,6,1>), the witness first provides a private reason with unit WY^3, and then, pressured by the questioning of the judge, the witness finally admits that the visa problem is one of the major reason.

6.2.1.3 The Cycling Development of Information

The cycling development of information refers to the reoccurrence or hovering of the same information which leads to the appearance of information vortex (Du 2009a: 42). Different from the horizontal or vertical development of information, where information flows smoothly either on the same information level or through different information levels, the cycling development of information is the result of information blocking. The information vortex is usually reveals the focus of the discourse or interlocutors.

In court hearings, the cycling development of information can be an effective way to find facts or resolve disputes. Here is an extract from Chapter 4, reproduced as Extract (80), in which the judge questions the witness about his signing on the written testimony.

(80)

01[法官]：<2,6,3,9,WF^{1}, C>你说工头带你们到工地签的字。<3,9,4,2,WY^{1}, b>为什么签字？	01[J]: You said that the foreman took you to the construction site to sign the name. **Why did you sign your name?**
02[证人]：<3,9,4,2,WY^{2}, a>工头领着去就签字了。	02[W]: **The foreman took me there and then I signed the name.**
03[法官]：<3,9,4,3,WY^{3}, b>为什么工头领着去就签了？	03[J]: **Why did you do that?**
04[证人]：<3,9,4,3,WY^{4}, a>他们让签就签字了。	04[W]: **They asked me to sign the name and I did what they asked me to do.**
05[法官]：<4,3,5,1,WF^{2}, b>你认识字吗？	05[J]: Can you read?
06[证人]：<4,3,5,1,WF^{3}, a>认识但是不多。	06[W]: Yes. But not very good at it.
07[法官]：<4,3,5,2,WF^{4}, b>你看到上边写了什么吗？	07[J]: Did you notice what was written on the paper?
08[证人]：<4,3,5,2,WF^{5}, a>没有看见。	08[W]: No.
09[法官]：<3,9,4,4,WY^{5}, b>为什么没有看见就签字了？	09[J]: **Why did you sign the name without knowing what was there?**
10[证人]：<3,9,4,4,WY^{6}, a>因为是工头领着去的，让签字就签字了。	10[W]: **Because we were taken there by the foreman. We just did what he asked.**

In this case, one of the major disputes is, as the plaintiff claims, whether the written testimony produced by the defendant is signed by the witnesses when they were under threat. In the extract, the judge questions one of the witnesses about the reason why he signed his name.

With unit WY^1 in 01, the judge activates the discourse space of the reasons why the witness signed his name. However, in 02 the witness provides no valuable information and thus makes no contribution to the development of the space. Therefore, in the same discourse space the judge repeats the question with unit WY^3 by questioning closely why the witness signed his name at the request of the foreman. The repeated questioning (WY^1 and WY^3) of the judge give rise to the first information vortex at the fourth information level. However, the witness's answer with unit WY^4 still contributes no information to the development of the discourse space.

In the following two turns (05 and 07), the judge closes up the discourse space by abandoning the topic about the signing of the testimony and instructs the flow of information to deeper levels to activate a new space of the witness's literacy. The two questions free the information from the information vortex and promote the smooth development of the new space.

It seems as if the information might continue to have a smooth development on the lower information levels in the new discourse space of the witness's literacy. However, the transitory smooth development is only a preparation for the re-emergence of the first space. After confirming with the two WF units (WF^3 and WF^5) that the witness had no idea about the content of the testimony, the judge instructs the information to flow back to the fourth level with unit WY^5 and rejoins the information vortex by reactivating the discourse space of the reasons why the witness signed his name. This time, the witness makes an important contribution to the development of the space with a cause-effect structure*因为是工头领着去的，让签字就签字了(Because we were taken there by the foreman. We just did what he asked.)*, which makes it clear that the foreman played an important role in the signing of the testimony.

We can see that the judge's manipulation of the cycling development of the discourse information helps to prove that the witnesses' signing of the testimony was not their real intention, thus promoting an agreement between him and the witness on the validity of the testimony.

In most cases, the lawsuit is concerned with more than one dispute. Some of the disputes are more important for the final resolution of the COI and therefore attract more attention of the court. The information concerning these disputes may have a cycling development through the whole discourse, as is in the following extract in which the plaintiff sues the defendant for plagiarizing his novel.

(81)

01[原告]：<2,11,3,13,WN[1]，a>证据1，我们提交的证据说明发表时间是07年11月底。	01[P]: Evidence 1 is to prove that the book was published at the end of November, 2007.
02[法官]：<2,11,3,14,WN[2]，b>认可被告方第一章内容是在07年11月底发表的？	02[J]: Do you agree with the defendant that the first chapter was published at the end of November 2007?
03[原告]：<2,11,3,14,WN[3], a>是的。	03[P]: Yes.
04[被告]：<2,11,3,15,WN[4], d>最初发表时间是07年10月份，<2,11,3,16,WR, d>发表在XX社区的XX栏目。	04[D]: It was first published in October, 2007, at XX Column of XX BBS.
……	…
05[法官]：<4,9,5,5,WN[5]，b>图书定稿最后完成时间？	05[J]: When was the last version finished?
06[被告]：<4,9,5,5,WN[6], d>是在07年10月份，10月23日左右。	06[D]: October, 2007. Around October 23rd.
07[法官]：<4,9,5,6,WN[7]，b>原告明确定稿完成时间？	07[J]: Does the plaintiff agree with the date?
08[原告]：<4,9,5,6,WN[8]，d>07年11月底。	08[P]: At the end of November 2007.
……	…
09[法官]：<2,16,3,33,WA[1]，b>原告方，被告所述10月份发表了作品的第一、二章，认可吗？	09[J]: Does the plaintiff agree with the defendant that the first two chapters were published in October?
10[原告]：<2,16,3,33,WA[2]，a>不认可。<3,33,4,20,WN[9]，d>是在07年11月20多号。<3,33,4,21,WN[10]，a>我们的作品在07年4月份已经给了吴X，<3,33,4,22,WF[1],a>他给了书商。<3,33,4,23,WF[2], a>10、11月份是在修改。	10[P]: No. It was around November 20th, 2007. We handed in our work to Wu X in April, 2007, who gave it to the publishing company, and revised it in October and November.
11[法官]：<4,21,5,12,WF[3]，b>原告之前发给吴X的邮件保留了吗？	11[J]: Has the plaintiff kept the emails to Wu X?
12[原告]：<4,21,5,12,WF[4], a>有保存。	12[P]: Yes.

One of the major disputes of the case, besides the similarity of the content of the novel and validity of the contract, is the publication date of the two drafts. The extract is from different phases of the court hearings, in which the information concerning the publication date has a cycling development through the whole discourse.

In the first part of the discourse, which happens in the cross-examining phase of the court hearings, the information flow forms the first information vortex on the third information level of the discourse (<2,11,3,13>, <2,11,3,14>, <2,11,3,15>). With unit WN^1 in 01 the plaintiff first activates the discourse space of the publication date of the book and makes a first contribution by defining it the end of November, 2007. But he does not specify which draft he refers to. Therefore, in 02 the judge instructs the information to flow back to the activated space by asking the plaintiff to confirm the specific draft with unit WN^2.

However, the plaintiff's contribution to the development of the space meets with blocks from the defendant, who proposes with unit WN^4 that the draft was first published on the internet in October, 2007. The defendant's challenge reinforces the cycling development of the information vortex by highlighting the dispute between the opposing parties.

In the second part of the discourse, which happens in the court debate, the information flow forms the second information vortex in the same discourse space of the publication date of the draft, which is reactivated by unit WN^5. This time, the information vortex develops on the lower information levels of the discourse (<4,9,5,5> and <4,9,5,6>). It can be seen that the judge's questioning is still the impetus that promotes the cycling development of the information in the space, because with units WN^5 and WN^7, the judge intends to solve the dispute over the publication date. But the two parties' answers with units WN^6 and WN^8 are still conflicting and make no contribution to its resolution.

In the third part of the discourse, the judge activates the same discourse space for a third time by asking the plaintiff's attitude towards the publication date proposed by the defendant (unit WA^1). The cycling development of the information rejoins the first information vortex in the first part of the discourse and makes the dispute more prominent.

It indicates that the confirmation of the publication date is of vital importance to the final resolution of the COI. This time, the plaintiff provides his correspondence with Wu X as new evidence, which helps to confirm the publication date proposed by the plaintiff.

It can be seen that, under the instruction of the judge, the cycling development of information can run through the whole discourse, forming information vortexes on different information levels, which lead to the resolution of disputes.

6.2.2 Intervention of Information Transference

According to Verschueren (1999), language use is a process in which interlocutors make intentional selections of the words, structures and intonations for the need of the communication. In court hearings, the selection is also closely concerned with information transference, in which the flow of information can be intervened by participants, who may re-organize the information according to their communicative purposes (Du 2009b).

In the following, I will have a discussion of how the intervention of information transference can help participants to resolve disputes in court hearings. The intervention will be analyzed from three aspects: information accretion, information loss and information reporting.

6.2.2.1 Information Accretion

Information accretion refers to the phenomenon that some information units drift away from the core information unit and, instead of contributing to the development of information, may block the smooth flow of discourse information (Du 2009a: 41). In court hearings, information accretion may cause difficulties for the efficient resolution of COI. Therefore, under such circumstances, the judge is obliged to take measures to eliminate the negative influence caused by information accretion, as is illustrated in the following extract.

(82)

01[法官]：<WN[1], b>什么时间签的合同？<HW, b>补充一下合同里营业税是如何约定的？

02[上诉人]：<WF[1], a>我自己每个月租2,000块，作为全部一块，包括一切税收，<WF[2], a>其它的你自己办。**<WF[3], a>**怎么知道他赖在我这个老人的头上，……，**<WF[4], a>**那他现在要结束的时候，他就说逃税，**<WF[5], a>**当时缴税使用现金来交的。"**<WF[6], a>**装修的越多，缴税就越多。**<WF[7], a>**阿姨啊，不如我少交一点好不好。"……。

03[法官]：<WT[1], a>上诉人，如果你讲一些和本案无关的话，就不要再说了，<WT[2], a>我们要你讲的是事实的补充，<WT[3], a>不是叫你在这里吵。

04[上诉人]：**<WF[8], a>**这些就是事实啊。**<WT[4], a>**我现在就是清晰的和你讲……

05[法官]：<WT[5], a>我们现在要你讲的不是这些……

06[上诉人]：**<WF[9], a>**他分明在骗我钱。**<WF[10], a>**我现在又没有钱。**<WF[11], a>**在这一点上，你今天打官司的行为，分明又在骗我钱，**<WF[12], a>**你根本就是蛮不讲理的……

07[法官]：<WT[6], a>上诉人，我和你严肃的讲，<WF[13], a>案件是有时间限制的，<WP[1], a>法庭问你什么，你就答什么，<WP[2], a>不是让你随便乱说。<WT[7], a>现在法庭是要问上诉人一个问题，<WN[2], b>你们是什么时候跟被上诉人一方签订协议的？

08[上诉人]：<WN[3], b>正式的日期应该是10月20日。

01[J]: When was the contract signed? Can you explain how sales tax is stipulated in the contract?

02[AT]: I rented the house for 2,000 yuan a month, as a whole, including all the tax. You would deal with the rest. **How could I know that he blamed it on me, the old woman… When he finished, he said he'd evade tax, which was paid in cash at that time. "The more I decorate, the more I'll pay the tax. Aunty, can I pay less?"…**

03[J]: Appellant, if you continue to talk irrelevantly, you can stop now. What the court asks for is supplementary statement to facts, not quarrels.

04[AT]: **These are the facts, and I want to make it clear…**

05[J]: These are not what the court needs…

06[AT]: **Obviously he was trying to coax money from me. I have no money. On this occasion, in this lawsuit, you're coaxing my money too. You're totally savage and absurd…**

07[J]: Appellant, now I'm talking to you seriously. We have a time limit here for the hearing. You should answer what the court asks. Stop talking nonsense. Now the court asks the appellant one question. When did you sign the contract with the appellee?

08[AT]: The valid date is October 20th.

The extract is from a court investigation, in which the judge tries to form a conceptualization about the signing of contract between the appellant and appellee. However, when answering the questions of the judge, the appellant provides excessive information which constitutes information accretion.

In 01 the judge activates the discourse space of the signing of the contract with two questions: one is the date of signing (WN^1) and the other, the provision on sales tax. These questions take on a very schematic view and create a discourse expectation on the information provided by the appellant. Namely, the appellant is expected to provide specific construal that is closely related to the discourse space.

As a response, the appellant in 02 manifests great specificity in her construal of the event. For example, with two WF units (WF^1 and WF^2), the appellant provides adequate answer to the second question by making it clear that the rent (2,000 yuan a month) includes the sales tax. These WF units make an adequate contribution to the development of the discourse space.

However, in the following discourse the appellant provides further information about the quarrel between her and the appellee[1]. On the surface, it seems that the information units in the bolded discourse in 02 are connected to the second question in the discourse space, since they all concern the topic of sales tax. However, on a deeper level, they are not consistent with the core information unit because it is *the provision on sales tax in the contract (合同里营业税是如何约定的)* that is cared about by the judge, not the private bargaining between the two opposing parties. Therefore, the information units in the bolded discourse of the appellant constitute information accretion that blocks the smooth development of information.

Recognizing the potential harm of the information accretion to the development of the discourse space, in 03 the judge gives his first instruction on the appellant's response with three WT units (WT^1, WT^2 and WT^3). The judge makes it clear with WT^1 that the appellant's answer is irrelevant, and instructs her to provide supplementary information about the facts of the case (WT^2).

1 The original discourse about the quarrel between the appellant and the appellee has 384 words. For the sake of space, I have only presented a small part of it.

Then from 04 to 07 the judge and the appellant are involved in an intense fight for the floor of speaking. In 04 the judge's instruction is overlooked by the appellant who intends to continue with the information accretion by adopting a hedge *我现在就是清晰的和你讲(I want to make it clear)*. In 05 the judge attempts to regain the floor and stop the information accretion. But his effort is failed by the appellant's interruption in 06 which continues with the appellant's accusation of the appellee's unlawful behavior (WF^9, WF^{10}, WF^{11} and WF^{12}).

The information accretion is finally stopped by the judge's interruption in 07. The two WP units (WP^1 and WP^2) make it clear that the appellant should provide information required by the court and thus clarifies the direction of the information flow. Based on the instruction, the appellant finally provides adequate information to the judge's question about the date of the signing of the contract, which satisfies the expectation of the discourse space.

We can see that information accretion can block the natural development of discourse information and cause difficulties to the resolution of COI. The judge's instruction can eliminate the information accretion and bring the information flow back to its normal track, which can promote the efficient resolution of COI.

Although information accretion may block the smooth flow of discourse information and cause problems for the final resolution of disputes, in some cases on the contrary, information accretion may promote the development of information and exert positive influence on the resolution of COI if it is performed cooperatively by participants.

(83)

01[法官]：<WF[1], b>原告，交通事故发生时，你是否向保险公司报险？
02[原告]：<WF[2], a>交通事故发生时，我们报险了。**<WP[1], a>**当时保险公司派来的定损员说需要办理批改。
03[法官]：<WF[3], b>被告，原告所说是否属实？
04[被告]：<WF[4], c>当时就是这么和原告说的。**<WF[5], a>**原告周一就到保险公司来办批改了。
05[法官]：<WF[6], b>被告，你们现在使用的商业险的保单是什么内容？
06[被告]：**<WF[7], a>**现在的商业保险的保单不需要办理批改手续，**<WC, a>**只要保险的标的危险程度没有增加就可以。
07[法官]：<WF[8], b>原告，你从王X来处购买车辆后，车辆的危险程度是否增加？
08[原告]：<WF[9], a>没有增加。**<WF[10], a>**我有驾照，**<WF[11], a>**以前也驾驶过车辆，**<WF[12], a>**车辆也是家庭自用。
09[法官]：<WF[13], b>被告，你方有证据证明原告购买车辆后其危险程度有增加吗？
10[被告]：<WF[14], a>我没有证据证明原告购买车辆后车辆的危险程度增加了，**<WF[15], c>**车辆危险程度没有增加。

01[J]: Plaintiff, did you report the traffic accident to the insurance company when it happened?
02[P]: Yes. We did when it happened. **The loss assessor of the insurance company said that the transfer of the insurance must be approved by the company.**
03[J]: Does the defendant agree with the plaintiff's statement?
04[D]: That's what was said to the plaintiff. **And he came to the company for approval the next Monday.**
05[J]: Defendant, what content is involved in your business insurance policy?
06[D]: **No approval is needed in the present insurance policy, as long as the risk of the insured object matter does not increase.**
07[J]: Plaintiff, did the risk of the car increase after you bought the car from Wang X?
08[P]: No. **I've got a license and have driven a car before, which was mainly for domestic use.**
09[J]: Defendant, do you have evidence to prove the risk increase after the car was bought by the plaintiff?
10[D]: We have no evidence to prove that. **The risk of the car does not increase.**

In this case, the defendant refuses to settle the insurance claims of the plaintiff for the reason that the transfer of the insurance needs to be approved by the insurance company. In the extract, when answering the questions of the judge, both litigants provide excessive information which constitutes information accretion.

With unit WF[1] in 01 the judge first activates the discourse space of the reporting of the accident, to which the plaintiff in 02 provides an affirmative answer as its space component. In addition to that, the plaintiff also quotes the remarks of the loss assessor *定损员说需要办理批改手续 (the insurance company said that the transfer of the insurance must be approved by the company)*, which activates a new space of the approval of the insurance transfer (WP[1]).

The new discourse space constitutes information accretion since it is obviously excessive to the yes/no question of the judge. However, instead of destructing the natural development of information, this information accretion is favorable to the information flow because it leads the information to the major dispute of the lawsuit.

After providing excessive information with unit WF[5] in 04 which demonstrates the plaintiff's application for the approval of the insurance transfer, in 06 the defendant takes a more specific view of construal in his elaboration of the conditions for the settlement of insurance claims (units WF[7] and WC). The defendant makes it clear that insurance claims would be settled if the risk of the insured object matter does not increase. The information accretion in 04 and 06 is performed cooperatively by the defendant, because these excessive answers provide valuable information for the resolution of the dispute.

Based on the information provided by the defendant about the conditions for the settlement of insurance claims, the judge asks the two litigants respectively in 07 and 09 whether the risk of the car increases after the transfer of its ownership. This time, as is shown by the information accretion in the litigants' answers in 08 and 10, the defendant arrives at a consensus with the plaintiff with unit WF[15] (category C) that the risk does not increase after the transfer of the ownership. This consensus means that the defendant accepts the validity of the insurance contract and agrees to make the payment.

It shows that information accretion, if conducted cooperatively, can help to promote the smooth development of discourse information, which in turn contributes to the final resolution of COI.

6.2.2.2 *Information Loss*

Information loss refers to the phenomenon that some information drops out of the information flow and dies away from the natural development of the discourse (Du 2009a: 41). Information loss is usually caused by the negligence of interlocutors who neglect the value of the information. However, in court hearings, information loss can be the result of litigants' deliberate selection for the sake of their interest pursuit.

(84)

01[法官]：<WA, b>被告，你对原告出示的证据真实性有没有异议？<WF^1, b>双方确实存在传真往来件？<WF^2, b>你的意见是双方在履行合同当中，除了书面约定，还进行了口头约定吗？	01[J]: Defendant, do you accept the authenticity of the evidence produced by the plaintiff? Are there really fax correspondences? Do you mean that besides the written contract you have entered into an oral agreement to guarantee the performance of the contract?
02[被告]：<WF^3, a>当时双方一致商定按口头约定履行。<WF^4, a>但失误就在我们没有把口头约定写进合同里。	02[D]: Both parties agreed to follow the oral agreement. But the mistake was that we didn't include the oral agreement in the contract.
03[法官]：<WF^5, b>双方口头怎么约定的？	03[J]: What was the oral agreement?
04[被告]：<WF^6, a>原告工作人员罗XX跟我们口头承诺在电视剧《暖春》的剧后插播该段广告……。	04[D]: Luo XX, one of the staff of the plaintiff, promised orally that the commercial would be broadcast after the TV series "Warm Spring"...

In this case, the two litigants are involved in a lawsuit of advertising contract. One of the major disputes of the case is the airtime of the TV commercial. The plaintiff proposes that the valid airtime of the TV commercial is the time stipulated in the contract. However, the defendant claims that the valid airtime is stipulated otherwise in an oral agreement.

In 01 the judge takes a very specific way of construal by asking three questions which concern the discourse space of the agreed airtime of the TV commercial. Question one (unit WA) concerns the defendant's attitude towards the authenticity of the evidence (fax correspondence) provided by the plaintiff. Question two (unit WF^1), although in different form, is the same with question one. In the third question (unit WF^2), the judge asks if they have entered into any oral agreement on the airtime of the TV commercial.

Of the three questions, the evidence provided by the plaintiff, namely, the fax correspondence (WA and WF[1]) is highlighted in the judge's construal, which shows that this evidence is of great importance to the final resolution of the COI.

However, in 02 the information in the first two questions is completely ignored by the defendant, who only provides answers with units WF[3] and WF[4] to the third question. Consequently, the information in the first two questions drops out of the information flow and therefore constitutes information loss. The information loss is the result of the defendant's intervention of the information flow, which results from the defendant's different perspective in his construal of the dispute, in that the evidence of fax correspondence, if accepted by the court, may place him into a very unfavorable position. In this way, the defendant intends to lighten the effect of the plaintiff's evidence and strengthen the effect of his own.

By emphasizing with unit WF[3] that the oral agreement between him and the plaintiff is actually the valid contract for the TV commercial, the defendant successfully shits the court's attention from the fax correspondence to the oral agreement. This can be demonstrated by the judge's questioning in 03 about the content of the oral agreement.

It shows that the information loss in the extract is the result of the defendant's intentional selection. Information loss can lead to the dropping out of the unfavorable information, from which the defendant may gain benefits in the final resolution of COI.

However, sometimes information loss may be a temporary phenomenon. It means that, with the intervention of litigants, some information may drop out of the information flow for a short time but later emerge again and rejoin the development of the discourse information. This is usually caused by the indispensible position of the information in the resolution of the dispute, as is demonstrated in the following extract.

(85)

01[法官]：<3,10,4,9,WF^1, b>分家单上的四丈二是多少米？<3,10,4,10,WY, b>你提供的证据和现在的数据是相矛盾的。	01[J]: What is the specific length of 4.2 zhangs in meter on the list of the property division? The evidence you produced contradicts with the present data.
02[原告]：<3,10,4,9,WF^2, a>13.23米。	02[P]: It is 13.23 meters.
……	…
03[法官]：<5,5,6,8,WF^3, a>测量的尺子有木匠尺和米尺，<5,5,6,9,WF^4, b>你们用的是哪个，<5,5,6,10,WA^1, b>被告认可吗？	03[J]: There are two kinds of measurements: carpentry rule and meter rule. Which one did you use? Does the defendant accept the measurement?
04[原告]：<5,5,6,9,WF^5, a>就是木匠尺。	04[P]: It was carpentry rule.
05[被告]：<5,5,6,10,WA^2, a>不认可。	05[D]: We don't accept carpentry rule.
06[法官]：<5,5,6,11,WF^6, b>第三人对四丈二发表意见？	06[J]: What's the third party's opinion about 4.2 zhangs?
07[第三人]：<5,5,6,11,WF^7, a>我们认为现有的文书都是在解放以后，采用的就是公认的米尺。	07[3rd P]: We think that all the documents were signed after China's liberation. Therefore, it should be the generally accepted as meter rule.

The extract is from a case of real estate partition, in which the property area of the house stipulated in the contract becomes the major dispute. In the extract, participants try to solve the issue of measurement, which is closely related to the definition of house property area.

With units WF^1 and WY in 01, the judge activates the discourse space of measurement standard by highlighting in his construal the inconsistency between the present data and that in the evidence provided previously by the plaintiff. However, in 02 the plaintiff only provides answer to the first question by making it clear that 4.2 zhangs equal 13.23 meters, and totally neglects the judge's request to explain the inconsistency. The information loss brought about by the plaintiff leaves vacancy in the discourse space that needs to be filled out later. It indicates that the inconsistency of the data may have negative effects on his interest pursuit in the resolution of COI and therefore is deliberately dropped by the plaintiff.

But different from Extract (84) where the lost information completely drops out of the information flow, in this extract the lost information reemerges at the lower information levels (<5,5,6,8>, <5,5,6,9> and <5,5,6,10>) in the subsequent discourse. In 03 the judge reactivates the discourse space by pointing out that the inconsistency is actually caused by the difference of measurement between carpentry rule and meter rule. With units WF^4 and WA^1, the judge further asks which rule should be accepted as the standard measurement. The reemergence of the lost information shows that the measurement inconsistency is still the focus of the judge's construal and is an issue of vital importance to the final resolution of the COI and therefore should be clarified.

Consequently, from 04 to 07, the litigants are involved in a debate over the standard measurement, which helps to fill out the vacancy left in the discourse space. The plaintiff insists that the carpentry rule should be accepted, while the defendant and the third party support the meter rule. In unit WF^7, the third party further points out that meter rule should be the generally accepted measurement standard since the contract was signed after China's liberation: *现有的文书都是在解放以后(all the documents were signed after China's liberation)*. The testimony of the third party adds strength to the court's final adoption of meter rule as the standard measurement.

It can be seen that information loss has a great influence on the normal development of discourse information. However, if the lost information is of significant importance to the resolution of the COI, it is inclined to reemerge in the subsequent discourse and make contributions to the final resolution of the COI.

6.2.2.3 Information Reporting

Since information transference is the communication of information between different interlocutors, the interpersonal meanings of information flow are also important aspects concerning the development of discourse information (Halliday & Matthiessen 2004). One of the interpersonal meanings is the persuasive effects of the discourse information (Du 2008). Among the various ways to realize persuasion, information reporting is frequently used by interlocutors to strengthen their persuasive power by intervening the normal flow of discourse information.

In court hearings, in order to gain a favorable position in the final resolution of the COI, litigants may, by reporting information from various sources, try to strengthen the persuasive power of his own information or weaken the persuasive power of the information of the opposing party.

(86)

01[原告]：<WT^1, A>在本次交通事故中，经XX队交警支队处理并认定，<WF^1, A>该肇事司机承担本次交通事故的全部责任，<WF^2, A>原告李**X**不负事故责任。<WT^2, A>交通事故发生后，经鉴定，<WF^3, A>原告李军的伤势构成十级，<WF^4, A>休息**6**个月，<WF^5, A>营养期**3**个月，<WF^6, A>护理**3**个月。	01[P]: As demonstrated by XX traffic police, in this traffic accident, **the taxi driver should take all the responsibility for the accident and Li X, the plaintiff, should not.** After the accident, according to the appraisal report, **Li X has suffered a ten-scale injury and should take 6 months' break, 3 months' nutrition and 3 months' nursery.**
02[法官]：<WT^3, A>被告XX交通集团股份有限公司发表答辩意见。	02[J]: The Defendant XX Transportation Company shall make a reply.
03[被告]：<WP^1, A>请法院查明本次交通事故的事故形成原因及过错归责方式，<WP^2, A>依法确定驾驶员唐XX与被告XX公司之间的行为的关系。	03[D]: We request the court to find out the cause of the traffic accident, ascertain the way of fault attribution and clarify the legal relation between the driver Tang XX and the defendant XX company.

This extract is from a case of traffic accident, in which the definition of responsibility for the accident and amount of compensation become prominent conceptual contents in the resolution of the COI.

In 01 the plaintiff makes his own definition of the responsibility for the accident and the injury incurred by the victim. In order to increase its persuasive power, the information is presented in reporting forms. The information reporting highlights a new participant in the context model schema generated thereby, namely, *XX队交警支队(XX traffic police)*, which is also the information source. The revelation of the information source in the context model schema guarantees the authenticity of the following WF units (WF^1 and WF^2), with which the plaintiff asserts that the defendant should assume all the responsibility for the traffic accident, while the victim should not.

Similarly, units WF^3 to WF^6 are also reported information about the injury the victim has suffered in the traffic accident. Here although a very vague process information element *经鉴定(according to the appraisal report)* is employed to refer to the information source, which defines no specific participant in the context model schema, the plaintiff indicates with unit WT^2 that the information is cited from a reliable organization.

Compared with the discourse of the plaintiff, the propositions in 03 are only the defendant's personal proposals for the disposition of the disputes. Due to the lack of support from other information sources, the WP units (WP^1 and WP^2) in the defendant's discourse seem to be groundless and less persuasive.

We can see that reported information strengthens the persuasive power of the claims of litigants and may help them to gain more benefits in the final resolution of the COI. Apart from that, in some cases, information can be reported to weaken the persuasive power of the opposing party, as is in the following extract.

(87)

01[被告]：<WC^1, a>如果原告配偶的收入像原告所说的这么高的话，<WP^1, a>那么以她的收入情况去请三四个人做护理是请得到的。<WC^2, a>那么按照她这样做的话，<WC^3, a>如果原告的损失存在的话，<WJ^1, a>存在明显的扩大损失。	01[D]: If the income of the plaintiff's spouse is as high as what the plaintiff described, she could have hired 3 or 4 people for the nursery. If that is true and if the plaintiff really suffers economic losses, his losses are obviously exaggerated.
02[原告]：**<WT, c>**刚才被告提到，**<WC^4, d>**既然廖**XX**的收入这么高，**<WP^2, d>**完全可以请两个雇工，就可以解决了，**<WE, d>**不会产生这么大的损失，**<WJ^2, d>**并且得出结论，是由于廖**XX**的护理，才造成了损失的扩大。<WA, a>那么原告对此说法也是无法予以认可的。<WF^1, a>试想出了交通事故以后，人受到伤害以后，最需要得到的是什么？<WF^2, a>除了治疗以外，应该最重要的是亲情的关爱和呵护。	02[P]: **The defendant just mentioned that, since Liao XX has such a high income, she could have hired some nurses, and things would have been done without incurring so many losses. The defendant moved on to conclude that it was due to the nursery given by Liao XX herself that the economic losses were enlarged.** We can't agree with the defendant on it. Just consider: what do people need most after they are injured? Apart from medical treatment, it should be the care and love of their family.

The extract is from the same case with Extract (86). In this extract, the plaintiff debates with the defendant over the amount of compensation damages. In 01 the defendant bases his conceptualization of compensation damages on the speech management strategy of logical reasoning by proposing that the plaintiff's economic loss is exaggerated. The ground for his reasoning is that the plaintiff's wife has the financial capacity to hire nursing workers but she did not.

The defendant's account in 01 constitutes an important component of the context model schema which is formed on the basis of the plaintiff's construal of the dispute. Taking on a contrastive perspective in the compensation responsibility, the plaintiff in 02 first conducts information reporting of the defendant's remarks, which is initiated by a WT unit *刚才被告提到(the defendant just mentioned)*. In the information reporting, units WC^4 and WP^2 correspond to units WC^1 and WP^1, and units WE and WJ^2 correspond to unit WJ^1 respectively in the defendant's discourse. The conformity of information units in the discourses of the two litigants forms cohesion and promotes the information flow on the discourse level.

However, in the following discourse the reported information is challenged by the plaintiff, which helps to hold it back from reaching the other participants, the judge in particular. With unit WA, the plaintiff expresses clearly his opposition to the reported information. The following two WF units (WF^1 and WF^2) make emotional appeals for his opposition. The plaintiff means that the care and love of the wife is the most valuable for the recovery of the victim. The emotional appeal conforms to the common pursuit of Chinese traditional value and is well-grounded, thus imposing a great challenge to the reported information.

The challenge of the plaintiff weakens the persuasive power of the reported information and imposes barriers to its normal development to the court. By setting back the defendant's attempt to diminish his economic losses, the plaintiff has increased his chance to get more benefits in the final resolution of the COI.

In short, information management is an important discursive strategy employed in court hearings to promote agreement between participants of lawsuit. This is usually realized by manipulation of information flow and engagement of information transference. Under the manipulation of participants, discourse information tends to have a horizontal, vertical or cycling development. The intervention of information transference can lead to information accretion, information loss or information reporting. With information management, litigants can help to clarify disputes or promote consensus in their own favors.

6.3 Cognitive Management

As was discussed previously, resolution of COI is also a cognitive process in which different interest appeals of litigants are negotiated and finally resolved. In court hearings, one of the major functions of the communication of information is to bring about changes in the attitudes of litigants, so that their positions of interest appeals can be modified or completely altered, which contributes to the final resolution of the COI.

In this section, I will analyze how the cognitive activities are managed by participants of lawsuits in the communication of information for the resolution of COI. During the analysis, the following three aspects will be touched upon: integration of information, assimilation of intentions and goals and reconciliation of construal phenomena.

6.3.1 Integration of Information

As was revealed in section 5.3.2 of Chapter 5, information sharing is one of the integral factors of context model schema that influence the negotiation of interest between different parties. Among the various information sharing categories, the information that enjoys a high degree of consensus is usually preferred by the court because it is the basis on which the conciliation or final judgment is made (Xu 2013). Therefore, in court hearings, one of the purposes of cognitive management is to achieve information integration between opposing parties either by reinforcing shared information or eliminating controversial information.

6.3.1.1 *Reinforcing Shared Information*

According to Du (2009b: 367), court hearing is an agreement-reaching process in which the opposing parties with different interest appeals define, negotiate and alter their communicative goals until the COI is finally resolved. Shared information is of great importance for the resolution of COI because it is the direct manifestation of agreement or consensus. Therefore, in court hearings, shared information, the information concerning the resolution of the major disputes in particular, is often reinforced by the court.

(88)

01[法官]：<WN^{1}, b>原告是何时受伤的？	01[J]: When was the plaintiff injured?
02[原告]：<WN^{2}, a>2009年4月9日。	02[P]: On April 9th, 2009.
03[法官]：<WY^{1}, b>原告什么原因受的伤？	03[J]: What caused your injury?
04[原告]：<WY^{2}, a>受被告雇佣卸木材，在卸到第九车时从车上摔下来导致腰部受伤。	04[P]: I was unloading wood for the defendants and injured my waist by falling down from the 9th truck.
05[法官]：<WA^{1}, b>原告所述是否属实？	05[J]: Is what the plaintiff said true?
06[被告1]：<WA^{2}, c>属实。	06[D1]: Yes.
07[被告2]：<WA^{3}, c>属实。	07[D2]: Yes.
08 [法官]：<WF^{1}, b>原告与二被告是什么关系？	08[J]: What is the relation between the plaintiff and the two defendants?
09 [原告]：<WF^{2}, a>雇佣关系，<WF^{3}, a>二被告雇佣我卸木材。	09[P]: Employment relation. The two defendants hired me to unload wood.
10 [被告1]：<WA^{4}, c>对。	10[D1]: Yes.
11 [被告2]：<WA^{5}, c>对。	11[D2]: Yes.
12 [法官]：<HW^{1}, b>原告工资的支付方式？	12[J]: Plaintiff, how were you paid?
13[原告]：<HW^{2}, a>被告每天支付原告50元。	13[P]: They paid me 50 yuan a day.
14[法官]：<WA^{6}, b>原告所述是否属实？	14[J]: Is what the plaintiff said true?
15[被告1]：<WA^{7}, c>属实。	15[D1]: Yes.
16[被告2]：<WA^{8}, c>属实。	16[D2]: Yes.

In this case, the plaintiff claims compensation for his injury which was caused during his work for the defendant. In the extract, the judge makes investigation about some of the important facts of the incident.

Information units in the first two turns (WN^1 and WN^2) concern the temporal setting of the context model. During the questioning, the judge does not ask the two defendants to make confirmation about the temporal setting, since, as background information in this case, the date of the plaintiff's injury is not indispensible to the final resolution of the COI.

In 03 the judge moves on to ask about the cause of the plaintiff's injury (WY^1), which constitutes trajectory in the cause-effect relation. In 04 the plaintiff makes it clear with unit WY^2 that he was injured by his falling down from the truck when he unloaded wood for the defendant. This information is of significant importance to the resolution of the COI because it establishes the trajectory-landmark relation between the plaintiff's injury and the defendant's employment and attributes compensation responsibility to the defendant.

Considering the importance of the information, in 05 the judge requests the two defendants to make confirmation by asking *原告所述是否属实(Is what the plaintiff said true)*. The defendant's answers in 06 and 07 turn the A-category information into shared information (category C). It indicates that the opposing parties have reached an agreement on the cause of the plaintiff's injury.

The two parties' confirmation gives rise to another important factor of the context model: the legal relationship between the opposing parties. In the previous questioning, this factor is backgrounded by the cause of the injury and is not in the participants' focus of attention. Since participant relation can legalizes the compensation claims, in 08 the judges foregrounds the information with the question *原告与二被告是什么关系(What is the relation between the plaintiff and the two defendants)*. Consequently, the legal relation is first elaborated by the plaintiff and then confirmed by the two defendants and becomes shared information.

In the same vein, from 12 to 16 the participants reach an agreement on the salary of the plaintiff, thus setting up a compensation standard for the final resolution of the COI.

We can see that, for every information unit provided by the plaintiff, the judge asks confirmation immediately from the defendants. This can help to reinforce the shared information between the opposing parties, which in turn contributes to the final resolution of the COI.

Apart from the judge's practice to reinforce shared information during the process of court investigation, shared information is also reinforced at the end of court investigation, in which shared information is usually presented in a summary form.

(89)

01[法官]：<WT,A>通过上述法庭调查，对于下列事实予以确认：<WF^{1},A>第一是唐XX于XX驾驶出租车将李X撞倒；<WF^{2},A>第二是，唐XX肇事后逃离现场，……，<WF^{3},A>被判处有期徒刑1年零6个月；<WF^{4},A>第三是，李X伤后即被送至XX医院救治，……，<WF^{5},A>被告XX交通公司为李X支付了医疗费是132,221元7毛。<WA^{1},b>对于上述事实认同吗？	01[J]: Through court investigation, the court confirms the following facts: Firstly, Tang XX, who drove a taxi, knocked Li X down on XX. Secondly, Tang XX ran away from the spot…and was imprisoned for one year and a half. Thirdly, after the accident Li X was sent to XX hospital for treatment. The defendant, XX Transportation Company paid 132,221.7 yuan for the medical treatment of Li X. Do the parties agree with the above facts?
02[原告]：<WA^{2},c>认可。	02[P]: Yes.
03[法官]：<WA^{3},b>被告公司认可吗？	03[J]: The transportation company?
04[被告1]：<WA^{4},c>认可。	04[D1]: Yes.
05[法官]：<WA^{5},b>保险公司认可吗？	05[J]: The insurance company?
06[被告2]：<WA^{6},c>认可。	06[D2]: Yes.

The extract is from the end of the court investigation, in which, after summarizing the major facts of the lawsuit, the judge asks confirmation from the participants.

The information units in 01 reflect different construal phenomena of the judge in her conceptualization of the traffic accident. Unit WF^{1} is a general description of the traffic accident, in which the defendant (the taxi driver) is put at the place of trajectory, indicating that he assumes more responsibility for the cause of the accident. Unit WF^2 focuses on the defendant's illegal act of hit-and-run and the punishment imposed on him thereof. It verifies the defendant's responsibility for the accident because, according to Article 92 of Law of the People's Republic of China on Road Traffic Safety, the vehicle driver who flees away from the scene after the occurrence of traffic accident shall take all the responsibility. Unit WF^5 highlights the specificity in the judge's construal of the defendant's effort to make compensation for the medical treatment.

After summarizing the major facts, the judge asks the participants to make confirmations with units WA^1, WA^3 and WA^5 respectively. The unanimous confirmation of the participants in 02, 04 and 06 reinforces the consensus in the shared information about the responsibility attribution, degree of disablement and appraisal costs. The consensus in the shared information constitutes the context model for participants' conceptualization of the dispute and provides an indispensible basis for the final resolution of the COI, either in the form of conciliation or judgment.

6.3.1.2 Eliminating Controversial Information

Apart from reinforcing shared information, another way to promote information integration between opposing parties is to eliminate controversial information. According to Du (2010), D-category information is the information type that enjoys the lowest degree of consensus. Actually, D-category information is the origin of disputes or controversies which generate obstacles for agreement reaching between opposing parties. Therefore, in court hearings, participants may try to eliminate the controversial information by increasing its credibility or acceptability. This can be achieved by the production of evidence or citation of articles of law, as is demonstrated in the following extract.

(90)

01[原告]：<WA^1, d>我们对决定书第二张照片“曹XX跨院应是分成两部分（分别是东半部和西半部）”有异议，<WB^1, a>被告做出决定没有依据。	01[P]: We disagree with the second picture in the written decision that “the courtyard of Cao XX should be divided into two parts (western and eastern parts)”. The written decision is groundless.
02[被告]：<WB^2, a>处理决定书及送达回证，证明被告做出决定后分别向原告及第三人送达的工作过程。<WB^3, a>复议决定书，证明复议机关维持了被告做出的处理决定，<WB^4, a>根据《中华人民共和国土地管理法》第十六条第二款。	02[D]: The written decision and its service can prove that the written decision was delivered to the plaintiff. The written decision of reconsideration can prove that the review organ has sustained the original disposal of the real estate, based on Paragraph 2 in Article 16 of the Law of Land Administration of the PRC.
03[法官]：<WA^2, b>原告你对被告所作处理决定所适用的法律有意见吗？	03[J]: Does the plaintiff object to the application of the law in the defendant’s disposal?
04[原告]：<WA^3, a>没有意见。	04[P]: No.
05[法官]：<WA^4, b>第三人对被告所作处理决定所适用的法律有意见吗？	05[J]: Does the third party object to the application of the law in the defendant’s disposal?
06[第三人]：<WA^5, a>没有意见。	06[3rd P]: No.

It is a case involving disputes over house property. In this extract, the defendant proposes that the disputed courtyard of Cao XX should be divided into two parts: western part and eastern part. However, this proposition is challenged by the plaintiff in 01, claiming that the defendant’s position is totally groundless (WB^1). The challenge has converted the knowledge status in participants’ context model schema into D-category. As a result, the way to dispose the courtyard (WA^1) becomes one of the major disputes in the conceptualization of participants.

On the part of the defendant, the plaintiff’s challenge with unit WB^1 activates the discourse space of burdens of proof in the context model, to which the defendant in 02 provides three space components (WB^2, WB^3 and WB^4). Unit WB^2 demonstrates that the written decision about the disposal of the courtyard was delivered to and received by the plaintiff. Unit WB^3 is a written decision of reconsideration, which proves that the review organ has sustained the original disposal of the real estate. It indicates that the plaintiff used to apply to the review organ for the reconsideration of the disposal of the real estate but was rejected. Unit WB[4] introduces the specific article of law *《中华人民共和国土地管理法》第十六条第二款(Paragraph 2 in Article 16 of the Law of Land Administration of the PRC)*, which provides legal basis for the written decision about the disposal of the real estate and the review decision.

Among the three pieces of evidence presented by the defendant, the legal provision is foregrounded in the construal of the judge, who believes that it may make more contributions to the resolution of the dispute since it is the most persuasive and is more likely to be accepted by the opposing parties. Therefore, in 03 and 05 the judge asks the plaintiff and the third party whether they have any objections to the application of law. The negative answers by the two parties in 04 and 06 show that they accept the application of law and also the validity of the first two evidences. As a result, the controversy concerning the disposal of the courtyard has been eliminated, which makes a good preparation for the resolution of the dispute.

In some instances, judges may play a decisive role in eliminating controversial information. During court hearings, besides giving instructions to guarantee the smooth trial of cases, judges may also engage in the cross-examination process by making comments on the evidence produced by litigants. Apart from other various functions, their engagement may help to eliminate controversies between opposing litigants.

(91)

01[法官]：<WF^1,b>监督站是否出正式报告了？	01[J]: Did the supervision station produce a formal report?
02[原告]：<WF^2, a>没有。<WY^1, a>我让他们给出报告，但他们说得经法院指派。	02[P]: No. I asked them to produce a report but they said there must be a court order.
03[法官]：<WC^1, A>既然原告找了种子监督站，<WP^1, A>那他们就应该给出报告。<WC^2, A>即使没有出报告，<WP^2, A>那也应提取土样。	03[J]: Since the plaintiff went to the supervision station, they should have produced a report. Even if there was no report, they should have take soil samples.
04[原告]：<WP^3, A>他们照相了。	04[P]: They took photos.
05[法官]：<WF^3, A>庄稼出苗率的问题，播种不是唯一的原因，<WF^4, A>还有温度、湿度、土地的质量以及人工管理等原因。<WB, A>从原告提供的证据来看，<WJ, A>不能判定就是被告播种的原因造成出苗率不齐而给原告造成了损失。	05[J]: Seed sowing is not the only factor that leads to the problem of seedling emergence. Other factors such as temperature, moisture, land quality and field tending are also possible causes. From the evidence produced by the plaintiff, no conclusion can be made that it was the defendant's sowing that led to the problem of seedling emergence.

In this case, the two opposing parties dispute over the real cause of the poor seedling emergence of the plaintiff. In the previous discourse, the plaintiff cites the testimony of the supervision station to prove that the non-separation of seeds and fertilizer caused by the defendant's mishandling is the major reason for the poor seedling emergence. However, the testimony is rejected by the defendant and becomes one of the major controversies in the resolution of the dispute. Therefore, in this extract, the judge questions the details of the testimony to determine its validity.

In 01 the written report about the cause of the poor seedling emergence is regarded as the main factor in the conceptualization of the judge to solve the dispute. After the plaintiff gives a negative answer in 02, the judge makes comments for the first time on the duties of the supervision station.

The judge points out that the supervision station should produce a written report (WP^1) or at least take soil samples (WP^2). It is evident that the judge has taken a different perspective in his construal of the validity of evidence. With the two WP units, the judge indicates that, without written or physical material, the testimony itself cannot be used as evidence against the defendant.

With the first piece of evidence rejected, in 03 the plaintiff further proposes that the supervision station has taken photos as evidence. However, the information again does not conform to the judge's construal of evidence validity and is therefore ignored and becomes lost information in the discourse.

In the following turn, the judge continues with his comment by elaborating the possible causes of the poor seedling emergence, which are prominent in the trajectory-landmark relation between factors and seedling emergence. With unit WF^3 and WF^4, the judge states clearly that besides the factor of sowing, other factors such as temperature, moisture and field tending are also possible causes of seedling problems. Based on the elaboration, the judge concludes with unit WJ that the testimony of the supervision station cannot be accepted as valid evidence against the defendant. As a result, the judge's comment eliminates the controversy on the cause of seedling problem and promotes the resolution of the dispute.

6.3.2 Assimilation of Intentions and Goals

As one of the important psychological factors that influence the process of interest negotiation, intentions and goals of participants of lawsuits also play important roles in the final resolution of COI. In court hearings, the assimilation of intentions and goals of opposing parties may help litigants to reach agreements on controversies, which in turn may lead to the resolution of disputes.

In the following case, the defendant's husband, who was an employee of the plaintiff's company, died on the job. According to the arbitration award, the plaintiff should assume the major part of the upbringing cost of the defendant's children. Refusing to accept the arbitration award as final, the plaintiff takes the defendant to court and requests her to assume the corresponding upbringing cost. In Extract 6–17, the judge tries to promote agreement between the opposing parties by assimilating their communicative goals.

(92)

01[法官]：<WB, A>根据《中华人民共和国民事诉讼法》第一百二十八条的规定，<WT^{1}, A>由法庭主持双方本着自愿合法的原则进行调解。<WA^{1}, b>各方当事人是否愿意调解？	01[J]: According to Article 128 of the Civil Procedure Law of the PRC, the court shall preside over the conciliation between the two parties by following the principle of mutual willingness. Do both parties agree to conciliate?
02[原被告]：<WA^{2}, a>同意调解。	02[P&D]: Yes.
03[法官]：<WA^{3}, C>双方当事人同意调解，<WT^{2}, A>由原告提出调解意见和方案。	03[J]: Both parties agree to conciliate. Now the plaintiff shall put forward his proposals.
04[原告]：<WP^{1}, A>要求被告承担一半的费用。	04[P]: I require that the defendant take half of the expenses.
05[法官]：<WT^{3}, A>被告对原告的调解意见和方案发表意见，<WT^{4}, A>或提出新的调解方案。	05[J]: Now the defendant shall declare his attitude towards the plaintiff's proposal or put forward new proposals.
06[被告]：<WA^{4}, d>不同意原告的方案，<WY, A>不能少那么多。<WP^{2}, A>要求原告一次性付清85,000元。	06[D]: I don't agree with the plaintiff's proposals. It's too less from what I've expected. I require that the plaintiff make a one-off payment of 85,000 yuan.
07[法官]：<WA^{5}, b>原告是否同意被告的调解方案？	07[J]: Does the plaintiff agree?
08[原告]：<WA^{6}, a>同意。	08[P]: Agree.

In the judge's conceptualization of the conciliation, the speech is well managed to achieve its utmost effect. For example, in 01 before asking whether the litigants agree to resolve the dispute in conciliation, the judge first cites the specific article of law *《中华人民共和国民事诉讼法》第一百二十八条的规定(Article 128 of the Civil Procedure Law of the PRC)* as the legal basis for the conciliation. Besides, unit WT^{1} makes a special mention that the conciliation will be conducted according to the principles of free will and legitimacy. These two units (WB and WT^{1}) provide an important legal foundation for the following conciliation and can help to make conciliation as a more acceptable way to resolve disputes.

With unit WA^{1}, the judge probes into the participants' willingness to conciliate, which constitutes the most important factor in the context model constructed. After the litigants express their willingness to conciliate in 02, the judge first instructs them to propose their conciliation attitudes, namely, to manifest his specific goals of communication.

These goals are elaborated in details, which reflect the specificity of the participants' construal of the conciliation. In 04 the plaintiff makes it clear with unit WP[1] that his goal is to request the defendant to assume half of the upbringing cost. As a response, in 06 the defendant proposes with unit WP[2] that the plaintiff should make a full payment of 85,000 yuan.

Compared with the original requests in the unpresented discourse, where the defendant asked for a payment of more than 120,000 yuan, both litigants have substantially modified their communicative goals in their construal of the dispute. The modification of goals makes preparation for the final agreement on the payment. Then in 07 when the judge asks the plaintiff whether he accepts the proposal of the defendant, the plaintiff makes another modification of the communicative goal and expresses his agreement (WA[6]). By far, on the basis of assimilation of intentions and goals, the two opposing parties have reached a final agreement on the payment, and thus brought the COI to a close.

In some cases, the assimilation of intentions and goals may be achieved by one party's dropping of claims or acceptance of the claims of the other party. The following is an example in which the two opposing parties negotiate over the ownership of the inherited house and finally reach an agreement about its segmentation.

(93)

01[原告]：<WF[1], A>被告未与原告协商，私自将原告分得的西侧36.50平方米房屋产权登记到被告的名下，<WF[2], A>并领取了房屋所有权证。	01[P]: Without negotiating with the plaintiff, the defendant privately transferred to him the ownership of the western half (36.50 m^2) divided to the plaintiff and got the property ownership certificate.
02[被告]：<WF[3], D>该房办照时，父亲说被告是长子，<WF[4], D>就落在被告的名下，<WF[5], D>省得以后过户费事。	02[D]: When applying for the certificate, our father said that, as the eldest son, the house should be transferred to my name so as to avoid the troubles in the ownership transfer.
……	……

03[原告]：<WF^{6}, D>当时按父母的意愿，这户房子是原、被告一家一半，<WP^{1}, D>现在我要求履行遗嘱协议，<WP^{2}, D>西侧36.50平方米的房屋归我所有。	03[P]: According to the will of our parents, the plaintiff and defendant each have property right to half of the house. Now I propose to execute the will by transferring the western half (36.50 m^{2}) of the house to my name.
04[法官]：<WT, A>现在由被告发言。	04[J]: Now the defendant shall state his opinion.
05[被告]：<WF^{7}, C>考虑到原、被告是兄弟，<WF^{8}, C>父亲生前有这个意愿，<WA, C>我同意原告的诉讼请求。	05[D]: Considering that we are brothers and the will of our father, I accept the request of the plaintiff.

The discourse in 01 and 02 takes place at the beginning of the court hearing. In the plaintiff's conceptualization in 01, he is entitled to the ownership of the house. This conceptualization is supported by his elaboration of the participants' intentions and relations between them in the context model.

The expression *原告分得的(divided to the plaintiff)* in unit WF^{1} defines the inheritance relation between him and his father, which legalizes his ownership of the house. Units WF^{1} and WF^{2} also present how the ownership of the house was transferred to the name of the defendant. The expressions such as *未与原告协商(without negotiating with the plaintiff)* and *私自(privately)* in unit WF^{1} reveal the plaintiff's intention to demonstrate that the transfer of the ownership is illegal and therefore invalid.

The defendant's conceptualization of the ownership of the house also draws on the participant relations in the context model. In 02 the defendant claims with three WF units that the transfer of the ownership of the house was actually conducted at the will of their father. These three WF units are diametrically opposed to those in the discourse of the plaintiff, transferring them into D-category information. The defendant intends to show that his ownership of the house is legitimate and protected by the law.

Insisting on the same conceptualization about the ownership of the house, the plaintiff in 03 has taken on a more specific perspective in his construal of the dispute by foregrounding the segmentation of the house (WF^{6}, WP^{1} and WP^{2}). He proposes that he should get the ownership of the western half of the house. These information units express the plaintiff's specific communicative goal in the lawsuit. As is indicated by the information sharing category (category D), the dispute over the ownership of the house is still one of the major controversies to be resolved.

On the part of the defendant, he has taken on a quite different perspective in construing the dispute, foregrounding a different relation between him and the plaintiff. In 05 the defendant first describes with unit WF^{7} the brotherhood between him and the plaintiff, thus assimilating his definition of participant relations and goals of lawsuit in the context model. The assimilation of goals provides basis for further consensus between the plaintiff and the defendant. As a result, with unit WF^{8} the defendant confirms the information of unit WF^{6} in the discourse of the plaintiff. Furthermore, the following WA unit expresses his consent to the plaintiff's claims. The defendant's dropping of claims promotes the final resolution of the COI.

6.3.3 Reconciliation of Construal Phenomena

As was discussed in section 5.3.3 of Chapter 5, the disputes or controversies between participants of lawsuits may be caused by the differences in their construal phenomena. Therefore, in court hearings, one of the important ways of cognitive management is to reconcile litigants' construal phenomena. The reconciliation of construal phenomena can help to promote the agreement reaching between opposing parties.

(94)

01[原告]：<WY^{1}，A>婚礼当天由于被告公司摄影师迟到，<WE^{1}，A>致使视频缺失了部分重要镜头。<WE^{2}，A>11月5日，我收到婚礼视频和摄影光盘后，发现摄影质量粗糙、人物模糊、画面失真。<WF^{1}，A>经与被告方多次沟通交涉，方知照片实为视频截图，<WY^{2}，A>摄影原片因摄影师失误已经丢失。	01[P]: On the wedding day, due to the late arrival of the photographer, some of the important wedding scenarios were missing. On November 5th, after I got the wedding video and discs, I found them to be in inferior quality with vague figures and distorted pictures. After I negotiated with the defendant for several times, I was told that the pictures were actually video screenshots because the original photos were lost due to the operational errors of the photographer.

02[被告]：<WF^{2}, C>我们的摄像师确实迟到了。<WY^{3}, A>我们公司的电脑被盗了，<WF^{3}, C>摄影原片也就丢失了。<WF^{4}, A>我们也十分了解原告的心情，<WF^{5}, A>但是我们确实也有苦衷，<WF^{6}, A>摄影原片丢失我们也不愿意。<WP^{1}, C>我们愿意赔礼道歉，<WP^{2}, C>也愿意退还摄影费用和摄像费用各1,000元，<WA, D>但是原告要求的精神损害赔偿金过高。

02[D]: The photographer did arrive late. The original photos were lost because our computer was stolen. We understand how the plaintiff feels. But we have our own difficulties and troubles. We also regret losing the original photos. We'd like to return 1,000 yuan of the shooting and photographing expenses. But the mental damages requested by the plaintiff are too high.

In this case, the defendant signed a contract with the plaintiff to record his wedding ceremony, but was later taken to court by the plaintiff for the poor quality of the videos and photos. In this extract, based on reconciliation of their construal on prominence, the two opposing parties arrive at an agreement on part of the compensation claims proposed by the plaintiff.

In the plaintiff's conceptualization in 01, the defendant is responsible for all the damages incurred to the plaintiff. The conceptualization is based on the elaboration of one of the participants in the context model, namely, the photographer of the wedding ceremony. Unit WY^{1} profiles the fault of the photographer: *被告公司摄影师迟到 (late arrival of the photographer)*, and together with unit WE^{1}, forms the first cause-effect relationship. Unit WY^{1} is trajectory; unit WE^{1} presents the severe consequence of the defendant's fault: *视频缺失了部分重要镜头 (some of the important wedding scenarios were missing)* and is landmark. Since trajectory is the factor more highlighted in a cause-effect relationship, the fact that the defendant was late for the wedding ceremony is what the plaintiff intends to emphasize.

Similarly, units WE^{2}, WF^{1} and WY^{2} constitute another cause-effect relationship, in which unit WY^{2} is profiled as trajectory. It shows that the defendant should assume the responsibility for the loss of the original photos, which led to the poor quality of the wedding videos and photos.

In 02 the defendant first confirms with unit WF^{3} (C-event) that the photographer did arrive late at the wedding ceremony. With this unit, the defendant also profiles his errors in work and arrives at a conciliation of construal with the plaintiff. Unit WF^{3} (category C) confirms the loss of the original photos. Although the defendant explains with unit WY^2 that the original photos were lost because the computer was stolen, there is still conciliation between the two parties about the severe consequence of the loss of the original photos. This conciliation is then clearly conveyed by unit WF^5, by which the defendant expresses his sympathy for the loss of the photos.

The following two WF units (WF^6 and WF^7) try to invite the plaintiff's attention to the hardship the defendant has met with. It is the defendant's effort to promote conciliation by changing the plaintiff's way of construal. Although no response is made by the plaintiff, the conciliation of construal phenomena reached so far finally leads to a certain agreement between the two parties. As is revealed by the two C-category units WP^1 and WP^2, the defendant agrees to make apologies and payments to the plaintiff for part of his economic losses.

In some situations, participants of lawsuits may also try to reconcile the construal of specificity. This usually happens when participants negotiate over the details of compensation. Their reconciliation of specificity in compensation provides a very important basis for the final resolution of the COI.

(95)

01[法官]：<WA^1, b>原告是否认可交通队的事故责任认定？	01[J]: Does the plaintiff accept the definition of accident liability made by the traffic police?
02[原告]：<WA^2, a>认可交通队做的责任认定。<WP^1, a>在交强险范围内，我按照1：9的比例承担。	02[P]: Yes. We agree to the ratio of 1:9 in the scope of compulsory insurance.
03[法官]：<WP^2, b>被告，你们认可的责任比例？	03[J]: What ratio does the defendant accept?
04[被告1]：<WP^3, a>应该是同等责任。<WP^4, a>张某和赵某应该各承担事故整体的25%责任，<WP^5, a>三原告占事故责任的50%。	04[D1]: We accept equal liability, with Zhang and Zhao each taking 25% of the liability and the three plaintiffs, 50% altogether.
05[被告2]：<WA^3, a>我们同意同等责任。	05[D2]: We accept equal liability.
06[法官]：<WA^4, b>你们是否同意1万元医疗费限额先用于李X及李小X的赔偿？	06[J]: Do you agree that the limited 1,000-yuan medical expense will be first used for the compensation for Li X and Li XiaoX?
07[原告]：<WA^5, a>同意。	07[P]: Agree.
08[被告1,2]：<WA^6, a>同意。	08[P]: Agree.

In the extract, the judge tries to conciliate participants' construal phenomena on the specificity of compensation reliability.

In 01 the judge's question (WA^1) points to the plaintiff's conceptualization of the police's definition of accident responsibility. Although being an important component of the context model, the police did not specify in their report the specific proportion of compensation taken by each litigant. Therefore, unit WA^1 mainly concerns the plaintiff's general construal in his assumption of compensation reliability.

After giving a positive answer with unit WA^2, the plaintiff proposes that he will take only one tenth of the compensation (WP^1). This proposition turns the generality of compensation reliability into the discussion of its specificity, which can produce more positive effects on the resolution of the dispute.

Following the construal of specificity, in 03 the judge asks the defendants to propose their attitudes towards the proportion of compensation. With this question, the judge intends to reach reconciliation on the construal of specificity between the opposing parties. However, the first defendant proposes that the principle of equal responsibility should be followed (WP^3), which means the plaintiffs should take half of the compensation responsibility (WP^4).

It can be seen that there is a great disparity in the specificity of compensation between the opposing parties. But at least this disparity can work as the basis on which the compensation responsibility can be renegotiated and reconciliated. Moreover, as a result of the reconciliation, a consensus is first arrived at between the two defendants (WA^3), which will contribute to the resolution of the dispute.

Considering that more efforts will be exerted on the conciliation of compensation proportion, in 06 the judge turns to the discussion of another specific issue concerning compensation: the allocation of the ten-thousand-yuan medical payment. This time all parties agree that the payment should be made to the two victims of Li X and Li XiaoX, thus resolving the dispute over the medical payment.

To sum up, together with the communication of information in court hearings, participants' cognitive activities are frequently managed for the resolution of COI. This is realized mainly by integration of information, assimilation of intentions and reconciliation of construal phenomena.

Integration of information can help to reinforce shared information and eliminate controversial information. Assimilation of intentions can lead to the modification of participants' litigation goals and makes preparation for the resolution of disputes. Reconciliation of construal phenomena can help participants to promote consensus on the details of disputes, which in turn contributes to the final resolution of COI.

6.4 Linguistic Management

From the perspective of cognitive linguistics, discourse is the result or outer manifestation of interlocutors' cognitive activities. In order to make a precise presentation of their cognition, interlocutors would try to manage the process of discourse production and comprehension. The discourse management model summarized by Tomlin et al. (1997) can be used to analyze how linguistic devices are employed by interlocutors to manage the production and comprehension of discourse.

Tomlin et al. (1997) proposes four threads of linguistic management: thematic management, referential management, focus management and rhetorical management. Among these four aspects, focus management involves more on the cognitive level about the prominence of information elements and has already been discussed in Section 5.3.3 of Chapter 5. Therefore, in this section, I will mainly focus on the analysis of the other three aspects.

6.4.1 Referential Management

As was discussed in sections 5.3.2 of Chapter 5 and 6.3.1 of Chapter 6, certain information or concepts are held in common or shared by both speakers and listeners. The shared information "forms part of the conceptual scaffolding on which speaker and listener depend for effective communication" (Tomlin et al. 1997: 77).

In court hearings, apart from cognitive management through which information can be integrated to ensure the reaching of consensus between opposing parties, information integration may also be realized on the linguistic level through referential management. For example, in Extract (36) (reproduced here as Extract (96)), when the plaintiff clarifies with explanatory information which part of his book was plagiarized by the defendant, the referents he employs play an important role in the information integration between the judge and the plaintiff.

(96)

01[法官]：<WF^{1}，C>"诉讼请求第二项，认为被告构成了抄袭"，<WF^{2}，b>抄袭的部分指的是哪一稿？ 02[原告]：<WF^{3}，a>修订稿的第一章。<WF^{4}，a>我方所陈述的事实部分，关于诉讼请求第二项，指我方作品修订稿的第一章，实际出版图书的第一章。<WF^{5}，a>在网上被被告抄袭，以自己的名义发表。	01[J]: "The second compensation request: the defendant's behavior has constituted plagiarism". **Which version** do you refer to as being plagiarized? 02[P]: **The first chapter of the revised version**. In our statement about the facts of the case, the second compensation request refers to **the first chapter of the revised version on our part, which is also the first chapter of the published version.** It was plagiarized by the defendant on the internet and published in his own name.

In 01 the judge meets with difficulty in his conceptualization of which part of the book is plagiarized by the defendant. This problem results from the vagueness in the plaintiff's reference to the cause of the dispute, which constitutes one of the important components of the discourse space of compensation request. Therefore, with units WF^{1} and WF^{2}, the judge profiles the cause of dispute as trajectory and asks for further explanation.

The judge's profiling of the vagueness forces the plaintiff to contribute a more specific construal of the cause of dispute by employing three different referential expressions. The first referential expression *修订稿的第一章(the first chapter of the revised version)* in unit WF^{3} makes it clear that it is the first chapter of the revised draft that is plagiarized. In this expression, the modifier *修订稿*(*the revised version*) sets a constraint on the version of the draft and thus makes the reference more precise.

Feeling that the first referential expression might still cause controversy, the plaintiff employs two other expressions to make further clarifications. In the second referential expression *我方作品修订稿的第一章(the first chapter of the revised version on our part)* in unit WF[4], the plaintiff adds another modifier *我方作品*(*the revised version on our part*). The modifier not only makes the reference more accurate but also highlights the plaintiff's undisputed ownership of the copyright to the plagiarized chapter. It can be seen that the first two referential expressions have one common referent, namely, the first chapter in the revised draft of the plaintiff.

In the third referential expression*实际出版图书的第一章(the first chapter of the published version)*, another modifier *实际出版图书* (*the published version*) is employed. We can see that although the plaintiff still employs *第一章*(*the first chapter*) to refer to the disputed chapter, it has a different referent from the first two referential expressions. With the third referential expression, the plaintiff actually refers to the first chapter published in the book of the defendant. This expression not only gives a precise definition of the specific chapter involved in the lawsuit, but also helps to prove the defendant's plagiarism.

It shows that with the three different referential expressions, the plaintiff clarifies the controversy caused by the vague reference in the judge's conceptualization, thus promoting information integration between the judge and the plaintiff.

In some cases, the participants' choice of referential expressions can reveal their relative positions or attitudes in the litigation. The employment of certain referential expression can promote conciliation between opposing parties.

(97)

01[原告]：<WF^{1}, D>起因是被告过错在先，<WY^{1}, D>因为被告种鱼草过界了。	01[P]: The incident was initiated by the fault of the defendant, who planted water shield across the line.
02[被告]：<WF^{2}, D>本案被告所产生的行为是正当防卫的，<WY^{2}, D>是因为原告无理取闹把被告种的鱼草拔了，<WF^{3}, D>实际上被告没有种过界。	02[D]: My behavior was legitimate defense, since the plaintiff uprooted my water shield for no particular reason. Actually the defendant didn't cross the line.
03[法官]：<WT, A>下面由原告、被告讲下你们的调解方案。	03[J]: Now the two parties can put forward your conciliation proposals.
04[原告]：<WF^{4}, C>我们是本村的，<WA^{1}, A>我也不希望有什么矛盾深化。<WP^{1}, A>我现在放弃营养费，其他的医疗费、交通费、误工费共计2,000多元由被告赔偿。	04[P]: We are from the same village. I don't want to intensify the conflict. I relinquish the nutrition fee. The defendant should pay 2,000 yuan for the medical, transportation expenses and loss in income.
05[被告]：<WP^{2}, A>对医疗费、交通费两项，我愿意承担一半，就是500元，……。	05[D]: I can only pay half of the medical and transportation expenses, namely, 500 yuan.
06[原告]：<WP^{3}, A>我最少要被告出800元及诉讼费。	06[P]: The defendant should pay at least 800 yuan plus litigation expense.
07[法官]：<WF^{5}, A>本案的诉讼费50元，减半收取是25元。<WA^{2}, b>被告你是否同意原告的意见？	07[J]: The litigation expense is 50 yuan. The court will only take half of it, namely, 25 yuan. Does the defendant agree?
08[被告]：<WA^{3}, a>我同意，<WP^{4}, A>我给825元给原告。	08[D]: Agree. I'll pay 825 yuan to the plaintiff.

In this case, the defendant is sued by the plaintiff for personal injury. After court investigation and debate, the two parties agree to enter into conciliation, which is manifested on the linguistic level by the referential expressions.

As is shown by the first two turns, before the opposing parties agree to solve the dispute in conciliation, they have conflicting conceptualizations of the disputes involved. This can be demonstrated by the referential expressions they employ to refer to each other: *原告(plaintiff)* and *被告(defendant)*. These expressions highlight in the context model the adversarial relationship between the two parties.

They also conform to the D-category of the information units in the first two turns.

However, their conceptualizations have changed after the two parties agree to solve the dispute in conciliation. This first reflects the modification in their construal of their identities. For example, the plaintiff emphasizes that the two opposing parties are from the same village, thus resulting in a different definition of participant relation in the context model. Consequently, the two parties both chose to refer to each other with other referential expressions. For the first time in 04 the plaintiff employs *我们(we)* to refer to the two opposing parties. This referential expression highlights the commonness between the plaintiff and defendant and provides a reasonable basis for his willingness to make compromise in the compensation claims.

Similarly, in the following two information units (WA^1 and WP^1), the plaintiff replaces *原告(plaintiff)* with *我(I)* to refer to himself. This alteration indicates that the plaintiff has changed his role from the adversarial antagonizer to the more cooperative negotiator. As a response, in the following turns, the defendant also employs *我(I)* to refer to himself when he negotiates and finally expresses his willingness to make the payment.

It can be seen that the use of such referential expressions as *我们(we)* and *我(I)* can help participants to arrive at agreement on certain issues of the lawsuit and promote the final resolution of COI in conciliation.

6.4.2 Thematic Management

According to Tomlin et al. (1997), discourse themes refer to those concepts or propositions that are more central or important to the development of the discourse than others. These concepts or propositions usually provide the framework around which the details of the discourse are emplaced (Tomlin et al. 1997: 83), and therefore can decide the direction of the flow of discourse information.

In court hearings, the judge is the person who is entitled with the power to have a general management of the themes of the whole discourse. This is usually achieved by the instructions given by judges.

(98)

01[法官]：<WT[1], A>现在开始法庭调查。<WT[2], A>首先由原告陈述起诉的事实、理由及诉讼请求。	01[J]: Now proceed to court investigation. The plaintiff shall first make statement about the facts, reasons and compensation requests.
02[法官]：<WT[3], A>下面由原被告分别进行举证质证。<WT[4], A>证据可以按照证明内容分组出示并阐述该证据要证明的内容。	02[J]: Now the plaintiff and defendant shall proceed to proof cross-examination. The evidence can be produced in groups according to the content it tries to prove.
03[法官]：<WT[5], A>下面进行法庭辩论。<WT[6], A>当事人应当依据法律规定阐述自己对案件的意见，<WT[7], A>不得对对方当事人进行人身攻击和侮辱。	03[J]: Now proceed to court debate. The parties shall express their attitudes towards the facts according to relevant provisions and are not allowed to attack or insult the opposing party.

This extract is instructions given by judges at different stages of court hearings. Each instruction activates a certain discourse space and imposes a thematic control on the information units that will flow into it as space constituents.

The instruction in 01, which activates the discourse space of the stage of court investigation, imposes a constraint on the theme of the plaintiff's discourse by limiting its content to *事实理由及诉讼请求 (facts, reasons and compensation claims)*. Unit WT[3] in 02 activates the cross-examination space. The following unit WT[4] takes on a specific construal perspective by making it clear that, after each group of evidence is produced, the content it aims to prove should be elaborated. In 03 after activating the discourse space of court debate, the judge imposes control on its theme with units WT[6] and WT[7], which also emphasize specificity. According to these WT units, litigants should elaborate their own attitudes towards facts of cases and should not make personal abuse or insult to the opposing party.

The thematic management carried out by judges in court hearings imposes constraints on the content around which participants make their negotiations or debates. It provides a preliminary foundation for the resolution of COI by focusing participants' attention on the important issues of cases.

However, in some instances, the thematic management of the judge may not be as effective as expected in that litigants may deviate from the set theme of the discourse in their own interest. Under such circumstances, the judge may try to regain his control over the discourse by repeating the theme, as is shown in the following extract.

(99)

01[法官]：<WC, A>原告，你要办理申请的话，要有营业执照。<WF^{1}, b>现在你是否有营业执照，<WF^{2}, b>或按法律法规申请办理营运证的其他手续?	01[J]: Plaintiff, you have to acquire a business license before making an application. Do you have a business license or have you gone through other necessary formalities?
02[原告]：<WF^{3}, a>我从被告处买到后，被告得把营运手续注销了，<WP^{1}, a>我可以重新申请营运证。<WF^{4}, a>每个车只有一个道路运输许可证。	02[P]: The defendant needs to log off the business license after I bought the truck so that I can reapply. Every truck can have only one permit.
03[法官]：<WF^{5}, b>我要问你是否有工商营业执照？	03[J]: I asked whether you'd got a business license issued by the administrative organ.
04[原告]：<WP^{2}, a>我买了车，正本副本和营运证都应该给我过户。<WP^{3}, a>他们应该把这些手续都给我注销了，<WP^{4}, a>我就可以重新申请了。	04[P]: I bought the truck. Therefore the original permit, the copy and the business license should have been transferred to me. They should've logged off all of the registrations so that I can reapply.
05[法官]：<WF^{6}, b>现在你是否有营业执照。	05[J]: Now do you have a business license or not?
06[原告]：<WF^{7}, a>我没有营业执照。	06[P]: No. I don't.

In this case, after purchasing a truck from the defendant, the plaintiff claims that the defendant is responsible to help him to apply for the road transport permit. In the extract, the relevant requirements the plaintiff has to meet before applying for the road transport permit has become prominent in the judge's conceptualization.

With unit WC in 01 the judge activates the discourse space of road transport permit, and provides two WF units as space constituents, which concern whether the plaintiff has a business license or has gone through other necessary formalities. The discourse space and its constituent WF units assign a fixed theme for the following discourse of the plaintiff.

However, in 02 it seems that the plaintiff has failed to form a proper conceptualization of the context model which is constructed based on the discourse space. Instead of highlighting the discourse theme of business license as required by the judge, the plaintiff profiles in his construal the logging off and application of road transport permit. The plaintiff intends to show that his failure in application of road transport permit is mainly caused by the nonperformance of the defendant. As a result, the three information units (WF^3, WP^1 and WF^4) in the plaintiff's discourse, although conforming to his own interest appeal, deviate from the discourse theme set by the judge in 01.

Therefore, in 03 the judge reformulates his question by employing a more formal referential expression *工商营业执照(business license issued by the administrative organ)*, hoping to pull the plaintiff back to the discussion of the theme of business license. However, for a second time, the judge's effort does not bear any fruit in that, in 04 the plaintiff continues with his accusation of the defendant's nonperformance in the application of the road transport permit.

Having no other choice, in 05 the judge repeats the former question about business license with unit WF^6 :*现在你是否有营业执照(Now do you have a business license or not)*, to which the plaintiff finally provides a negative answer with unit WF^7.

The analysis shows that, due to the difference in communicative goals, there are conflicts in the choosing of discourse themes between different parties. The judge's successful thematic management can help to find facts of cases which may contribute to the final resolution of dispute.

6.4.3 Rhetorical Management

Among the various definitions of rhetoric, Gill & Whedbee (1997: 157) define rhetoric as a type of instrumental discourse through which a speaker may reinforce or alter the understandings of listeners. Tomlin et al. (1997) go one step further by labeling rhetorical management as one of the components of linguistic management in discourse production, since rhetorical management influences the effect of information transference and the realization of communicative purposes.

In court hearings, rhetorical management is also an effective strategy frequently used by participants to promote consensus between opposing parties, which can be achieved by persuading litigants to accept the conflicting attitudes of each other. This is usually realized through three modes of proof originally proposed by Aristotle: logos, pathos and ethos (Gill & Whedbee 1997).

Ethos refers to ethical appeal used to establish the speaker as honest, fair and knowledgeable about the subject matter. In court hearings one way to make ethical appeal is to expose or emphasize the identity of participants of lawsuit. As was revealed in Section 5.2.2.1 of Chapter 5, litigants may resort to the identity of information source to increase the acceptability or reliability of the testimony, thus hoping to generate consensus in the court or opposing party.

Apart from identity, ethical appeal also concerns the personal character of the participants or witnesses, through which such good characters as honesty and wide knowledge can be proved.

(100)

01[被代]：<WF[1], A>被告平日为人正直，<WF[2], A>乐于助人，<WF[3], A>与邻里之间关系和睦。<WY, A>原告在此次事故中所受到的伤害也是因被告的善良和热心导致的。<WA[1], A>因此，我们同意原告关于治疗费和误工费的请求，<WP, A>但有关精神抚慰金的请求希望在法庭主持下予以调解。
02[法官]：<WA[2], b>原告意见？
03[原代]：<WA[3], a>同意调解。

01[DA]: The defendant is honest, helpful and in very good terms with his neighbors. The injury the plaintiff suffered in the incident was caused by the kindness and warmheartedness of the defendant. Therefore, we accept the plaintiff's request for compensation for medical expenses and time off from work. We hope the court can conciliate the plaintiff's request for mental damages.
02[J]: Does the plaintiff agree to conciliate?
03[PA]: Agree.

In this case, the defendant was sued for causing injury to the plaintiff when driving him home. In the above extract, the attorney highlights in his conceptualization the good character of the defendant. This conforms to the prominence of the participant component in the context model, which is constructed based on his specific construal of the defendant.

The attorney first employs three WF units (WF^1, WF^2 and WF^3) to elaborate the good character of the defendant. Unit WF^1 describes the integrity of the defendant; unit WF^2 depicts his willingness to help others; and unit WF^3 talks about his harmonious relationship with neighbors. These WF units help to prove that the injury to the plaintiff was not caused by the subjective intention of the defendant but by his kindness and warmheartedness (WY^1). Based on these information units, the attorney first expresses his consensus to accept the plaintiff's request for medical expenses and time off from work (WA) and then expresses his willingness to conciliate over the plaintiff's request for compensation for mental suffering with unit WP. The WP unit makes preparation for the following consensus in unit WA^3, in which the plaintiff agrees to resolve the dispute in conciliation.

It can be seen that litigants' ethical appeal about their personal characters can help to increase the persuasive power of their testimony and promote consensus between opposing parties.

Another mode of proof frequently used in court hearings is logical appeals, which refer to the strategic use of logic or evidence to convince an audience. In the following case, the defendant, who is the people's government of Jin XX Town, was sued by the plaintiff for improperly handling the land dispute between the plaintiff and a third party. In the following extract, the judge concludes that the defendant's decision in handling the land dispute is reasonable and well-grounded and therefore should be sustained. In the judgment, in order to promote consensus between the opposing parties, the judge has imposed efficient rhetorical management on the logos of the discourse information.

(101)

[法官]：<WT[1]，A>本案中，被告在处理原告与第三人土地使用权争议过程中，依法立案，<WT[2], A>向当事人送达相关法律文书。<HW，A>经向有关证人调查，<WF, C>查明第三人现东跨院北院墙系其原北正房后檐墙的事实，<WA[1], C>对此原告亦予以承认。<WT[3]，D>被告以此墙作为确定双方土地使用界线的参照物，<WB[1], C>并结合当地院落构造的乡俗做出被诉处理决定，<WA[2], A>认定事实清楚、适用法律正确，<WB[2], C>符合《土地管理法》三十五条规定，<WP, A>应予维持。

[J]: In this case, the defendant has followed the legal procedures during the hearing of the case where the plaintiff and the third party are involved in the land dispute. The relevant documents were also delivered to the parties. Based on the investigation from the witnesses, it has been found out that the north wall of the eastern courtyard of the third party was the back wall of the former principal room, which is confirmed by the plaintiff. Using the north wall as the boundary line and based on the local custom, the defendant entered into a decision to resolve the dispute, with facts fully proved and laws applied correctly. The decision also conforms to Article 35 of the Land Management Law and therefore should be sustained.

In this extract, the judge forms a conceptualization that the defendant's decision in handling the land dispute should be sustained (WP[1]). This decision is based on the elaboration of two components of the context model: participants and knowledge status. In presenting the behaviors of the defendant, the judge draws on logical appeals to justify his validity.

In 01 the judge first introduces briefly with two WT units (WT[1] and WT[2]) the procedure the defendant followed when handling the land dispute. The WT units show that the case filing and the delivery of the relevant documents are in conformity with law. The two WT units justify the defendant's subsequent activities in the handling of the dispute.

Then with unit WF, the judge presents the most important fact ascertained by the defendant about the disputed wall. The WF unit is supported by two explanatory information units: units HW and WA[1]. Unit HW reveals that the fact is ascertained based on the deposition of the litigants and witnesses and the scene investigation. The information sharing category (category C) of unit WA[1] shows that, by introducing the plaintiff's attitude towards the disputed wall, the judge highlights the consensus arrived at between the opposing parties during court investigation. The consensus indicates that the plaintiff has already agreed to the fact ascertained by the defendant, namely, to use the north wall as the boundary line between the real estates of the plaintiff and the third party (WT^{3}).

Moreover, the judge also provides two bases for the rationality of using the north wall as the boundary line. Unit WB^{1} demonstrates that the defendant's decision conforms to the local custom; unit WB^{2} makes it clear that the decision is in accordance with the specific principles stipulated in the relevant provisions: *土地管理法第三十五条规定(Article 35 of the Land Management Law)*. Based on the two WB units, the judge concludes with a WA unit (WA^{2}) that in the defendant's decision facts have been ascertained clearly and laws applied correctly, and therefore the original decision should be upheld (WP).

The above analysis shows that the judge mainly appeals to logos to justify the defendant's decision in handling the land dispute. By justifying the legal procedure, the plaintiff's consensus and the customary and legal bases, the judge successfully upholds the defendant's decision against the plaintiff.

The last mode of proof often employed by litigants in court hearings is emotional appeals, which target the emotions of the audience to create resonance or sympathy, as is in the following extract.

(102)

01[原告]：<WF^{1}， A>婚礼照片是具有人生象征意义的特定纪念物品，<WF^{2}， A>不仅记录了婚姻美好的开始，<WF^{3}， A>还记录了众多亲友的祝福，<WF^{4}， A>人生历史意义重大。	01[P]: Wedding photos are a special souvenir of symbolic meanings. They record not only the beauty of the wedding, but also the blessings of relatives and friends and therefore are particularly meaningful.
02[原告]：<WF^{5}， A>这张照片是我丈夫一家的全家福，<WF^{6}, A>有40多口人，<WF^{7}, A>其中有多位家里的长辈，<WF^{8}, A>以后可能再也没有机会将这么多人聚集在一起照全家福了。	02[P]: This is a family portrait of my husband, with over 40 people in it. Among them, there are several seniorities of the family, who may never have the chance to gather for a family portrait.

03[原告]：<WE, A>被告公司的行为给我们造成了难以弥补的物质和精神损失，<WP^{1}, A>因此我请求法院判令被告违约，<WP^{2}, A>退还摄影费用和摄像费用1,000元，<WP^{3}, A>支付精神损害赔偿金3万元，<WP^{4}, A>并在被告公司网站首页公开赔礼道歉30天。

03[P]: The defendant's behavior has incurred irretrievable physical and mental losses on us. I hope the court can recognize the infringement of the defendant and order him to refund 1,000 yuan of shooting and photographing expenses, pay 30 thousand yuan as mental damages and apologize to the plaintiff on the homepage of the defendant's website for 30 days.

In this case, the plaintiff sued the photographer for losing the photos for the wedding ceremony. Before proposing his requests for compensation in 03, the plaintiff tries to increase the persuasive power of his testimony by resorting to emotional appeals.

In 01 the plaintiff employs four WF units to emphasize the importance of the wedding photos. In unit WF^{1}, the plaintiff employs *具有人生象征意义的特定纪念物品(a special souvenir of symbolic meanings)* to describe the nature of these photos. In units WF^{2} and WF^{3}, the plaintiff uses*婚姻美好的开始(the beauty of the wedding)* and*众多亲友的祝福(the blessings of relatives and friends)* to create resonance in the judge and the defendant. In 02 the plaintiff focuses on the importance of the wedding photo to the whole family by describing it as *全家福(family portrait)* (WF^{5}), which has a significant meaning to those elders since their old age does not allow them too much time to take photos together.

On the basis of the above emotional appeals, the plaintiff specifies his compensation requests with four WP units (WP^{1}, WP^{2}, WP^{3} and WP^{4}) in 03. These emotional appeals help to generate consensus in the defendant about the plaintiff's compensation requests.

In short, litigants tend to employ linguistic management as an important strategy to generate agreement between opposing parties. Among the various kinds of linguistic management, referential management, thematic management and rhetorical management are the most frequently used ones. Referential management can help to facilitate information integration in discourse. Sometimes, the employment of such referential expressions that designate commonness between opposing parties can promote consensus or even conciliation. Thematic management can help judges to have an effective control over the topics or themes of the whole discourse, which provides a preliminary basis for the final resolution of COI. Moreover, rhetorical management can help to persuade litigants to accept the conflicting attitudes of each other and thus promote consensus between opposing parties.

6.5 Summary

In this chapter, I have analyzed how discourse is managed by participants of litigation to reach agreements between opposing parties, which in turn facilitates the final resolution of COI. The analysis has been conducted from three aspects: information management, cognitive management and linguistic management. On the basis of data analysis, it has been found that information management is mainly realized through manipulation of information flow and intervention of information transference. The manipulation of information flow can lead to a horizontal, vertical or cycling development of discourse information; and the intervention of information transference can lead to information accretion, information loss or information reporting, with which litigants can help to clarify disputes or promote consensus in their own favors.

Through cognitive management, participants can exert influence on the cognitive activities of each other, which is usually realized by integration of information, assimilation of intentions and reconciliation of construal phenomena. Cognitive management can help to reinforce shared information, eliminate controversial information, modify participants' litigation goals and prepares for the final resolution of disputes.

It has also been found that agreement between opposing parties can be generated through linguistic management. This is usually realized by referential management, thematic management and rhetorical management. Linguistic management can help to facilitate information integration, designate commonness or persuade litigants to accept the conflicting attitudes of each other and thus promote the final resolution of COI.

7 Conclusion

In this chapter, I will summarize the major findings of the research and then draw conclusions in which the three research questions raised at the very beginning of this book will be answered. Furthermore, I will have a discussion of the implications of this study for judicial practice and academic studies. Finally, the limitations of this study and suggestions for further research projects in the future will be put forward.

7.1 Summary of the Major Findings

Under the guidance of the theoretical framework constructed in Chapter 3, in Chapters 4 to 6, I have analyzed features of discourse information in interest appeal, factors influencing interest negotiation and how discourse is managed to reach agreement between opposing parties. Based on the data analysis, this study comes up with the following major findings.

Firstly, it is found that discourse information serves as the major medium in the whole process of the resolution of COI in Chinese civil court hearings. During interest appeal, information in the discourse of litigants manifests different features of distribution, combination and development.

1) Litigants mainly resort to three kinds of discourse information to facilitate their interest appeals in court hearings: subjective information, objective information and explanatory information.
2) Subjective information is frequently used by litigants to make claims or counterclaims during interest appeal, during which WA, WI, WJ and WP are the most often used information units.

   a) WP and WA are the most frequently used subjective information units during litigants' claiming of damage compensation. Combined with other information types, they can help to express litigants' compensation requests or reveal their attitudes or positions in COI.
   b) When attributing fault, WI units tend to be combined with WF, WE or WB units to attribute intentional fault, while pseudo-WF units are often employed to attribute negligent fault.
   c) WJ and WP units are often used to assert unlawful acts of opposing parties. WJ units tend to be combined with WF, WB or WY units to prove the performance of unlawful acts, while WP units are inclined to be used to demonstrate the nonperformance of legal obligations.
3) Objective information is mainly used by litigants to provide basis for their claims or requests. Among the different information units, WF, WB and WE units are the most frequently used ones.
   a) WF and WO units are often used by litigants to clarify background of litigation, especially the legal relationship between opposing parties.
   b) WF and WE units are frequently employed to present cause of litigation. In most cases, they are combined with other objective information units (WB, WO, WN, WR) to introduce course of infringement and facts of harm.
   c) WB units are the most frequently used objective information units to provide ground for claims. They are either combined with such subjective information units as WA, WI or WJ to present legal ground or combined with WF units to introduce evidential ground.
4) Explanatory information is often used by litigants to ensure the reasonableness of their arguments or requests in interest appeal. It helps them to make interpretations, elaborate connections and eliminate uncertainties.
   a) Explanatory information ranges widely from subjective to objective information units, since it provides explanations to both of the types.

   b) Explanatory information units are usually presented in question-answer forms either between judges and litigants or between litigants themselves.
   c) Although explanatory information units are mainly provided by litigants, they are usually first initiated by judges in the form of court instructions or questions.

Secondly, it is found that interest negotiation in Chinese court hearings is mainly a cognitive process that involves the processing of discourse information. Altogether, three kinds of factors are recognized as indispensable components that influence the processing of discourse information in interest negotiation: sociological, psychological and discursive factors.

1) The interest negotiation in court hearings is mainly a sociological process in which the elements of settings and participants can influence the distribution of discourse information and the final production and interpretation of discourse.
2) The major function of settings is to impose temporal and spatial constraints on the discourses in interest negotiation or to organize the information about the temporal and spatial properties of these discourses.
   a) Temporal settings are usually used to organize or impose constraint on the sequence of communicative actions in court hearings.
   b) Spatial settings can be employed to narrow interpersonal gap, influence the word choice or speaking manners of participants in litigation.
3) Social identities and social relations of participants can activate the associated social values or social beliefs, which in turn help to increase the acceptability and reliability of the testimony or evidence produced by litigants.
4) Interest negotiation in court hearings is also a psychological process which involves such cognitive factors as intentions and goals of participants, information sharing and construal phenomena.
   a) In order to gain the support of the court for their compensation requests, litigants tend to reveal explicitly or make

necessary modifications of their intentions or goals of litigation.

b) In those cases where the intentions or goals of litigation are expressed vaguely, judges can have an active interference with the process of interest negotiation to make them explicit.
c) Information sharing categories manifest diverse features both in their mutual manifestness and acceptability, which can influence the whole process of interest negotiation.
d) In court hearings, information sharing categories can be mutually transformed, which can either generate new disputes or promote consensus between opposing parties.
e) The process of interest negotiation is under great influence of litigants' construal phenomena. They can make their presentations specifically or schematically, choose to either foreground or background the same discourse information, profile the same relationship differently or assume different perspectives on the same event involved in the lawsuit.

5) Such discursive factors as the activation and integration of discourse spaces and discourse expectations also exert considerable influence on the process of interest negotiation in court hearings.
   a) The activation of discourse spaces prepares litigants for their contribution of information units and also imposes constraint on the order of their appearance in those spaces.
   b) The successful integration of discourse spaces facilitates the court to ascertain the major disputes between opposing parties, while the unsuccessful or inadequate integration of discourse spaces prevents the interest negotiation from achieving any desirable results.
   c) Discourse expectations can help to reveal litigants' basic positions or attitudes in court hearings and thus promote the final outcome of interest negotiation.

Thirdly, it is found that, in order to promote agreement between opposing parties, litigants in Chinese civil court hearings tend to impose information management, cognitive management and linguistic management on their own discourse or the discourse of other participants.

1) Information management is mainly realized by manipulation of information flow and engagement of information transference between participants of litigation.
2) The manipulation of information flow can lead to a horizontal, vertical or cycling development of discourse information. The intervention of information transference between participants of litigation can lead to information accretion, information loss or information reporting. Information management can help litigants to clarify disputes or promote consensus in their own favors.
3) Through cognitive management, participants of litigation can exert influence on the cognitive activities of each other. This is usually realized by integration of discourse information, assimilation of intentions or goals of litigation and reconciliation of construal phenomena.
    a) Integration of information can help to reinforce shared information or eliminate controversial information between opposing parties.
    b) Assimilation of intentions can help litigants to modify their basic goals of litigation and prepares for the resolution of COI in the form of conciliation.
    c) Reconciliation of construal phenomena can facilitate participants to arrive at consensus on the details of disputes, which in turn contributes to the final resolution of COI.
4) Linguistic management is also an effective strategy to promote agreement between opposing parties. It is usually realized by referential management, thematic management and rhetorical management.
    a) Referential management can help to facilitate information integration and designate commonness between opposing parties.
    b) Through thematic management, judges can impose an effective control over the topics or themes of the whole

discourse, which provides a preliminary basis for the final resolution of COI.

c) Rhetorical management can help to persuade litigants to accept the conflicting attitudes of each other and thus promote consensus between opposing parties.

7.2 Answers to Research Questions

Based on the above major findings, I will draw conclusions that intend to answer the three research questions raised at the very beginning of the study.

Firstly, it is found that discourse information in litigants' appeal for interest (subjective information, objective information and explanatory information) can be employed to realize different functions. Subjective information (WA, WI, WJ and WP) is mainly used by litigants to make claims or counterclaims during interest appeal. It helps to claim damage compensation, attribute fault or assert unlawful act. Objective information (mainly WF, WB and WE) is frequently used by litigants to provide basis for their claims or requests. It is usually combined with other information units to clarify background of litigation, elaborate cause of lawsuit and provide ground for claims. By helping litigants to make interpretations, elaborate connections and eliminate uncertainties, explanatory information is often used by litigants to ensure the reasonableness of their arguments or requests in interest appeal.

Secondly, it is found that sociological, psychological and discursive factors play indispensible roles in the negotiation of interest between opposing litigants. Among the sociological factors, settings, identities and relations of participants can influence the distribution of discourse information and the final production and interpretation of discourse. Such psychological factors as intentions and goals of participants, information sharing and construal phenomena can influence the acceptability of the testimony of participants, modify their goals of litigation and make preparations for conciliation. Discursive factors can impose constraint on the order of the appearance of discourse information, help the court to ascertain the major disputes between opposing parties, reveal litigants' basic positions or attitudes in court hearings and thus promote the final outcome of interest negotiation.

Thirdly, it is found that litigants tend to impose information management, cognitive management and linguistic management on their own discourse or the discourse of other participants to promote agreement between opposing litigants. Information management is mainly realized by manipulation of information flow and engagement of information transference between participants of litigation. Cognitive management mainly involves integration of discourse information, assimilation of intentions or goals of litigation and reconciliation of construal phenomena. Linguistic management is often realized by referential management, thematic management and rhetorical management.

Based on data analysis instructed by the theoretical framework constructed in Chapter 3, we are now in a position to conclude that resolution of COI in Chinese civil court hearings is realized through the collaborative effort of participants in lawsuits, in light of their appropriate processing of discourse information, by considering the relevant factors influencing interest negotiation and effectively managing the discourse to promote agreement.

7.3 Implications

This book is an interdisciplinary research involving the issues of language and law. Therefore, there are two major implications drawn from the study: theoretical implications for forensic linguistics and legal studies, and practical implications for participants of litigation in Chinese court hearings.

Theoretically, the "rocket model" constructed in this book proves to be a practical and effective linguistic framework for the description, analysis and interpretation of resolution of COI in Chinese civil court hearings. According to the framework, resolution of COI in court hearings is not only a discursive practice, but also a cognitive practice involving the processing of discourse information. Therefore, the theoretical framework incorporates the comprehensive findings of the DIT on discourse information, which makes the exploration of resolution of COI in court hearings more practical and systematical. Moreover, it also gains insights from the relevant new findings in cognitive linguistics, the context model and the discourse management model from the socio-cognitive approach to specify the major factors that influence the process of resolution of COI in court hearings.

It is hoped that this framework contributes to the research of forensic linguistics, especially to the analysis of discourse in court hearings. It is also hoped that the framework promotes the further development and application of the DIT. Furthermore, it may also shed light on the study of resolution of COI in other situations such as criminal court hearings.

Practically, this book is helpful for both litigants and judges to gain a better understanding of the process of resolution of COI and thus increase the efficiency of its resolution. The findings concerning features of discourse information in interest appeal, factors influencing interest negotiation and strategies to perform efficient management on discourse to facilitate agreement can help participants in lawsuits become more aware of the importance of discourse information and the factors that influence interest negotiation and agreement reaching during the resolution of COI. More importantly, by taking the perspective of discourse information theory, this study can provide linguistic references to enhance judicial efficiency.

7.4 Limitations and Suggestions for Further Research

This study has so far drawn satisfactory conclusions to the research questions and accomplished the general research objective. It is, undoubtedly, far from exhaustive and not free from limitations.

Firstly, during the transcription of the data, some linguistic features such as stress, intonation, pause and gesture cannot be shown in writing. Besides, discourse makers like "eh" and "ah" which are significant for linguistic research are omitted in some of the transcriptions of the data. This limitation renders this study to draw mainly on the written documents, which may not be able to reveal the entire process of COI.

The second limitation concerns the analysis of factors influencing interest negotiation. Apart from the three kinds of factors that have been identified, other factors such as demographic and cultural features of participants are left unexplored.

The limitations of the study indicate that there is spacious room for further research. Here are some suggestions. First of all, more linguistic features should be revealed in the transcription of the data. Such multimodal semiotics as gesture and gaze should be considered in order to reveal more interpersonal meanings in resolution of COI. Secondly, to avoid subjectivity in analysis, field work is highly recommended. Field research like interviewing participants of lawsuits can be taken to test the cognitive reality of the findings of the study.

Moreover, since resolution of COI in court hearings is a complicated process involving a wide range of factors, it is preferable to observe how such factors as age, sex, education and cultural background influence resolution of COI.

References

Amsterdam, Anthony G. / Bruner, Jerome 2000. *Minding the law*. Cambridge: Harvard University Press.

Bennett, W. Lance / Feldman, Martha S. (1981). *Reconstructing Reality in the Courtroom.* New Brunswick: Rutgers University Press.

Berk-seligson, Susan 1990. Bilingual Court Proceedings: The Role of the Court Interpreter. In Levi, Judith N. / Walker, Anne G. (eds) *Language in the Judicial Process*. New York: Plenum Press, 155–201.

Biber, Douglas / Conrad, Susan / Reppen, Randi 1998. *Corpus Linguistics: Investigating Language Structure and Use*. Cambridge: Cambridge University Press.

Bodenheimer, Edgar 1962. *Jurisprudence: The Philosophy and Method of the Law*. Cambridge: Harvard University Press.

Brewer, Neil / Williams, Kipling D. 2005. *Psychology and Law: An Empirical Perspective*. New York: The Guilford Press.

Brigham, John C. 1981. The Accuracy of Eyewitness Evidence: How Do Attorneys See it?. *The Florida Bar Journal.* 55: 714–721.

Brigham, John C. / Wolfskeil, Melissa P. 1983. Opinions of Attorneys and Law Enforcement Personnel on the Accuracy of Eyewitness Identification. *Law and Human Behavior.* 7/4, 337–349.

Brown, Gillian / Yule, George 1983. *Discourse Analysis*. Cambridge: Cambridge University Press.

Chafe, Wallace 1979. The Flow of Thought and the Flow of Language. In Givon, Talmy (ed.) *Discourse and Syntax.* New York: Academic Press, 159–181.

Chafe, Wallace 1980. *The Pear Stories: Cognitive, Cultural, and Linguistic Aspects of Narrative Production*. Norwood: Ablex Publishing Company.

Chafe, Wallace 1987. Cognitive Constraints on Information Flow. In Tomlin, Russell (ed.) *Coherence and Grounding in Discourse.* Amsterdam: John Benjamins, 21–51.

Chafe, Wallace 1994. *Discourse, Consciousness, and Time: The Flow and Displacement of Conscious Experience in Speaking and Writing*. Chicago: University of Chicago Press.

Chen, Jian 2010. 对斗争与和谐的关系的思考: 兼论正确处理构建和谐社会进程中的利益冲突 (Reflections on the Relation between Fight and Harmony: A Study on the Proper Handling of COI during the Construction of Harmonious Society). 探索 *(Probe)*. 5: 188–192.

Chen, Jinshi 2011. 控辩审关系的建构: 法官庭审语篇处理的框架分析 *(The Construction of Prosecution-Defense-Judge Relationship: A Frame Analysis of Judges' Courtroom Discourse Processing)*. Beijing: Science Press.

Chen, Yong / Feng, Zhe 2008. 法官角色的理性化分析与诠释 (A Pragmatic Analysis and Reinterpretation of the Roles of Judges). 河北师范大学学报哲学社会科学版*(Journal of Hebei Normal University: Philosophy and Social Sciences Edition)*. 5: 62–65.

Collett, Peter 1989. Time and Action. In Roger, Derek / Bull, Peter (eds) *Conversation: An Interdisciplinary Perspective.* Clevedon, UK: Multilingual Matters, 218–237.

Conley, John M. / O'Barr, William M. 1998. *Just Words: Law, Language, and Power*. Chicago: The University of Chicago Press.

Conley, John M. / O'Barr, William M. / Lind, E. Allan 1978. The Power of Language: Presentational Style in the Courtroom. *Duke Law Journal.* 6, 1375–1399.

Cotterill, Janet 2003. *Language and Power in Court: A Linguistic Analysis of the O. J. Simpson Trial*. New York: Palgrave Macmillan.

Coulthard, Malcolm / Johnson, Alison 2007. *An Introduction to Forensic Linguistics: Language in Evidence*. London & New York: Routledge.

Du, Jiang / Zou, Guoyong 2003. 德国"利益法学"思潮述评 (Review on Jurisprudence of Interests in Germany). 法学论坛 *(Legal Forum)*. 6: 91–94.

Du, Jinbang 2007. 法律语篇树状信息结构研究 (A Study of the Tree Information Structure of Legal Discourse). 现代外语 *(Modern Foreign Languages)*. 1: 40–50.

Du, Jinbang 2008. 司法语篇隐性说服研究 (A Study on Implicit Persuasion in Legal Discourse). 现代外语 *(Modern Foreign Languages)*. 3: 253–262.
Du, Jinbang 2009a. 论语篇中的信息流动 (Information Flow in Discourse). 外国语 *(Journal of Foreign Languages)*. 3: 36–43.
Du, Jinbang 2009b. 从法庭问答的功能看庭审各方交际目标的实现 (A Study of the Functions of Courtroom Questioning and Answering and Participants' Communicative Objective Attainment). 现代外语 *(Modern Foreign Languages)*. 4: 360–368.
Du, Jinbang 2010. 从处置类信息的处理看法庭语篇说理的实现 (Realization of Persuasive Reasoning in Courtroom Discourse: From the Perspective of Transaction-oriented Information Processing). 现代外语*(Modern Foreign Languages)*. 4: 363–370.
Du, Jinbang 2012. Application of multimodal information corpus techniques in legal English teaching. *International Journal of Law, Language and Discourse*. 2/4, 19–38.
Du, Jinbang 2014. 法律语篇信息研究 *(On Legal Discourse Information)*. Beijing: People's Publishing House.
Drew, Paul 1990. Strategies in the Contest between Lawyer and Witness in Cross-examination. In Levi, Judith N. / Walker, Anne G. (eds) *Language in the Judicial Process*. New York: Plenum Press, 39–64.
Eades, Diana 1997. Language in Court: the Acceptance of Linguistic Evidence about Indigenous Australians in the Criminal Justice System. *Australian Aboriginal Studies*. 1, 15–27.
Fan, Yu 2007. 纠纷解决的理论与实践 *(Theories and Practices of Resolution of Conflicts)*. Beijing: Tsinghua University Press.
Fauconnier, Gilles 1994. *Mental Spaces: Aspects of Meaning Construction in Natural Languages*. Cambridge: Cambridge University Press.
Fiske, Alan Page 1992. The Four Elementary Forms of Sociality: Framework for a Unified Theory of Social Relations. *Psychological Review*. 99/4, 689–723.
Foley, Linda Anderson 1993. *A Psychological View of the Legal System*. Madison, WI: Brown & Benchmark.
Ge, Yunfeng 2011. 庭审会话的机构性特征研究 (A Study on the Institutional Features of Courtroom Conversation). 广东外语外贸大

学学报 *(Journal of Guangdong University of Foreign Studies)*. 5: 70–75.

Ge, Yunfeng 2013. 法庭问话中的信息获取研究：语篇信息处理视角 *(Solicitation of Desired Information in Courtroom Questioning: A Discourse Information Processing Perspective)*. Jinan: Shandong University Press.

Gibbons, John 2003. *Forensic Linguistics: An Introduction to Language in the Justice System*. Oxford: Blackwell Publishing Ltd.

Gill, Ann / Whedbee, Karen 1997. Rhetoric. In van Dijk, Teun A. (ed.) *Discourse as Structure and Process (Volume I)*. London: Sage Publications, 157–184.

Green, Georgia M. 1990. Linguistic Analysis of Conversation as Evidence Regarding the Interpretation of Speech Events. In Levi, Judith N. / Walker, Anne G. (eds) *Language in the Judicial Proces*. New York: Plenum Press, 247–277.

Gries, Stefan Thomas 2003. *Multifactorial Analysis in Corpus Linguistics: A Study of Particle Placement*. London: Continuum.

Halliday, Michael A. K. 1967. Notes on Transitivity and Theme in English (Part II). *Journal of Linguistics*. 3/2, 199–244.

Halliday, Michael A. K. 1978. *Language as Social Semiotics: The Social Interpretation of Language and Meaning*. Baltimore: University Park Press.

Halliday, Michael A. K. / Matthiessen，Christian 2004. *An Introduction to Functional Gramma*. London: Edward Arnold.

Hao, Yun 2007. 利益理论比较研究 *(A Comparative Study on Interest Theory)*. Shanghai：Fudan University Press.

Harder, Peter 1996. *Functional Semantics: A Theory of Meaning, Structure and Tense in English*. Berlin: Mouton de Gruyter.

Harris, Sandra 1989. Defendant Resistance to Power and Control in Court. In Coleman, Hywel (ed.) *Working with Language: A Multidisciplinary Consideration of Language Use in Work Contexts*. Berlin: de Gruyter, 131–64.

Harris, Sandra 1994. Ideological Exchanges in British Magistrates Courts. In Gibbons, John (ed.) *Language and the Law*. London: Longman, 156–70.

Huang, Huiming 2007. 利益法学的源流及其意义 (The Origin and Significance of Jurisprudence of Interests). 云南社会科学 *(Social Sciences in Yunnan)*. 6: 76–80.

Jackson, Bernard S. 1991. Narrative Models in Legal Proof. In Papke, David R. (ed.) *Narrative and the Legal Discourse: A Reader in Storytelling and the Law.* Liverpool: Deborah Charles Publications, 158–178.

Jacquemet, Marco 1996. *Credibility in Court: Communicative Practices in the Camorra Trials*. Cambridge: Cambridge University Press.

Jensen, Marie 1995. Linguistic Evidence Accepted in the Case of a Non-native Speaker of English. In Eades, Diana (ed.) *Language in Evidence.* Sydney: University of New South Wales Press, 127–146.

Jiang, Weiqun 2010. 民事诉讼法 *(On Civil Procedure Law)*. Beijing: Peking University Press.

Johnson, Michael G. 1990. Language and Cognition in Products Liability. In Levi, Judith N. / Walker, Anne G. (eds) *Language in the Judicial Process*. New York: Plenum Press, 291–308.

Kapardis, Andreas 2010. *Psychology and Law: A Critical Introduction (3rd Edition)*. Cambridge: Cambridge University Press.

Kennedy, Graeme 1998. *An Introduction to Corpus Linguistics*. London: Longman.

Kress, Gunther / van Leeuwen, Theo 2006. *Reading Images: The Grammar of Visual Design*. London: Routledge.

Lambrecht, Knud 1994. *Information Structure and Sentence Form: Topic, Focus and the Mental Representations of Discourse Referents*. Cambridge: Cambridge University Press.

Langacker, Ronald W. 1987. *Foundations of Cognitive Grammar, Volume I: Theoretical Prerequisites*. Stanford: Stanford University Press.

Langacker, Ronald W. 1991. *Foundations of Cognitive Grammar, Volume II: Descriptive Application.* Stanford: Stanford University Press.

Langacker, Ronald W. 2001. Discourse in Cognitive Grammar. *Cognitive Linguistics.* 12/2, 143–188.

Langacker, Ronald W. 2008. *Cognitive Grammar: A Basic Introduction.* Oxford: Oxford University Press.

Levelt, Willem J. M. 1989. *Speaking: From Intention to Articulation*. London: The MIT Press.
Levi, Judith N. / Walker, Anne G. 1990. *Language in the Judicial Process*. New York: Plenum Press.
Levi, Judith N. (1990). The Study of Language in the Judicial Process. In Levi, Judith N. / Walker, Anne G. (eds), *Language in the Judicial Process*, 3–35. New York: Plenum Press.
Li, Yuekai 2013. *The Study of Testimonial Verification Modes: Mappings and Integrations of Courtroom Discourse Information*. PhD Dissertation: Guangdong University of Foreign Studies.
Liu, Yunliang 1999. 论诉讼公正标准 (On the Standard of Litigation Justice). 海南大学学报社会科学版*(Social Science Journal of Hainan University)*. 3: 85–89.
Loftus, Elizabeth F. 1996. *Eyewitness Testimony*. Cambridge: Harvard University Press.
Lv, Shilun / Sun, Wenkai 2000. 赫克的利益法学 (Heck's Jurisprudence of Interests). 求是学刊 *(Seeking Truth)*. 6: 61–67.
Lu, Pinghui 2003. 论现阶段我国社会利益冲突的法律控制 (On China's Legal Control of Conflict of Interest at the Present Stage). 政治与法律 *(Political Science and Law)*. 2: 21–27.
Maley, Yon 1994.The Language of the Law. In Gibbons, John (ed.) *Language and the Law.* London: Longman Group UK Limited, 11–50.
Martin, James R. 1985. Process and Text: Two Aspects of Human Semiosis. In Benson, James D. / Greaves, William S. (eds) *Systemic Perspectives on Discourse: Selected Theoretical Papers from the 9th International Systemic Workshop*. Norwood: Ablex Publishing Company, 248–274.
Marx, Karl / Engels, Friedrich 1956. 马克思恩格斯全集(第一卷) *(Karl Marx and Frederick Engels (Volume 1))*. Beijing: People's Press.
Maynard, Douglas W. 1984. *Inside Plea Bargaining: The Language of Negotiation*. New York: Plenum Press.
Maynard, Douglas W. 1990. Narratives and Narrative Structure in Plea Bargaining. In Levi, Judith N. / Walker, Anne G. (eds) *Language in the Judicial Process*. New York: Plenum Press, 65–95.
Munsterberg, Hugo 1908. *On the Witness Stand: Essays on Psychology and Crime*. New York: AMS Press.

Nuyts, Jan 2007. Cognitive Linguistics and Functional Linguistics. In Geeraerts, Dirk / Cuyckens, Hubert (eds) *Handbook of Cognitive Linguistics*. Oxford: Oxford University Press, 543–565.

O'Barr, William M. / Conley, John M. 1990. Litigant Satisfaction Versus Legal Adequacy in Small Claims Court Narratives. In Levi, Judith N. / Walker, Anne G. (eds) *Language in the Judicial Process*. New York: Plenum Press, 97–131.

Onesti, Cristina / Ge, Yunfeng 2012. 意大利法律语料库的建设 (Construction of an Italian Legal Corpus). 广东外语外贸大学学报 *(Journal of Guangdong University of Foreign Studies)*. 3: 42–48.

Prince, Ellen 1981. Towards a Taxonomy of Given-new Information. In Cole, Peter (ed.) *Radical Pragmatics*. New York: Academic Press, 223–254.

Prince, Ellen 1990. On the Use of Social Conversation as Evidence in a Court of Law. In Levi, Judith N. / Walker, Anne G. (eds) *Language in the Judicial Proces*. New York: Plenum Press, 279–289.

Renkema, Jan 2004. *Introduction to Discourse Studies*. Amsterdam/ Philadelphia: John Benjamin's Publishing Company.

Sanford, Anthony J. / Garrod, Simon C. 1981. *Understanding Written Language: Explorations of Comprehension beyond the Sentence*. Chichester: John Wiley & Sons.

Schank, Roger / Abelson, Robert 1977. *Scripts, Plans, Goals, and Understanding: An Inquiry into Human Knowledge Structures*. Hillsdale, New Jersey: Lawrence Erlbaum Associates, Inc.

Shuy, Roger W. 1993. *Language Crimes: The Use and Abuse of Language Evidence in the Courtroom*. Oxford: Blackwell.

Sik, Ota 1962. *Economics, Interests and Politics*. Prague: State Publishing House.

Simon, Thomas W. 2001. *Law and Philosophy: An Introduction with Readings*. New York: The McGraw-Hill Companies, Inc.

Sinclair, John 1991. *Corpus, Concordance, Collocation*. Oxford: Oxford University Press.

Sun, Li 2013. 事实重构的法律语言学研究 *(Forensic Linguistic Study on Criminal Event Reconstruction in Witness Statements)*. Kaifeng: Henan University Press.

Sun, Xiaoyuan 2008. 利益协调导论: 科学发展观视野中的利益协调研究 *(Introduction to Interest Negotiation: A Study on Interest*

Negotiation from the perspective of Scientific Outlook on Development). Nanjing: Southeast University Press.
Tang, Jia 2003. 建立我国法官阐明义务制度初探(On the Construction of the System of Judges' Clarification Obligation in China). 行政与法*(Public Administration & Law)*. 5: 66–67.
Tajfel, Henri / Turner, John 1986. The Social Identity Theory of Intergroup Behavior. In Austin, William / Worchel, Stephen (eds) *Psychology of Intergroup Relations*. Chicago: Nelson, 7–24.
Talmy, Leonard 2000. *Toward a Cognitive Semantics Volume I: Concept Structuring Systems.* Cambridge: the MIT Press.
Tapp, June L. 1977. Psychology and Law: A Look at the Interface. In Sales, Bruce D. (ed) *Psychology in the Legal Process*. New York: Spectrum, 1–15.
Tomlin, Russell S. / Forrest, Linda / Pu, Ming M. / Kim, Myung Hee 1997. Discourse Semantics. In van Dijk, Teun (ed.) *Discourse as Structure and Process*. London: Sage Publications, 63–111.
Van Dijk, Teun A. 2006. Discourse, Context and Cognition. *Discourse Studies*. 8/1, 159–177.
Van Dijk, Teun A. 2008. *Discourse and Context: A Socio-cognitive Approach*. Cambridge: Cambridge University Press.
Van Dijk, Teun A. 2009. *Society and Discourse: How Social Contexts Influence Text and Talk*. Cambridge: Cambridge University Press.
Verschueren, Jef 1999. *Understanding Pragmatics*. New York: Oxford University Press.
Wang, Liming 2004. 侵权行为法研究 *(On Tort Liability Law)*. Beijing: Renmin University Press.
Wang, Weiguang 2010. 利益论 *(On Interest)*. Beijing：China Social Sciences Press.
Wang, Yin 2003. 认知语言学与语篇分析: Langacker的语篇分析观 (Cognitive Linguistics and Discourse Analysis: Langacker's Perspective of Discourse Analysis). 外语教学与研究 *(Foreign Language Teaching and Research)*. 2: 83–88.
Wang, Yin 2007. 认知语言学 *(Cognitive Linguistics)*. Shanghai: Shanghai Foreign Language Education Press.
Wells, Gary L. / Loftus, Elizabeth F. 1984. Eyewitness Research: Then and Now. In Wells, Gary L. / Loftus, Elizabeth F (eds) *Eyewitness*

Testimony: Psychological Perspectives. New York: Cambridge University Press, 1–11.
Wodak, Ruth 1985. The Interaction between Judge and Defendant. In van Dijk, Teun A. (ed.) *Handbook of Discourse Analysis Volume 4: Discourse Analysis in Society*. London: Academic Press, 181–91.
Xia, Jinwen / Shi, Changqing 2006. 交涉与合意：论诉讼的本质 (Negotiation and Conciliation: The Nature of Litigation). 南京社会科学 *(Social Sciences in Nanjing)*. 9: 98–106.
Xiong, Yuemin 2008. 民事诉讼中法院的法律观点指出义务: 法理、规则与判例(On Courts' Obligation of Clarification of Legal Opinions in Civil Litigations: Jurisprudence, Rules and Cases). 中国法学 *(China Legal Science)*. 4: 119–127.
Xu, Youping 2013. 语篇信息视角下的中国法院调解说服实现研究 *(Realization of Persuasion in Chinese Court Conciliation: The Discourse Information Approach)*. Beijing: Science Press.
Xue, Chengyou 2008. 法治视角下的利益冲突问题 (Conflict of Interest from the Perspective of Rule of the Law). 广东青年干部学院学报 *(Journal of Guangdong College of Young Cadres)*. 4: 71–74.
Yang, Lixin 2005. 侵权法论 *(On Tort Law)*. Beijing: People's Court Press.
Zhang, Wenxian 1999. 法理学 *(Jurisprudence)*. Beijing: Higher Education Press.
Zhang, Xiaoming 2002. 伟大的共谋: 市场经济条件下的利益关系研究 *(The Great Scheme: A Study on Interest Relations in Market Economy Conditions)*. Beijing: China Renmin University Press.
Zhang, Wenshun 2010. 操纵证券市场民事责任构成要件的研究 (A Study on the Key Components of Civil Liability of Security Market Manipulation). 法制与社会 *(Legal System and Society)*. 12: 118–119.
Zhao, Junfeng 2011. 法律语篇信息结构及语言实现研究: 汉英语篇对比分析 *(On the Information Structure and Its Linguistic Realization in Legal Discourse: A Chinese-English Contrastive Discourse Analysis)*. Beijing: Science Press.
Zhao, Zhenjiang 1998. 法律社会学 *(Sociology of Law)*. Beijing: Peking University Press.

Zhu, Weiyi 2008. 中国社会阶层利益冲突的法律调整机制 (On the Legal Adjustment Mechanism of Conflict of Interest between Social Stratums). 江苏社会科学 *(Social Sciences in Jiangsu)*. 4: 158–164.

Zwaan, Rolf A. / Radvansky, Gabriel A. 1998. Situation Models in Language Comprehension and Memory. *Psychological Bulletin.* 123/4, 162–185.

Appendix I Transcription Conventions

?	**Inquiring intonation**
!	**Exclamation intonation**
,	**Continuation**
.	**Falling, stopping intonation**
...	**Omission of the content**
(0.5)	**Timed pause**
(word)	**Comments made by the researcher**
‖	**Overlappings**
⊥	**Self-repair of wording**
▲▼	**The start and end of interruption**
J	**The judge(s)**
P	**The plaintiff**
D	**The defendant**
W	**Witness**
PA	**The plaintiff's attorney**
DA	**The defendant's attorney**
AT	**Appellant**
AE	**Appellee**

Appendix II List of Abbreviations

CDS	Current Discourse Space
CLIPS	Corpus for Legal Information Processing System
COI	Conflict of Interest
DIT	The Discourse Information Theory
SFL	Systemic Functional Linguistics
The Tree Model	The Tree Information Structure Model
KN	Kernel Proposition
HW	How
WA	What Attitude
WB	What Basis
WC	What Condition
WE	What Effect
WF	What Fact
WG	What Change
WI	What Inference
WJ	What Conclusion
WN	When
WO	Who
WP	What Disposal
WR	Where
WT	What Thing
WY	Why

Index

Linguistic Insights

Studies in Language and Communication

This series aims to promote specialist language studies in the fields of linguistic theory and applied linguistics, by publishing volumes that focus on specific aspects of language use in one or several languages and provide valuable insights into language and communication research. A cross-disciplinary approach is favoured and most European languages are accepted.

The series includes two types of books:

- **Monographs** – featuring in-depth studies on special aspects of language theory, language analysis or language teaching.
- **Collected papers** – assembling papers from workshops, conferences or symposia.

Each volume of the series is subjected to a double peer-reviewing process.

Vol. 1 Maurizio Gotti & Marina Dossena (eds)
Modality in Specialized Texts. Selected Papers of the 1st CERLIS Conference.
421 pages. 2001. ISBN 3-906767-10-8 · US-ISBN 0-8204-5340-4

Vol. 2 Giuseppina Cortese & Philip Riley (eds)
Domain-specific English. Textual Practices across Communities and Classrooms.
420 pages. 2002. ISBN 3-906768-98-8 · US-ISBN 0-8204-5884-8

Vol. 3 Maurizio Gotti, Dorothee Heller & Marina Dossena (eds)
Conflict and Negotiation in Specialized Texts. Selected Papers of the 2nd CERLIS Conference.
470 pages. 2002. ISBN 3-906769-12-7 · US-ISBN 0-8204-5887-2

Vol. 4 Maurizio Gotti, Marina Dossena, Richard Dury, Roberta Facchinetti & Maria Lima
Variation in Central Modals. A Repertoire of Forms and Types of Usage in Middle English and Early Modern English.
364 pages. 2002. ISBN 3-906769-84-4 · US-ISBN 0-8204-5898-8

Editorial address:

Prof. Maurizio Gotti Università di Bergamo, Dipartimento di Lingue, Letterature Straniere e Comunicazione, Piazza Rosate 2, 24129 Bergamo, Italy
Fax: +39 035 2052789, E-Mail: m.gotti@unibg.it

Vol. 5 Stefania Nuccorini (ed.)
Phrases and Phraseology. Data and Descriptions.
187 pages. 2002. ISBN 3-906770-08-7 · US-ISBN 0-8204-5933-X

Vol. 6 Vijay Bhatia, Christopher N. Candlin & Maurizio Gotti (eds)
Legal Discourse in Multilingual and Multicultural Contexts.
Arbitration Texts in Europe.
385 pages. 2003. ISBN 3-906770-85-0 · US-ISBN 0-8204-6254-3

Vol. 7 Marina Dossena & Charles Jones (eds)
Insights into Late Modern English. 2nd edition.
378 pages. 2003, 2007.
ISBN 978-3-03911-257-9 · US-ISBN 978-0-8204-8927-8

Vol. 8 Maurizio Gotti
Specialized Discourse. Linguistic Features and Changing Conventions.
351 pages. 2003, 2005.
ISBN 3-03910-606-6 · US-ISBN 0-8204-7000-7

Vol. 9 Alan Partington, John Morley & Louann Haarman (eds)
Corpora and Discourse.
420 pages. 2004. ISBN 3-03910-026-2 · US-ISBN 0-8204-6262-4

Vol. 10 Martina Möllering
The Acquisition of German Modal Particles. A Corpus-Based Approach.
290 pages. 2004. ISBN 3-03910-043-2 · US-ISBN 0-8204-6273-X

Vol. 11 David Hart (ed.)
English Modality in Context. Diachronic Perspectives.
261 pages. 2003. ISBN 3-03910-046-7 · US-ISBN 0-8204-6852-5

Vol. 12 Wendy Swanson
Modes of Co-reference as an Indicator of Genre.
430 pages. 2003. ISBN 3-03910-052-1 · US-ISBN 0-8204-6855-X

Vol. 13 Gina Poncini
Discursive Strategies in Multicultural Business Meetings.
2nd edition. 338 pages. 2004, 2007.
ISBN 978-3-03911-296-8 · US-ISBN 978-0-8204-8937-7

Vol. 14 Christopher N. Candlin & Maurizio Gotti (eds)
Intercultural Aspects of Specialized Communication.
2nd edition. 369 pages. 2004, 2007.
ISBN 978-3-03911-258-6 · US-ISBN 978-0-8204-8926-1

Vol. 15 Gabriella Del Lungo Camiciotti & Elena Tognini Bonelli (eds)
Academic Discourse. New Insights into Evaluation.
234 pages. 2004. ISBN 3-03910-353-9 · US-ISBN 0-8204-7016-3

Vol. 16 Marina Dossena & Roger Lass (eds)
Methods and Data in English Historical Dialectology.
405 pages. 2004. ISBN 3-03910-362-8 · US-ISBN 0-8204-7018-X

Vol. 17 Judy Noguchi
The Science Review Article. An Opportune Genre in
the Construction of Science.
274 pages. 2006. ISBN 3-03910-426-8 · US-ISBN 0-8204-7034-1

Vol. 18 Giuseppina Cortese & Anna Duszak (eds)
Identity, Community, Discourse. English in Intercultural Settings.
495 pages. 2005. ISBN 3-03910-632-5 · US-ISBN 0-8204-7163-1

Vol. 19 Anna Trosborg & Poul Erik Flyvholm Jørgensen (eds)
Business Discourse. Texts and Contexts.
250 pages. 2005. ISBN 3-03910-606-6 · US-ISBN 0-8204-7000-7

Vol. 20 Christopher Williams
Tradition and Change in Legal English. Verbal Constructions in Prescriptive Texts.
2nd revised edition. 216 pages. 2005, 2007. ISBN 978-3-03911-444-3.

Vol. 21 Katarzyna Dziubalska-Kolaczyk & Joanna Przedlacka (eds)
English Pronunciation Models: A Changing Scene.
2nd edition. 476 pages. 2005, 2008. ISBN 978-3-03911-682-9.

Vol. 22 Christián Abello-Contesse, Rubén Chacón-Beltrán, M. Dolores López-Jiménez & M. Mar Torreblanca-López (eds)
Age in L2 Acquisition and Teaching.
214 pages. 2006. ISBN 3-03910-668-6 · US-ISBN 0-8204-7174-7

Vol. 23 Vijay K. Bhatia, Maurizio Gotti, Jan Engberg & Dorothee Heller (eds)
Vagueness in Normative Texts.
474 pages. 2005. ISBN 3-03910-653-8 · US-ISBN 0-8204-7169-0

Vol. 24 Paul Gillaerts & Maurizio Gotti (eds)
Genre Variation in Business Letters. 2nd printing.
407 pages. 2008. ISBN 978-3-03911-681-2.

Vol. 25 Ana María Hornero, María José Luzón & Silvia Murillo (eds)
Corpus Linguistics. Applications for the Study of English.
2nd printing. 526 pages. 2006, 2008. ISBN 978-3-03911-726-0

Vol. 26 J. Lachlan Mackenzie & María de los Ángeles Gómez-González (eds)
Studies in Functional Discourse Grammar.
259 pages. 2005. ISBN 3-03910-696-1 · US-ISBN 0-8204-7558-0

Vol. 27 Debbie G. E. Ho
Classroom Talk. Exploring the Sociocultural Structure of Formal ESL Learning.
2nd edition. 254 pages. 2006, 2007. ISBN 978-3-03911-434-4

Vol. 28 Javier Pérez-Guerra, Dolores González-Álvarez, Jorge L. Bueno-Alonso & Esperanza Rama-Martínez (eds)
'Of Varying Language and Opposing Creed'. New Insights into Late Modern English.
455 pages. 2007. ISBN 978-3-03910-788-9

Vol. 29 Francesca Bargiela-Chiappini & Maurizio Gotti (eds)
Asian Business Discourse(s).
350 pages. 2005. ISBN 3-03910-804-2 · US-ISBN 0-8204-7574-2

Vol. 30 Nicholas Brownlees (ed.)
News Discourse in Early Modern Britain. Selected Papers of CHINED 2004.
300 pages. 2006. ISBN 3-03910-805-0 · US-ISBN 0-8204-8025-8

Vol. 31 Roberta Facchinetti & Matti Rissanen (eds)
Corpus-based Studies of Diachronic English.
300 pages. 2006. ISBN 3-03910-851-4 · US-ISBN 0-8204-8040-1

Vol. 32 Marina Dossena & Susan M. Fitzmaurice (eds)
Business and Official Correspondence. Historical Investigations.
209 pages. 2006. ISBN 3-03910-880-8 · US-ISBN 0-8204-8352-4

Vol. 33 Giuliana Garzone & Srikant Sarangi (eds)
Discourse, Ideology and Specialized Communication.
494 pages. 2007. ISBN 978-3-03910-888-6

Vol. 34 Giuliana Garzone & Cornelia Ilie (eds)
The Use of English in Institutional and Business Settings.
An Intercultural Perspective.
372 pages. 2007. ISBN 978-3-03910-889-3

Vol. 35 Vijay K. Bhatia & Maurizio Gotti (eds)
Explorations in Specialized Genres.
316 pages. 2006. ISBN 3-03910-995-2 · US-ISBN 0-8204-8372-9

Vol. 36 Heribert Picht (ed.)
Modern Approaches to Terminological Theories and Applications.
432 pages. 2006. ISBN 3-03911-156-6 · US-ISBN 0-8204-8380-X

Vol. 37 Anne Wagner & Sophie Cacciaguidi-Fahy (eds)
Legal Language and the Search for Clarity / Le langage juridique et la quête de clarté.
Practice and Tools / Pratiques et instruments.
487 pages. 2006. ISBN 3-03911-169-8 · US-ISBN 0-8204-8388-5

Vol. 38 Juan Carlos Palmer-Silveira, Miguel F. Ruiz-Garrido &
Inmaculada Fortanet-Gómez (eds)
Intercultural and International Business Communication.
Theory, Research and Teaching.
2nd edition. 343 pages. 2006, 2008. ISBN 978-3-03911-680-5

Vol. 39 Christiane Dalton-Puffer, Dieter Kastovsky, Nikolaus Ritt &
Herbert Schendl (eds)
Syntax, Style and Grammatical Norms. English from 1500–2000.
250 pages. 2006. ISBN 3-03911-181-7 · US-ISBN 0-8204-8394-X

Vol. 40 Marina Dossena & Irma Taavitsainen (eds)
Diachronic Perspectives on Domain-Specific English.
280 pages. 2006. ISBN 3-03910-176-0 · US-ISBN 0-8204-8391-5

Vol. 41 John Flowerdew & Maurizio Gotti (eds)
Studies in Specialized Discourse.
293 pages. 2006. ISBN 3-03911-178-7

Vol. 42 Ken Hyland & Marina Bondi (eds)
Academic Discourse Across Disciplines.
320 pages. 2006. ISBN 3-03911-183-3 · US-ISBN 0-8204-8396-6

Vol. 43 Paul Gillaerts & Philip Shaw (eds)
The Map and the Landscape. Norms and Practices in Genre.
256 pages. 2006. ISBN 3-03911-182-5 · US-ISBN 0-8204-8395-4

Vol. 44 Maurizio Gotti & Davide Giannoni (eds)
New Trends in Specialized Discourse Analysis.
301 pages. 2006. ISBN 3-03911-184-1 · US-ISBN 0-8204-8381-8

Vol. 45 Maurizio Gotti & Françoise Salager-Meyer (eds)
Advances in Medical Discourse Analysis. Oral and Written Contexts.
492 pages. 2006. ISBN 3-03911-185-X · US-ISBN 0-8204-8382-6

Vol. 46 Maurizio Gotti & Susan Šarcević (eds)
Insights into Specialized Translation.
396 pages. 2006. ISBN 3-03911-186-8 · US-ISBN 0-8204-8383-4

Vol. 47 Khurshid Ahmad & Margaret Rogers (eds)
Evidence-based LSP. Translation, Text and Terminology.
584 pages. 2007. ISBN 978-3-03911-187-9

Vol. 48 Hao Sun & Dániel Z. Kádár (eds)
It's the Dragon's Turn. Chinese Institutional Discourses.
262 pages. 2008. ISBN 978-3-03911-175-6

Vol. 49 Cristina Suárez-Gómez
Relativization in Early English (950-1250). the Position of Relative Clauses.
149 pages. 2006. ISBN 3-03911-203-1 · US-ISBN 0-8204-8904-2

Vol. 50 Maria Vittoria Calvi & Luisa Chierichetti (eds)
Nuevas tendencias en el discurso de especialidad.
319 pages. 2006. ISBN 978-3-03911-261-6

Vol. 51 Mari Carmen Campoy & María José Luzón (eds)
Spoken Corpora in Applied Linguistics.
274 pages. 2008. ISBN 978-3-03911-275-3

Vol. 52 Konrad Ehlich & Dorothee Heller (Hrsg.)
Die Wissenschaft und ihre Sprachen.
323 pages. 2006. ISBN 978-3-03911-272-2

Vol. 53 Jingyu Zhang
The Semantic Salience Hierarchy Model. The L2 Acquisition of Psych Predicates
273 pages. 2007. ISBN 978-3-03911-300-2

Vol. 54 Norman Fairclough, Giuseppina Cortese & Patrizia Ardizzone (eds)
Discourse and Contemporary Social Change.
555 pages. 2007. ISBN 978-3-03911-276-0

Vol. 55 Jan Engberg, Marianne Grove Ditlevsen, Peter Kastberg & Martin Stegu (eds)
New Directions in LSP Teaching.
331 pages. 2007. ISBN 978-3-03911-433-7

Vol. 56 Dorothee Heller & Konrad Ehlich (Hrsg.)
Studien zur Rechtskommunikation.
322 pages. 2007. ISBN 978-3-03911-436-8

Vol. 57 Teruhiro Ishiguro & Kang-kwong Luke (eds)
Grammar in Cross-Linguistic Perspective.
The Syntax, Semantics, and Pragmatics of Japanese and Chinese.
304 pages. 2012. ISBN 978-3-03911-445-0

Vol. 58 Carmen Frehner
Email – SMS – MMS
294 pages. 2008. ISBN 978-3-03911-451-1

Vol. 59 Isabel Balteiro
The Directionality of Conversion in English. A Dia-Synchronic Study.
276 pages. 2007. ISBN 978-3-03911-241-8

Vol. 60 Maria Milagros Del Saz Rubio
English Discourse Markers of Reformulation.
237 pages. 2007. ISBN 978-3-03911-196-1

Vol. 61 Sally Burgess & Pedro Martín-Martín (eds)
English as an Additional Language in Research Publication and Communication.
259 pages. 2008. ISBN 978-3-03911-462-7

Vol. 62 Sandrine Onillon
Pratiques et représentations de l'écrit.
458 pages. 2008. ISBN 978-3-03911-464-1

Vol. 63 Hugo Bowles & Paul Seedhouse (eds)
Conversation Analysis and Language for Specific Purposes.
2nd edition. 337 pages. 2007, 2009. ISBN 978-3-0343-0045-2

Vol. 64 Vijay K. Bhatia, Christopher N. Candlin & Paola Evangelisti Allori (eds)
Language, Culture and the Law.
The Formulation of Legal Concepts across Systems and Cultures.
342 pages. 2008. ISBN 978-3-03911-470-2

Vol. 65 Jonathan Culpeper & Dániel Z. Kádár (eds)
Historical (Im)politeness.
300 pages. 2010. ISBN 978-3-03911-496-2

Vol. 66 Linda Lombardo (ed.)
Using Corpora to Learn about Language and Discourse.
237 pages. 2009. ISBN 978-3-03911-522-8

Vol. 67 Natsumi Wakamoto
Extroversion/Introversion in Foreign Language Learning.
Interactions with Learner Strategy Use.
159 pages. 2009. ISBN 978-3-03911-596-9

Vol. 68 Eva Alcón-Soler (ed.)
Learning How to Request in an Instructed Language Learning Context.
260 pages. 2008. ISBN 978-3-03911-601-0

Vol. 69 Domenico Pezzini
The Translation of Religious Texts in the Middle Ages.
428 pages. 2008. ISBN 978-3-03911-600-3

Vol. 70 Tomoko Tode
Effects of Frequency in Classroom Second Language Learning.
Quasi-experiment and stimulated-recall analysis.
195 pages. 2008. ISBN 978-3-03911-602-7

Vol. 71 Egor Tsedryk
Fusion symétrique et alternances ditransitives.
211 pages. 2009. ISBN 978-3-03911-609-6

Vol. 72 Cynthia J. Kellett Bidoli & Elana Ochse (eds)
English in International Deaf Communication.
444 pages. 2008. ISBN 978-3-03911-610-2

Vol. 73 Joan C. Beal, Carmela Nocera & Massimo Sturiale (eds)
Perspectives on Prescriptivism.
269 pages. 2008. ISBN 978-3-03911-632-4

Vol. 74 Carol Taylor Torsello, Katherine Ackerley & Erik Castello (eds)
Corpora for University Language Teachers.
308 pages. 2008. ISBN 978-3-03911-639-3

Vol. 75 María Luisa Pérez Cañado (ed.)
English Language Teaching in the European Credit Transfer System. Facing the Challenge.
251 pages. 2009. ISBN 978-3-03911-654-6

Vol. 76 Marina Dossena & Ingrid Tieken-Boon van Ostade (eds)
Studies in Late Modern English Correspondence. Methodology and Data.
291 pages. 2008. ISBN 978-3-03911-658-4

Vol. 77 Ingrid Tieken-Boon van Ostade & Wim van der Wurff (eds)
Current Issues in Late Modern English.
436 pages. 2009. ISBN 978-3-03911-660-7

Vol. 78 Marta Navarro Coy (ed.)
Practical Approaches to Foreign Language Teaching and Learning.
297 pages. 2009. ISBN 978-3-03911-661-4

Vol. 79 Qing Ma
Second Language Vocabulary Acquisition.
333 pages. 2009. ISBN 978-3-03911-666-9

Vol. 80 Martin Solly, Michelangelo Conoscenti & Sandra Campagna (eds)
Verbal/Visual Narrative Texts in Higher Education.
384 pages. 2008. ISBN 978-3-03911-672-0

Vol. 81 Meiko Matsumoto
From Simple Verbs to Periphrastic Expressions: The Historical Development of Composite Predicates, Phrasal Verbs, and Related Constructions in English.
235 pages. 2008. ISBN 978-3-03911-675-1

Vol. 82 Melinda Dooly
Doing Diversity. Teachers' Construction of Their Classroom Reality.
180 pages. 2009. ISBN 978-3-03911-687-4

Vol. 83 Victoria Guillén-Nieto, Carmen Marimón-Llorca & Chelo Vargas-Sierra (eds)
Intercultural Business Communication and Simulation and Gaming Methodology.
392 pages. 2009. ISBN 978-3-03911-688-1

Vol. 84 Maria Grazia Guido
English as a Lingua Franca in Cross-cultural Immigration Domains.
285 pages. 2008. ISBN 978-3-03911-689-8

Vol. 85 Erik Castello
Text Complexity and Reading Comprehension Tests.
352 pages. 2008. ISBN 978-3-03911-717-8

Vol. 86 Maria-Lluisa Gea-Valor, Isabel García-Izquierdo & Maria-José Esteve (eds)
Linguistic and Translation Studies in Scientific Communication.
317 pages. 2010. ISBN 978-3-0343-0069-8

Vol. 87 Carmen Navarro, Rosa Mª Rodríguez Abella, Francesca Dalle Pezze & Renzo Miotti (eds)
La comunicación especializada.
355 pages. 2008. ISBN 978-3-03911-733-8

Vol. 88 Kiriko Sato
The Development from Case-Forms to Prepositional Constructions in Old English Prose.
231 pages. 2009. ISBN 978-3-03911-763-5

Vol. 89 Dorothee Heller (Hrsg.)
Formulierungsmuster in deutscher und italienischer Fachkommunikation. Intra- und interlinguale Perspektiven.
315 pages. 2008. ISBN 978-3-03911-778-9

Vol. 90 Henning Bergenholtz, Sandro Nielsen & Sven Tarp (eds)
Lexicography at a Crossroads. Dictionaries and Encyclopedias Today, Lexicographical Tools Tomorrow.
372 pages. 2009. ISBN 978-3-03911-799-4

Vol. 91 Manouchehr Moshtagh Khorasani
The Development of Controversies. From the Early Modern Period to Online Discussion Forums.
317 pages. 2009. ISBN 978-3-3911-711-6

Vol. 92 María Luisa Carrió-Pastor (ed.)
Content and Language Integrated Learning. Cultural Diversity.
178 pages. 2009. ISBN 978-3-3911-818-2

Vol. 93 Roger Berry
Terminology in English Language Teaching. Nature and Use.
262 pages. 2010. ISBN 978-3-0343-0013-1

Vol. 94 Roberto Cagliero & Jennifer Jenkins (eds)
Discourses, Communities, and Global Englishes
240 pages. 2010. ISBN 978-3-0343-0012-4

Vol. 95 Facchinetti Roberta, Crystal David, Seidlhofer Barbara (eds)
From International to Local English – And Back Again.
268 pages. 2010. ISBN 978-3-0343-0011-7

Vol. 96 Cesare Gagliardi & Alan Maley (eds)
EIL, ELF, Global English. Teaching and Learning Issues
376 pages. 2010. ISBN 978-3-0343-0010-0

Vol. 97 Sylvie Hancil (ed.)
The Role of Prosody in Affective Speech.
403 pages. 2009. ISBN 978-3-03911-696-6

Vol. 98 Marina Dossena & Roger Lass (eds)
Studies in English and European Historical Dialectology.
257 pages. 2009. ISBN 978-3-0343-0024-7

Vol. 99 Christine Béal
Les interactions quotidiennes en français et en anglais. De l'approche comparative à l'analyse des situations interculturelles.
424 pages. 2010. ISBN 978-3-0343-0027-8

Vol. 100 Maurizio Gotti (ed.)
Commonality and Individuality in Academic Discourse.
398 pages. 2009. ISBN 978-3-0343-0023-0

Vol. 101 Javier E. Díaz Vera & Rosario Caballero (eds)
Textual Healing. Studies in Medieval English Medical, Scientific and Technical Texts.
213 pages. 2009. ISBN 978-3-03911-822-9

Vol. 102 Nuria Edo Marzá
The Specialised Lexicographical Approach. A Step further in Dictionary-making.
316 pages. 2009. ISBN 978-3-0343-0043-8

Vol. 103 Carlos Prado-Alonso, Lidia Gómez-García, Iria Pastor-Gómez &
David Tizón-Couto (eds)
New Trends and Methodologies in Applied English Language Research.
Diachronic, Diatopic and Contrastive Studies.
348 pages. 2009. ISBN 978-3-0343-0046-9

Vol. 104 Françoise Salager-Meyer & Beverly A. Lewin
Crossed Words. Criticism in Scholarly Writing?
371 pages. 2011. ISBN 978-3-0343-0049-0.

Vol. 105 Javier Ruano-García
Early Modern Northern English Lexis. A Literary Corpus-Based Study.
611 pages. 2010. ISBN 978-3-0343-0058-2

Vol. 106 Rafael Monroy-Casas
Systems for the Phonetic Transcription of English. Theory and Texts.
280 pages. 2011. ISBN 978-3-0343-0059-9

Vol. 107 Nicola T. Owtram
The Pragmatics of Academic Writing.
A Relevance Approach to the Analysis of Research Article Introductions.
311 pages. 2009. ISBN 978-3-0343-0060-5

Vol. 108 Yolanda Ruiz de Zarobe, Juan Manuel Sierra &
Francisco Gallardo del Puerto (eds)
Content and Foreign Language Integrated Learning.
Contributions to Multilingualism in European Contexts
343 pages. 2011. ISBN 978-3-0343-0074-2

Vol. 109 Ángeles Linde López & Rosalía Crespo Jiménez (eds)
Professional English in the European context. The EHEA challenge.
374 pages. 2010. ISBN 978-3-0343-0088-9

Vol. 110 Rosalía Rodríguez-Vázquez
The Rhythm of Speech, Verse and Vocal Music. A New Theory.
394 pages. 2010. ISBN 978-3-0343-0309-5

Vol. 111 Anastasios Tsangalidis & Roberta Facchinetti (eds)
Studies on English Modality. In Honour of Frank Palmer.
392 pages. 2009. ISBN 978-3-0343-0310-1

Vol. 112 Jing Huang
Autonomy, Agency and Identity in Foreign Language Learning and Teaching.
400 pages. 2013. ISBN 978-3-0343-0370-5

Vol. 113 Mihhail Lotman & Maria-Kristiina Lotman (eds)
Frontiers in Comparative Prosody. In memoriam: Mikhail Gasparov.
426 pages. 2011. ISBN 978-3-0343-0373-6

Vol. 114 Merja Kytö, John Scahill & Harumi Tanabe (eds)
Language Change and Variation from Old English to Late Modern English.
A Festschrift for Minoji Akimoto
422 pages. 2010. ISBN 978-3-0343-0372-9

Vol. 115 Giuliana Garzone & Paola Catenaccio (eds)
Identities across Media and Modes. Discursive Perspectives.
379 pages. 2009. ISBN 978-3-0343-0386-6

Vol. 116 Elena Landone
Los marcadores del discurso y cortesía verbal en español.
390 pages. 2010. ISBN 978-3-0343-0413-9

Vol. 117 Maurizio Gotti & Christopher Williams (eds)
Legal Discourse across Languages and Cultures.
339 pages. 2010. ISBN 978-3-0343-0425-2

Vol. 118 David Hirsh
Academic Vocabulary in Context.
217 pages. 2010. ISBN 978-3-0343-0426-9

Vol. 119 Yvonne Dröschel
Lingua Franca English. The Role of Simplification and Transfer.
358 pages. 2011. ISBN 978-3-0343-0432-0

Vol. 120 Tengku Sepora Tengku Mahadi, Helia Vaezian & Mahmoud Akbari
Corpora in Translation. A Practical Guide.
135 pages. 2010. ISBN 978-3-0343-0434-4

Vol. 121 Davide Simone Giannoni & Celina Frade (eds)
Researching Language and the Law. Textual Features and Translation Issues.
278 pages. 2010. ISBN 978-3-0343-0443-6

Vol. 122 Daniel Madrid & Stephen Hughes (eds)
Studies in Bilingual Education.
472 pages. 2011. ISBN 978-3-0343-0474-0

Vol. 123 Vijay K. Bhatia, Christopher N. Candlin & Maurizio Gotti (eds)
The Discourses of Dispute Resolution.
290 pages. 2010. ISBN 978-3-0343-0476-4

Vol. 124 Davide Simone Giannoni
Mapping Academic Values in the Disciplines. A Corpus-Based Approach.
288 pages. 2010. ISBN 978-3-0343-0488-7

Vol. 125 Giuliana Garzone & James Archibald (eds)
Discourse, Identities and Roles in Specialized Communication.
419 pages. 2010. ISBN 978-3-0343-0494-8

Vol. 126 Iria Pastor-Gómez
The Status and Development of N+N Sequences in
Contemporary English Noun Phrases.
216 pages. 2011. ISBN 978-3-0343-0534-1

Vol. 127 Carlos Prado-Alonso
Full-verb Inversion in Written and Spoken English.
261 pages. 2011. ISBN 978-3-0343-0535-8

Vol. 128 Tony Harris & María Moreno Jaén (eds)
Corpus Linguistics in Language Teaching.
214 pages. 2010. ISBN 978-3-0343-0524-2

Vol. 129 Tetsuji Oda & Hiroyuki Eto (eds)
Multiple Perspectives on English Philology and History of Linguistics.
A Festschrift for Shoichi Watanabe on his 80th Birthday.
378 pages. 2010. ISBN 978-3-0343-0480-1

Vol. 130 Luisa Chierichetti & Giovanni Garofalo (eds)
Lengua y Derecho. líneas de investigación interdisciplinaria.
283 pages. 2010. 978-3-0343-0463-4

Vol. 131 Paola Evangelisti Allori & Giuliana Garzone (eds)
Discourse, Identities and Genres in Corporate Communication.
Sponsorship, Advertising and Organizational Communication.
324 pages. 2011. 978-3-0343-0591-4

Vol. 132 Leyre Ruiz de Zarobe & Yolanda Ruiz de Zarobe (eds)
Speech Acts and Politeness across Languages and Cultures.
402 pages. 2012. 978-3-0343-0611-9

Vol. 133 Thomas Christiansen
Cohesion. A Discourse Perspective.
387 pages. 2011. 978-3-0343-0619-5

Vol. 134 Giuliana Garzone & Maurizio Gotti
Discourse, Communication and the Enterprise. Genres and Trends.
451 pages. 2011. ISBN 978-3-0343-0620-1

Vol. 135 Zsuzsa Hoffmann
Ways of the World's Words.
Language Contact in the Age of Globalization.
334 pages 2011. ISBN 978-3-0343-0673-7

Vol. 136 Cecilia Varcasia (ed.)
Becoming Multilingual.
Language Learning and Language Policy between Attitudes and Identities.
213 pages. 2011. ISBN 978-3-0343-0687-5

Vol. 137 Susy Macqueen
The Emergence of Patterns in Second Language Writing.
A Sociocognitive Exploration of Lexical Trails.
325 pages. 2012. ISBN 978-3-0343-1010-9

Vol. 138 Maria Vittoria Calvi & Giovanna Mapelli (eds)
La lengua del turismo. Géneros discursivos y terminología.
365 pages. 2011. ISBN 978-3-0343-1011-6

Vol. 139 Ken Lau
Learning to Become a Professional in a Textually-Mediated World.
A Text-Oriented Study of Placement Practices.
261 pages. 2012. ISBN 978-3-0343-1016-1

Vol. 140 Sandra Campagna, Giuliana Garzone, Cornelia Ilie & Elizabeth Rowley-Jolivet (eds)
Evolving Genres in Web-mediated Communication.
337 pages. 2012. ISBN 978-3-0343-1013-0

Vol. 141 Edith Esch & Martin Solly (eds)
The Sociolinguistics of Language Education in International Contexts.
263 pages. 2012. ISBN 978-3-0343-1009-3

Vol. 142 Forthcoming.

Vol. 143 David Tizón-Couto
Left Dislocation in English. A Functional-Discoursal Approach.
416 pages. 2012. ISBN 978-3-0343-1037-6

Vol. 144 Margrethe Petersen & Jan Engberg (eds)
Current Trends in LSP Research. Aims and Methods.
323 pages. 2011. ISBN 978-3-0343-1054-3

Vol. 145 David Tizón-Couto, Beatriz Tizón-Couto, Iria Pastor-Gómez & Paula Rodríguez-Puente (eds)
New Trends and Methodologies in Applied English Language Research II.
Studies in Language Variation, Meaning and Learning.
283 pages. 2012. ISBN 978-3-0343-1061-1

Vol. 146 Rita Salvi & Hiromasa Tanaka (eds)
Intercultural Interactions in Business and Management.
306 pages. 2011. ISBN 978-3-0343-1039-0

Vol. 147 Francesco Straniero Sergio & Caterina Falbo (eds)
Breaking Ground in Corpus-based Interpreting Studies.
254 pages. 2012. ISBN 978-3-0343-1071-0

Vol. 148 Forthcoming.

Vol. 149 Vijay K. Bhatia & Paola Evangelisti Allori (eds)
Discourse and Identity in the Professions. Legal, Corporate and Institutional Citizenship.
352 pages. 2011. ISBN 978-3-0343-1079-6

Vol. 150 Maurizio Gotti (ed.)
Academic Identity Traits. A Corpus-Based Investigation.
363 pages. 2012. ISBN 978-3-0343-1141-0

Vol. 151 Priscilla Heynderickx, Sylvain Dieltjens, Geert Jacobs, Paul Gillaerts & Elizabeth de Groot (eds)
The Language Factor in International Business.
New Perspectives on Research, Teaching and Practice.
320 pages. 2012. ISBN 978-3-0343-1090-1

Vol. 152 Paul Gillaerts, Elizabeth de Groot, Sylvain Dieltjens, Priscilla Heynderickx & Geert Jacobs (eds)
Researching Discourse in Business Genres. Cases and Corpora.
215 pages. 2012. ISBN 978-3-0343-1092-5

Vol. 153 Yongyan Zheng
Dynamic Vocabulary Development in a Foreign Language.
262 pages. 2012. ISBN 978-3-0343-1106-9

Vol. 154 Carmen Argondizzo (ed.)
Creativity and Innovation in Language Education.
357 pages. 2012. ISBN 978-3-0343-1080-2

Vol. 155 David Hirsh (ed.)
Current Perspectives in Second Language Vocabulary Research.
180 pages. 2012. ISBN 978-3-0343-1108-3

Vol. 156 Seiji Shinkawa
Unhistorical Gender Assignment in Lahamon's *Brut.* A Case Study of a Late Stage in the Development of Grammatical Gender toward its Ultimate Loss.
186 pages. 2012. ISBN 978-3-0343-1124-3

Vol. 157 Yeonkwon Jung
Basics of Organizational Writing: A Critical Reading Approach.
151 pages. 2014. ISBN 978-3-0343-1137-3.

Vol. 158 Bárbara Eizaga Rebollar (ed.)
Studies in Linguistics and Cognition.
301 pages. 2012. ISBN 978-3-0343-1138-0

Vol. 159 Giuliana Garzone, Paola Catenaccio, Chiara Degano (eds)
Genre Change in the Contemporary World. Short-term Diachronic Perspectives.
329 pages. 2012. ISBN 978-3-0343-1214-1

Vol. 160 Carol Berkenkotter, Vijay K. Bhatia & Maurizio Gotti (eds)
Insights into Academic Genres.
468 pages. 2012. ISBN 978-3-0343-1211-0

Vol. 161 Beatriz Tizón-Couto
Clausal Complements in Native and Learner Spoken English. A corpus-based study with Lindsei and Vicolse. 357 pages. 2013. ISBN 978-3-0343-1184-7

Vol. 162 Patrizia Anesa
Jury Trials and the Popularization of Legal Language. A Discourse Analytical Approach.
247 pages. 2012. ISBN 978-3-0343-1231-8

Vol. 163 David Hirsh
Endangered Languages, Knowledge Systems and Belief Systems.
153 pages. 2013. ISBN 978-3-0343-1232-5

Vol. 164 Eugenia Sainz (ed.)
De la estructura de la frase al tejido del discurso. Estudios contrastivos español/italiano.
305 pages. 2014. ISBN 978-3-0343-1253-0

Vol. 165 Julia Bamford, Franca Poppi & Davide Mazzi (eds)
Space, Place and the Discursive Construction of Identity.
367 pages. 2014. ISBN 978-3-0343-1249-3

Vol. 166 Rita Salvi & Janet Bowker (eds)
Space, Time and the Construction of Identity.
Discursive Indexicality in Cultural, Institutional and Professional Fields.
324 pages. 2013. ISBN 978-3-0343-1254-7

Vol. 167 Shunji Yamazaki & Robert Sigley (eds)
Approaching Language Variation through Corpora. A Festschrift in Honour of Toshio Saito.
421 pages. 2013. ISBN 978-3-0343-1264-6

Vol. 168 Franca Poppi
Global Interactions in English as a Lingua Franca. How written communication is changing under the influence of electronic media and new contexts of use.
249 pages. 2012. ISBN 978-3-0343-1276-9

Vol. 169 Miguel A. Aijón Oliva & María José Serrano
Style in syntax. Investigating variation in Spanish pronoun subjects.
239 pages. 2013. ISBN 978-3-0343-1244-8

Vol. 170 Inés Olza, Óscar Loureda & Manuel Casado-Velarde (eds)
Language Use in the Public Sphere. Methodological Perspectives and Empirical Applications
564 pages. 2014. ISBN 978-3-0343-1286-8

Vol. 171 Aleksandra Matulewska
Legilinguistic Translatology. A Parametric Approach to Legal Translation.
279 pages. 2013. ISBN 978-3-0343-1287-5

Vol. 172 Maurizio Gotti & Carmen Sancho Guinda (eds)
Narratives in Academic and Professional Genres.
513 pages. 2013. ISBN 978-3-0343-1371-1

Vol. 173 Madalina Chitez
Learner corpus profiles. The case of Romanian Learner English.
244 pages. 2014. ISBN 978-3-0343-1410-7

Vol. 174 Chihiro Inoue
Task Equivalence in Speaking Tests.
251 pages. 2013. ISBN 978-3-0343-1417-6

Vol. 175 Gabriel Quiroz & Pedro Patiño (eds.)
LSP in Colombia: advances and challenges.
339 pages. 2014. ISBN 978-3-0343-1434-3

Vol. 176 Catherine Resche
Economic Terms and Beyond: Capitalising on the Wealth of Notions.
How Researchers in Specialised Varieties of English Can Benefit from Focusing on Terms.
332 pages. 2013. ISBN 978-3-0343-1435-0

Vol. 177 Forthcoming.

Vol. 178 Cécile Desoutter & Caroline Mellet (dir.)
Le discours rapporté: approches linguistiques et perspectives didactiques.
270 pages. 2013. ISBN 978-3-0343-1292-9

Vol. 179 Ana Díaz-Negrillo & Francisco Javier Díaz-Pérez (eds)
Specialisation and Variation in Language Corpora.
341 pages. 2014. ISBN 978-3-0343-1316-2

Vol. 180 Pilar Alonso
A Multi-dimensional Approach to Discourse Coherence. From Standardness to Creativity.
247 pages. 2014. ISBN 978-3-0343-1325-4

Vol. 181 Alejandro Alcaraz-Sintes & Salvador Valera-Hernández (eds)
Diachrony and Synchrony in English Corpus Linguistics.
393 pages. 2014. ISBN 978-3-0343-1326-1

Vol. 182 Runhan Zhang
Investigating Linguistic Knowledge of a Second Language.
207 pages. 2015. ISBN 978-3-0343-1330-8

Vol. 183 Hajar Abdul Rahim & Shakila Abdul Manan (eds.)
English in Malaysia. Postcolonial and Beyond.
267 pages. 2014. ISBN 978-3-0343-1341-4

Vol. 184 Virginie Fasel Lauzon
Comprendre et apprendre dans l'interaction. Les séquences d'explication en classe de français langue seconde.
292 pages. 2014. ISBN 978-3-0343-1451-0

Vol. 185 Forthcoming.

Vol. 186 Wei Ren
L2 Pragmatic Development in Study Abroad Contexts
256 pages. 2015. ISBN 978-3-0343-1358-2

Vol. 187 Marina Bondi & Rosa Lorés Sanz (eds)
Abstracts in Academic Discourse. Variation and Change.
361 pages. 2014. ISBN 978-3-0343-1483-1

Vol. 188 Giuditta Caliendo
Rethinking Community. Discourse, Identity and Citizenship in the European Union.
240 pages. 2017. ISBN 978-3-0343-1561-6

Vol. 189 Paola Evangelisti Allori (ed.)
Identities in and across Cultures.
315 pages. 2014. ISBN 978-3-0343-1458-9

Vol. 190 Erik Castello, Katherine Ackerley & Francesca Coccetta (eds).
Studies in Learner Corpus Linguistics. Research and Applications for Foreign Language Teaching and Assessment.
358 pages. 2015. ISBN 978-3-0343-1506-7

Vol. 191 Ruth Breeze, Maurizio Gotti & Carmen Sancho Guinda (eds)
Interpersonality in Legal Genres.
389 pages. 2014. ISBN 978-3-0343-1524-1

Vol. 192 Paola Evangelisti Allori, John Bateman & Vijay K. Bhatia (eds)
Evolution in Genre. Emergence, Variation, Multimodality.
364 pages. 2014. ISBN 978-3-0343-1533-3

Vol. 193 Jiyeon Kook
Agency in Arzt-Patient-Gesprächen. Zur interaktionistischen Konzeptualisierung von Agency
271 pages. 2015. ISBN 978-3-0343-1666-8

Vol. 194 Susana Nicolás Román & Juan José Torres Núñez (eds)
Drama and CLIL. A new challenge for the teaching approaches in bilingual education.
170 pages. 2015. ISBN 978-3-0343-1629-3

Vol. 195 Alessandra Molino & Serenella Zanotti (eds)
Observing Norm, Observing Usage. Lexis in Dictionaries and in the Media.
430 pages. 2015. ISBN 978-3-0343-1584-5

Vol. 196 Begoña Soneira
A Lexical Description of English for Architecture. A Corpus-based Approach.
267 pages. 2015. ISBN 978-3-0343-1602-6

Vol. 197 M Luisa Roca-Varela
False Friends in Learner Corpora. A corpus-based study of English false friends in the written and spoken production of Spanish learners.
348 pages. 2015. ISBN 978-3-0343-1620-0

Vol. 198 Rahma Al-Mahrooqi & Christopher Denman
Bridging the Gap between Education and Employment. English Language Instruction in EFL Contexts.
416 pages. 2015. ISBN 978-3-0343-1681-1

Vol. 199 Rita Salvi & Janet Bowker (eds)
The Dissemination of Contemporary Knowledge in English. Genres, discourse strategies and professional practices.
171 pages. 2015. ISBN 978-3-0343-1679-8

Vol. 200 Maurizio Gotti & Davide S. Giannoni (eds)
Corpus Analysis for Descriptive and Pedagogical Purposes. ESP Perspectives.
432 pages. 2014. ISBN 978-3-0343-1516-6

Vol. 201 Ida Ruffolo
The Perception of Nature in Travel Promotion Texts. A Corpus-based Discourse Analysis.
148 pages. 2015. ISBN 978-3-0343-1521-0

Vol. 202 Ives Trevian
English suffixes. Stress-assignment properties, productivity, selection and combinatorial processes.
471 pages. 2015. ISBN 978-3-0343-1576-0

Vol. 203 Maurizio Gotti, Stefania Maci & Michele Sala (eds)
Insights into Medical Communication.
422 pages. 2015. ISBN 978-3-0343-1694-1

Vol. 204 Carmen Argondizzo (ed.)
European Projects in University Language Centres. Creativity, Dynamics, Best Practice.
371 pages. 2015. ISBN 978-3-0343-1696-5

Vol. 205 Aura Luz Duffé Montalván (ed.)
Estudios sobre el léxico. Puntos y contrapuntos.
502 pages. 2016. ISBN 978-3-0343-2011-5

Vol. 206 Maria Pavesi, Maicol Formentelli & Elisa Ghia (eds)
The Languages of Dubbing. Mainstream Audiovisual Translation in Italy.
275 pages. 2014. ISBN 978-3-0343-1646-0

Vol. 207 Ruth Breeze & Inés Olza (eds)
Evaluation in media discourse. European perspectives.
268 pages. 2017. ISBN 978-3-0343-2014-6

Vol. 208 Vijay K. Bhatia & Maurizio Gotti (eds)
Arbitration Discourse in Asia.
331 pages. 2015. ISBN 978-3-0343-2032-0

Vol. 209 Sofía Bemposta-Rivas, Carla Bouzada-Jabois, Yolanda Fernández-Pena, Tamara Bouso, Yolanda J. Calvo-Benzies, Iván Tamaredo (eds)
New trends and methodologies in applied English language research III. Synchronic and diachronic studies on discourse, lexis and grammar processing.
280 pages. 2017. ISBN 978-3-0343-2039-9

Vol. 210 Francisco Alonso Almeida, Laura Cruz García & Víctor González Ruiz (eds)
Corpus-based studies on language varieties.
285 pages. 2016. ISBN 978-3-0343-2044-3

Vol. 211 Juan Pedro Rica Peromingo
Aspectos lingüísticos y técnicos de la traducción audiovisual (TAV).
177 pages. 2016. ISBN 978-3-0343-2055-9

Vol. 212 Maria Vender
Disentangling Dyslexia. VenderPhonological and Processing Deficit in Developmental Dyslexia.
338 pages. 2017. ISBN 978-3-0343-2064-1

Vol. 213 Zhilong Xie
Bilingual Advantages. Contributions of Different Bilingual Experiences to Cognitive Control Differences Among Young-adult Bilinguals.
221 pages. 2016. ISBN 978-3-0343-2081-8

Vol. 214 Larissa D'Angelo
Academic posters. A textual and visual metadiscourse analysis.
367 pages. 2016. ISBN 978-3-0343-2083-2

Vol. 215 Evelyne Berger
Prendre la parole en L2. Regard sur la compétence d'interaction en classe de langue.
246 pages. 2016. ISBN 978-3-0343-2084-9

Vol. 216 David Lasagabaster and Aintzane Doiz (eds)
CLIL experiences in secondary and tertiary education: In search of good practices.
262 pages. 2016. ISBN 978-3-0343-2104-4

Vol. 217 Elena Kkese
Identifying Plosives in L2 English: The Case of L1 Cypriot Greek Speakers.
317 pages. 2016. ISBN 978-3-0343-2060-3

Vol. 218 Sandra Campagna, Elana Ochse, Virginia Pulcini & Martin Solly (eds)
Languaging in and across Communities: New Voices, New Identities. Studies in Honour of Giuseppina Cortese.
507 pages. 2016. ISBN 978-3-0343-2073-3

Vol. 219 Adriana Orlandi & Laura Giacomini (ed.)
Defining collocation for lexicographic purposes. From linguistic theory to lexicographic practice.
328 pages. 2016. ISBN 978-3-0343-2054-2

Vol. 220 Pietro Luigi Iaia
Analysing English as a Lingua Franca in Video Games. Linguistic Features, Experiential and Functional Dimensions of Online and Scripted Interactions.
139 pages. 2016. ISBN 978-3-0343-2138-9

Vol. 221 Dimitrinka G. Níkleva (ed.)
La formación de los docentes de español para inmigrantes en distintos contextos educativos.
390 pages. 2017. ISBN 978-3-0343-2135-8

Vol. 222 Katherine Ackerley, Marta Guarda & Francesca Helm (eds)
Sharing Perspectives on English-Medium Instruction.
308 pages. 2017. ISBN 978-3-0343-2537-0

Vol. 223 Juana I. Marín-Arrese, Julia Lavid-López, Marta Carretero, Elena Domínguez Romero, Mª Victoria Martín de la Rosa & María Pérez Blanco (eds)
Evidentiality and Modality in European Languages. Discourse-pragmatic perspectives.
427 pages. 2017. ISBN 978-3-0343-2437-3

Vol. 224 Gilles Col
Construction du sens : un modèle instructionnel pour la sémantique.
292 pages. 2017. ISBN 978-3-0343-2572-1

Vol. 225 Ana Chiquito & Gabriel Quiroz (eds)
Pobreza, Lenguaje y Medios en América Latina.
362 pages. 2017. ISBN 978-3-0343-2142-6

Vol. 226 Xu Zhang
English Quasi-Numeral Classifiers. A Corpus-Based Cognitive-Typological Study.
360 pages. 2017. ISBN 978-3-0343-2818-0

Vol. 227 María Ángeles Orts, Ruth Breeze & Maurizio Gotti (eds)
Power, Persuasion and Manipulation in Specialised Genres. Providing Keys to the Rhetoric of Professional Communities.
368 pages. 2017. ISBN 978-3-0343-3010-7

Vol. 228 Maurizio Gotti, Stefania Maci & Michele Sala (eds)
Ways of Seeing, Ways of Being: Representing the Voices of Tourism.
453 pages. 2017. ISBN 978-3-0343-3031-2

Vol. 229 Forthcoming.

Vol. 230 Anca-Cristina Sterie
Interprofessional interactions at the hospital. Nurses' requests and reports of problems in calls with physicians.
371 pages. 2017. ISBN 978-3-0343-2734-3

Vol. 231 Xiaodong Zhang
Understanding Chinese EFL Teachers' Beliefs and Practices in the Textbook-Based Classroom.
189 pages. 2017. ISBN 978-3-0343-3053-4

Vol. 232 Manuela Caterina Moroni & Federica Ricci Garotti (Hrsg.)
Brücken schlagen zwischen Sprachwissenschaft und DaF-Didaktik.
345 pages. 2017. ISBN 978-3-0343-2667-4

Vol. 233 Dimitrinka Georgieva Níkleva
Necesidades y tendencias en la formación del profesorado de español como lengua extranjera
401 pages. 2017. ISBN 978-3-0343-2946-0

Vol. 234 Forthcoming.

Vol. 235 Francisco Salgado-Robles
Desarrollo de la competencia sociolingüística por aprendices de español en un contexto de inmersión en el extranjero
241 pages. 2018. ISBN 978-3-0343-2323-9

Vol. 236 Maria Chiara Janner
Sguardi linguistici sulla marca. Analisi morfosintattica dei nomi commerciali in italiano
345 pages. 2017. ISBN 978-3-0343-2667-4

Vol. 237 Bárbara Herrero Muñoz-Cobo & Otman El Azami Zalachi
La primavera del árabe marroquí.
192 pages. 2017. ISBN 978-3-0343-3104-3

Vol. 238 Consuelo Pascual Escagedo
El papel del oyente en la construcción de la conversación espontánea de estudiantes italianos en su interlengua y en su lengua materna
295 pages. 2017. ISBN 978-3-0343-3186-9

Vol. 239 Stefania M. Maci
The MS Digby 133 *Mary Magdalene*. Beyond scribal practices: language, discourse, values and attitudes.
336 pages. 2017. ISBN 978-3-0343-3256-9

Vol. 240 Eliecer Crespo-Fernández
Taboo in Discourse. Studies on Attenuation and Offence in Communication.
326 pages. 2018. ISBN 978-3-0343-3018-3

Vol. 241–242 Forthcoming.

Vol. 243 Yunfeng Ge
Resolution of Conflict of Interest in Chinese Civil Court Hearings. A Perspective of Discourse Information Theory.
302 pages. 2018. ISBN 978-3-0343-3313-9

Vol. 244 Carla Vergaro
Illocutionary Shell Nouns in English
322 pages. 2018. ISBN 978-3-0343-3069-5

Vol. 245 Paolo Frassi
L'adjectif en français et sa définition lexicographique.
270 pages. 2018. ISBN 978-3-0343-3394-8

www.ingramcontent.com/pod-product-compliance
Ingram Content Group UK Ltd.
Pitfield, Milton Keynes, MK11 3LW, UK
UKHW020839290926
15470UKWH00004B/1439

9 783034 333139